Functional Family Therapy in Clinical Practice

Functional Family Therapy in Clinical Practice

An Evidence-Based Treatment Model for Working With Troubled Adolescents

Thomas L. Sexton

Routledge
Taylor & Francis Group
New York   London

Routledge
Taylor & Francis Group
270 Madison Avenue
New York, NY 10016

Routledge
Taylor & Francis Group
27 Church Road
Hove, East Sussex BN3 2FA

© 2011 by Taylor and Francis Group, LLC
Routledge is an imprint of Taylor & Francis Group, an Informa business

Printed in the United States of America on acid-free paper
10 9 8 7 6 5 4 3 2 1

International Standard Book Number: 978-0-415-99691-4 (Hardback) 978-0-415-99692-1 (Paperback)

Library of Congress Cataloging-in-Publication Data

Sexton, Thomas L., 1953-
    Functional family therapy in clinical practice : an evidence-based treatment model for working with troubled adolescents / by Thomas Sexton.
        p. cm.
    Includes bibliographical references and index.
    ISBN 978-0-415-99691-4 (hardback : alk. paper) -- ISBN 978-0-415-99692-1 (pbk. : alk. paper)
    1. Functional Family Therapy (Program) 2. Behavior therapy for teenagers--United States. 3. Family psychotherapy--United States. I. Title.

RJ505.B4S49 2010
618.92'89142--dc22
                                                                    2010007097

Visit the Taylor & Francis Web site at
http://www.taylorandfrancis.com

and the Routledge Web site at
http://www.routledgementalhealth.com

Dedication

To the families that seek help from FFT and the community organizations that implement FFT. I am humbled by the strength, resilience, and tenacity with which you face sometimes overwhelming odds. Each day I learn from you how FFT works in the real world.

To my colleagues (N.O., J.B.), who joined me on the journey that made this contribution to the FFT model possible.

To J.F.A. for the mentorship, collegiality, and opportunity to be part of the FFT history.

To Matt and Astrid. You teach, inspire, support, and show me the meaning of family every day.

Thomas Sexton
Bloomington, Indiana

Contents

SECTION I   An Introduction to Functional Family Therapy: A Dynamic Evolution of Theory, Science, and Practice

SECTION II   The Practice of FFT

SECTION III Translating FFT Into Community Settings

Foreword

Twenty-five to thirty years ago, there were no methods of family or couple therapy that had accumulated enough research evidence to qualify as "empirically supported" by today's standards. Currently, there are a substantial and impressive number of approaches to family and couple therapy that have deservingly earned the reputation of being "empirically supported." Some of these, especially in the couples' domain, are "broad-spectrum" in that they are provided for dealing with a very wide array of important relationship difficulties. Others, especially in the family domain, have been developed for more targeted clinical problems of great mental health significance. Within this select latter group, none has earned as lofty a position in the history of family therapy as Functional Family Therapy (FFT).

Many family therapies have come and gone, often fading when their creators leave us. But FFT has come and *grown* over the last 35 years. Undoubtedly the only major school of family therapy that has been grounded in an unending reciprocal relationship between research and practice, FFT has been dedicated not merely to its clinical principles, but also to scientifically demonstrating its effectiveness and efficacy long before it was stylish to have such concerns. And, unlike some empirically supported psychotherapies, whether focused on families, couples or individuals, the practice of FFT has always been grounded in the "real world" of people struggling with problems of genuine clinical significance. And more recently, FFT has gone where few other therapies have dared to go: into the "outerspace" clinics of the world—far beyond the academic settings where it had its beginnings—to demonstrate convincingly its cross-cultural potency. Given its longevity and its repeated and varied demonstrations of efficacy, it is not an exaggeration to say that FFT is truly unique in the world of family therapy.

What is it that has allowed FFT to grow, prosper, and become such a compelling approach to working with families faced with very challenging and disheartening adolescent behavior disorders?

FFT is a very sophisticated approach to working with families, at once both refined and complex. So, others might well identify different attributes of FFT that explain its increasing visibility and influence in the field. For me, there is an awesome trifecta of attributes of FFT that warrant its special place in the world of family therapy; indeed, in the wider world of all psychotherapies: FFT is grounded in solid psychological science, it is eminently teachable, and it requires therapist creativity.

FFT systematically incorporates into its evolving clinical theorizing and practice development advances in the psychological sciences of systems theory, epidemiology, developmental psychopathology, and clinical intervention research focused on both outcome and process. As a result, FFT focuses its understanding of core family processes and its use of particular therapeutic strategies and interventions on the most telling protective and risk factors involved in adolescent behavioral disturbances.

Given the clarity of its conceptual model of how adolescent behavior disorders develop, and what is called for to improve the family interactions that maintain such problems, it is not surprising that FFT is unusually teachable. But FFT is not merely teachable in the important sense that, unlike most family therapies, it defines both the necessary phases of therapeutic engagement and the necessary subtasks within these phases. FFT spells out with decided precision and coherence not only how to practice as a therapist, but also how to effectively supervise the practice of FFT, and how to assure the institutional quality of its practice. There is no other method of family therapy that can boast that.

But, lest you think that FFT's teachability may be the kind that renders the FFT therapist a manual-driven robot, not to worry. The central concept of "relational functions" in family relationships absolutely requires two things. First, in FFT, the therapist must always be not merely respectful of, but even deeply in tuned with, the unique psychological "culture" of each individual family and each of its members. In this profoundly clear way, FFT is inherently sensitive to differences of race, religion, ethnic identity, social class and the like. Second, this functional emphasis also absolutely requires that the therapist be strategically flexible, open, and, indeed, downright creative in helping family members find, or develop, new and more collaborative ways to maintain their individual relational goals and preferences, while enhancing the overall functioning of the family as a whole.

Although FFT's effectiveness is well researched and its technical aspects well articulated, this is not a "therapy by the numbers." FFT is an exquisite synergistic blend of clinical science and clinical attunement, and *Functional Family Therapy in Clinical Practice* is a most welcome, long-overdue contribution.

Alan S. Gurman, Ph.D.
Emeritus Professor of Psychiatry
University of Wisconsin School of Medicine and Public Health

Preface

Functional Family Therapy (FFT) has been a major family therapy approach for working with externalizing adolescents for more than 30 years. The first (and only) book on FFT, by Alexander and Parsons, appeared in 1982. Since that time, chapters on the FFT model have appeared in the most prestigious publications in the field, including Gurman and Kniskern's *Handbook of Family Therapy* (Barton & Alexander, 1981), *Comprehensive Handbook of Psychotherapy* (Alexander & Sexton, 2002; Sexton & Alexander, 2002), Sexton, Weeks, and Robbins's *Handbook of Family Therapy* (Sexton & Alexander, 2003), *The Handbook of Clinical Family Therapy* (Sexton & Alexander, 2006), and the *Handbook of Family Psychology* (Sexton, 2009). These publications demonstrate FFT's importance as a major theoretical and conceptual model in the field of family psychology. FFT has been designated by the Center for the Study and Prevention of Violence as a Blueprint Program for the successful treatment of delinquency, violence, and co-occurring problems for high-risk youth (Alexander, Pugh, Parsons, & Sexton, 2000).

The clinically rich, theoretically integrative, and systematic nature of the FFT clinical model along with its repeated demonstrations of successful outcomes with at-risk adolescents and their families has led to widespread community-based application in many settings with a wide range of clients (Alexander, Holzworth-Munroe, & Jameson, 1994; Sexton & Alexander, 2002; Sexton, Alexander, & Mease, 2004). Functional Family Therapy is now being extensively used in mental health and social service treatment systems in the United States and internationally to treat one of the most difficult clinical problems: externalizing behavior disorders of adolescents. At-risk adolescents are often viewed as treatment-resistant and unmotivated, with few effective treatment options available. These youths represent the most common clinical referrals in mental health systems, and youths who enter the juvenile justice system require significant resources and attention.

Because of its systematic clinical model, scientific research, supervision and training protocols, dissemination and implementation process, and quality improvement system, FFT appeals to practitioners, service providers, and communities seeking ways to help at-risk youth. In addition, its cultural sensitivity and ability to address the problems of diverse clients make it particularly valuable. In mental health systems

FFT is a primary treatment program for a wide range of problem youth (from early-entry first offenders to serious offenders and high-end youth) and their families in various contexts (Alexander, Sexton, & Robbins, 2002; Alexander & Sexton, 2002). In juvenile justice settings FFT is often a prevention program, where it is effective in diverting the trajectory of at-risk adolescents away from the mental health and justice systems (Alexander, Robbins, & Sexton, 2000). Across settings a wide range of interventionists including social workers, psychologists, counselors, and marriage and family therapists use FFT. In each of these settings FFT illustrates the successful integration of science and practice in a way that has important social consequences and very personal human impact. Because of its widespread application, it also represents a unique movement in the history of psychological interventions in which the strong theory and science of a powerful intervention model are being systematically moved into the world of clinical practice.

The FFT Story

Behind any clinical model's accomplishments, statistics, and publications there is a story. In the case of FFT it is a story of a set of ideas that grew over time into a comprehensive approach to working with some of the most difficult youth in the juvenile justice, mental health, and family services systems.

I am a family psychologist and family therapist with a passion for helping adolescents and families in their struggles. I have always had a keen interest in what helps people change, how a mere conversation between a client/family and a helper/therapist can, when done well, change the course of a person's life. But I had never found a model that was theoretically sound enough and sufficiently evidence-based to give me confidence that it could consistently produce change.

This discontent changed more than a decade ago when I learned about and then became actively involved in helping develop and disseminate the clinical model of FFT. FFT met my criteria: It was theoretically sound, research-based, and clinically powerful. The unique feature of the model, though, is its openness. FFT is built on core principles and clinical practices that are, by intention, open to new and evolving ideas in the field. The progenitor of FFT, James Alexander, believed that to remain relevant, clinical models must be dynamic, evolutionary, and ever-growing while at the same time retaining their core, their identity, and their center. This is a remarkable vision, particularly in light of our field's history of clinical models with great potential dying because the charismatic progenitor was unwilling or unable to pass the approach on to a new generation and incorporate new ideas. As long as this principle remains, FFT will be alive, clinically relevant, and an active and practiced model rather than a chapter in a book on the history of our field.

It is in the spirit of continuing the dynamic evolutional growth of FFT that I offer this book, built on a decade of scholarship and clinical practice. It presents a comprehensive and systematic guide to FFT's clinical practice, service delivery system, theoretical principles, and mechanism of therapeutic change. Section I provides an important historical context for the origins of FFT, its role in the evidence-based practice movement, the clinical problems addressed by FFT, and its theoretical and scientific foundations. Section II is devoted to clinical applications, and Section III describes the way in which FFT is used in clinical and real community-based practice settings, the outcomes of these efforts, and the clinical supervision process needed to make this dissemination successful. Because the goal here is to create a book that is consistent with the core principles of FFT—clinically relevant, theoretically sound, and scientifically based—each chapter contains a systematic discussion of the topic, the theoretical perspective that serves as the foundation, and illustrative clinical examples that demonstrate the manner in which these principles are applied in FFT.

At its heart, the Functional Family Therapy model—and this book—is about adolescents with behavior problems, their families, and their honest struggle to find a way to resolve the problems in their life. FFT seeks to acknowledge, appreciate, respect, and understand these clients individually, working *with* them instead of *on* them. For clinicians who are pasionate about engaging with these clients in one of the most intimate journeys possible, that of therapeutic change, FFT is a map, a guide, a set of well-grounded principles from which to make the contingent and immediate decisions that must occur in successful therapy.

I have been privileged to work with the model's progenitor, James Alexander, and a group of curious and dedicated developers (Parsons, Barton, Waldron, Robbins, and Turner, among others) who have helped articulate the clinical model, develop the dissemination process, study FFT in real clinical settings, and build ongoing service delivery systems. While the model will change again in the future, its strength remains practitioners who realize that a successful model helps translate theory into the "room" of clinical practice.

An Introduction to Functional Family Therapy: A Dynamic Evolution of Theory, Science, and Practice

G OOD CLINICAL WORK GOES WELL beyond empathetic listening and providing a safe and trusting relationship. The task involves assessing the internal life of the client (or, more complexly, a family or couple) while at the same time guiding and facilitating a relationally based interpersonal and relational journey through various stages on the way to a change that makes a difference in the client's life. No wonder clinicians seek clinical practice models to serve as a guide.

We have a long history of such models in family and couples therapy. Charismatic pioneers found effective, principle-based ways of working in relational systems; researchers have identified models that work, mechanisms of change, and core factors of successful clinical work. Now we have a new generation of evidence-based models—approaches that are theoretically based and clinically relevant while at the same time likely to produce good outcomes for clients.

Functional Family Therapy is a clinical model for helping adolescents with behavior difficulties and their families. At a theoretical level, FFT describes clinical change as a process moving a particular sequence of phases with the aim of helping the family achieve their goals effectively and efficiently. On the clinical level, FFT provides an effective map to follow, offering practical interventions and skills tailored to a particular client's situation. Most importantly, it is a way to organize information to understand the client context in order to engage with a client and act in the most purposeful, effective, and efficient manner, helping the client move in a positive and developmentally appropriate way forward through life's challenges. On a scientific level, FFT seems to consistently produce positive results with diverse clients in a variety of treatment and cultural settings.

This book is the story of the clinical model of FFT. This is not a history book detailing the many contributions of the developers of FFT or a treatise on the various stages of theoretical developments. Instead, it is a book about the clinical model—an inside description and understanding of a complex family therapy treatment model that has proved to produce good outcomes with some of the most difficult adolescent behavioral problems, a model that has emerged through a remarkable evolution over the last 35 years. It is a "change model" in its broad sense, at the level of principles that guide the therapy, supervision, dissemination, and training. In addition, there are specific "in the room" ways of working that have also become fine-tuned over the years of delivering, teaching, and implementing FFT. It is also the story of a dynamic and "evolving" model. Clearly FFT has its basics—those have been part of each of the 30 or more publications over the last 35 years. What makes it a story of evolution is that the articulations of these basics have grown to accommodate and assimilate new ideas, particularly ideas about the recursive and relational nature of what goes on "between the people" in therapy. Thus, the story is one where the articulations change and the model grows with new ideas, new people, new insights from clinical practice, supervision, research, and knowledge of the changing theoretical world around the FFT clinical model. The current FFT model is one that is based on the core principles developed early on, built on the process and clinical experience, to become more integrative into current theory and "real life" experiences in delivering the model at a therapist, supervisor, or organizational level.

This section of the book contains three chapters aimed at introducing FFT and the context within which it was developed and works: the behavioral problems of adolescents. Chapter 1 reviews the wide-ranging and complex clinical problems of adolescents, and the changing landscape of clinical models intended to help this set of clients. Within that story lies the evolution of FFT from a simple idea to a set of principles and now to a comprehensive model of practice that speaks to real-world clinical issues. The model that emerged is one that is client-centered, process-focused, and specific yet clinically flexible and adaptable. This is a critical context for understanding FFT for FFT is designed to address the primary risk and protective factors that impact youth and families.

Chapter 2 examines the theoretical foundations of FFT: the conceptual assumptions regarding the client, roles in therapy, and the focus of therapeutic attention and change. These principles form the foundation of clinical decision making in FFT therapy. Chapter 3 sets forth the clinical change model, describing the principles and structure of FFT as it unfolds in the room between therapist and family. Section II is built on this theoretical background and brings a more detailed discussion of each phase of FFT with real clinical examples used to illustrate the way FFT "thinks," the way it "works," and the "process" it takes.

1

The Evolution of Functional Family Therapy: From Traditional Theory to Evidence-Based Practice

The story of Functional Family Therapy (FFT) is a story not unlike that of an adolescent with troubles or a provider looking for solutions—it is a story of evolution and change, challenges and successes. It is the story of a clinical model that has now been extensively used in multiple contexts (rural and urban) with diverse clients, with a range of adolescent problem behaviors, in a number of organizational contexts, by thousands of practitioners all trained and supervised in this model. That database of clinical experiences has helped the practice of FFT evolve. The theoretical principles have taken on clinically relevant meanings, real clinical challenges have been tested and examined, and the change mechanisms of the FFT model have been appropriately revised and refined. It is this circular interaction of theoretical development and real clinical practice that has pushed FFT to become a strong clinical model in the last decade. The clinical application of FFT is the topic of this book.

Like many theoretical models, FFT began within its own small context (University of Utah) organized around its progenitor (James F. Alexander). The richness of the academic context that was created in Utah drew a generation of students who learned about FFT and a smaller group who along with other professionals (like myself) made contributions to the FFT approach in different ways. We all shared Jim's passion for helping kids, and we were all dedicated to finding out what works. Over the last decade FFT has been systematically implemented in clinics, mental health systems with diverse clients, and a variety of other service delivery contexts. Thousands of social workers, psychologists, family therapists, and behavior specialists have been trained to do FFT, actively supervised, and clinically monitored. Therapists, family members, and policy makers have found that when implemented well, with tools to aid in ongoing quality improvement, FFT can replicate research results in real-life clinical settings.

The Dynamic Evolution of FFT

Like any good idea, FFT was influenced by a number of different people and different perspectives, assimilated and incorporated new views and perspectives as they emerged, and changed in its articulation as more was learned from the research and from the clinical treatment room.

Initially developed by James Alexander and Bruce Parsons in the late 1960s, FFT was first applied to youth in juvenile justice contexts, and it focused on one of the critical issues of this population: engagement in the treatment process. Alexander and Parsons's interest was to find a way to work with kids whom no one else knew how to help. Jim was a young professor with strong roots in a family systemic perspective dedicated to accountability, research, and model articulation. Bruce, a graduate student, was a creative therapist and insightful observer. They went into the task with the core of an idea—motivation and engagement as a central goal in treatment. Albeit a seemingly obvious point from our perspective today, at the time it was a novel idea. Their work resulted in the initial version of the FFT clinical model that focused on a two-phase process of therapy (engagement and client motivation) and education (specific behavioral interventions).

Origins

The first major articulation of the core principles of FFT was Bruce Parsons (Alexander & Parsons, 1973, 1982). Later built on by Cole Barton and Jim Alexander (1976, 1980), FFT was included as one of the "second generation" of family therapy models in the historic *Handbook of Family Therapy* (Gurman & Kniskern, 1981). Cole, one of Jim's students, brought a unique way of looking at the relational connections between people that went beyond the prevailing view at the time, which focused on structure. Combining Cole's view with Alexander's dynamic theoretical background, this work was groundbreaking because it introduced a theory of relational functions to describe the role of individual psychological process in the systematic patterns and relationship among family members. At about the same time, Jim and Bruce published the first and only other FFT book. In 1988, Jim developed the anatomy of intervention model (AIM), which advanced the field by systematically dividing treatment into phasic goals that were matched with specific therapist behaviors. This was a significant step in that, for the first time, the role of the therapist was linked to specific goals and tasks across the different phases of the treatment model.

It is also important to note the important contribution of the simultaneous research processes that went on at the University of Utah during the early days of FFT. Alexander, in partnership with Charles Turner, a master biostatistician, formed a team that was able to meld theory genius with the statistical modeling needed to map the change process. The results were a number of important scientific findings regarding the role of gender, the way in which therapist structure and support functioned, the impact of reframing (Robbins, Alexander, & Turner, 2000), and the role of family negativity in the early stages of therapy, among other things. There is no doubt that the merger of this type of clinically based science and the theory made it possible for FFT to become established and grow as a viable treatment model.

Expansion

In the last decade FFT moved out of the Utah lab and became integrated into real-life clinical practice. This spurred the further articulation and growth of the clinical model. The phase task analysis, or PTA (Alexander, Pugh, Parsons, & Sexton, 2000; Sexton & Alexander, 2000), separates therapy into three phases, with intervention and assessment activities associated with real-life clinical strategies for accomplishing phase change goals. This development drew on the constant and complex relational process that plays out between psychologist and family in treatment. PTA helped further define FFT as a systemic, relational, and individualized clinical process most visible in intense in-the-room dynamics, moving forward through specific and predictable phases in which treatment outcomes built on one another, ultimately resulting in positive behavior change. This helped FFT move from a traditional stage-based model (assessment, treatment), like that used in the medical model approaches to psychotherapy, to a dynamic and more clinically focused approach in which the "around-and-around" interactions of the therapist and family are the therapeutic opportunities through which to pursue the change mechanisms. These clinically based applications of FFT with real families in real clinical settings are the topic of Section II.

The dissemination and transportation of FFT into a myriad of community settings brought an opportunity to test the clinical model in a variety of real-life settings. The clinical and theoretical lessons learned were significant, and solidified the relational process as the core of FFT. It is one thing to practice a model in a small sheltered academic setting and quite another to bring a model to real community settings with actual therapists working with a wide variety of youths. Current work in FFT is still fueled by actual clinical practice, which has been invaluable in further articulating and developing the model's clinical breadth. The products of these developments are the subjects of Section III.

Systematization

The most recent evolutionary change in FFT involved the development of systematic protocols for the clinical model and supervision, the creation of a systematic training plan, and the development of a computer-based quality improvement and case planning system. Placing a real-time feedback tool in the hands of clinicians provided a built-in means to capture outcome research and process-based research data that help improve the clinical application of the model. These efforts resulted in:

- a manual-driven approach to clinical supervision (Sexton, Alexander, & Gilman 2004)
- a computer-based quality assurance and improvement system to promote transportation to community settings (Sexton, 2008; Sexton & Alexander, 2000, 2004, 2006)
- a systematic approach to training and community dissemination (Sexton & Alexander, 2004)
- training organizations (FTT Associates, FFT inc.) and university research (Center for Adolescent and Family Studies, Indiana University; Oregon Research Institute, University of Oregon) and university-based training institutes (Functional Family Training Institute, Indiana University).
- The development of a quality improvement system brought research and practice together in real clinical practice settings. The outcomes of this development are discussed in detail in the final section of the book.

FFT as a Response to the Complexity of Adolescents With Behavior Problems

FFT is specifically designed to help youths who have acting-out behavior problems, and their families. Such problems are most often termed "conduct disorders." Conduct disorders include a broad range of externalizing behaviors that encompass school problems, drug use and abuse, violence, delinquency, and oppositional defiant behavior, among others (Kazdin, 2003). If we consider these behaviors as problems just for the individual adolescent, we seriously underestimate their scope. These problem behaviors significantly impact the individual's family, peers, school, and community. The child welfare, juvenile justice, and mental health systems within the community each apply their own labels to similar problem behaviors; which label sticks often depends on which system(s) the kid encounters first.

Range, Rate, and Prevalence of Behavior Problems

Estimates indicate that approximately 10% of American youth ages 10–17 will become involved in the juvenile justice system, with a lasting impact on their lives. For example, while the majority of such youths are placed on probation or sanctioned with fines, about one-fourth will enter some form of residential placement in a given year, and many of these youths will remain incarcerated into their early adult years. Considering those with a history in the juvenile justice system, 12% of formerly incarcerated youth will obtain a high school diploma or GED by young adulthood, compared with a national average of 14%. Only about 30% were either in school or had a job after their release. Delinquent youths are seven times more likely to have a history of unemployment and welfare dependence as an adult, and they are more likely to divorce and bear children outside of marriage. Ultimately, these youths are much more likely to be rearrested at some point in their lives (Chung et al., 2005).

The social costs of untreated mental health concerns and juvenile delinquent behavior are likewise considerable. Estimates of the overall costs of crime in the United States range from $300 billion to over $1 trillion (Andersen, 1995; Miller, Cohen, & Rossman, 1993). Considering that adolescents are estimated to be responsible for approximately 20–30% of all crime, the total costs of juvenile crime are estimated to be between $60 billion and $300 billion annually (Greenwood, Model, Rydell, & Chiesa, 1996). These losses are more than economic, however, as violence-related illness, disability, and premature death pose considerable burdens to families and communities (Dahlberg, 1998; Miller et al., 1993).

Juvenile delinquency is not just a social phenomenon. A sizable majority—from 60% to 85%—of youths classified as delinquents are diagnosed with at least one form of psychopathology, and frequently more than one mental health disorder (Teplin, Abram, McClelland, Dulcan, & Mericle, 2002; Robertson, Robertson, Dill, Husain, & Undesser, 2004; Abrantes, Hoffman, & Anton, 2005; Dixon, Howie, & Starling, 2004; Domalanta, Risser, Roberts, & Hale Risser, 2003; Pliszka et al., 2003). Different studies provide different measures of the prevalence of specific disorders, partially as a function of the composition (for example, the gender distribution) of the sample studied (Dixon et al., 2004; Teplin et al., 2002; Rosenblatt, Rosenblatt, & Biggs, 2000).

Measurements may be inconsistent, but the underlying issues are not. Externalizing disorders, substance abuse, and affective disorders are consistently the categories identified in the current literature describing juvenile delinquents. For example, a recent study of a large sample of ethnically diverse juvenile detainees in an urban juvenile justice system found that:

- More than 40% of both genders met criteria for either conduct disorder or oppositional defiant disorder
- Around 50% of both genders met criteria for substance abuse
- More than 20% of males and 25% of females met criteria for an affective disorder (Teplin et al., 2002)

In other samples, rates of conduct disorder were as high as 60% in both genders and up to 91% in females (Pliszka et al., 2000; Dixon et al., 2004). To make these statistics yet more worrisome, conduct disorder has been found to be likely comorbid with substance abuse disorders (Abrantes et al., 2005; Pliszka, Sherman, Barrow, & Irick, 2000), and depression and anxiety (Neighbors, Kempton, & Forehand, 1992; Dixon et al., 2004; Ulzen & Hamilton, 1998). Furthermore, polysubstance abuse (Neighbors et al., 1992) and a diagnosis of major depression (Domalanta et al., 2003) often accompany the mental health symptoms of adolescents. In fact, Neighbors et al. (1992) found that juvenile delinquents using multiple substances had more symptoms of and were more likely to be diagnosed with conduct disorder, depression, and anxiety than nonusers. Domalanta et al. (2003) found that of more than 1,000 juvenile detainees, those who met criteria for major depression had a slightly higher likelihood (3%) of multiple substance abuse than those with milder depressive disorder.

Youth tagged as "behavior problems" actually represent a complex clinical profile; the adolescent in question may be experiencing a wide range of developmental, emotional, and behavioral problems. Kazdin (2004) differentiates diagnosable psychiatric disorders (such as anxiety, mood, substance-related, adjustment, and disruptive behavior disorders) from risky or problem behaviors (such as substance use, school suspension, and truancy) and delinquency (unlawful acts). In addition, it may be difficult to identify behavior disorders because to some extent they overlap with behaviors that occur within normal adolescent development—for example, fighting, withdrawing, disagreeing, and standing up to authority figures.

Youth who come into contact with FFT are typically labeled as having one of the following three types of problems:

- *Externalizing disorders.* These are the classic acting-out behaviors aimed at other people and features of the environment. They include oppositional, hyperactive, aggressive, and antisocial behaviors. There are numerous categories of psychiatric diagnosis, including attention-deficit and disruptive disorders, that encompass such behaviors. Adolescents referred to the mental health and juvenile justice systems are most likely to exhibit externalizing behavior disorders, which is not surprising, as their acting out impacts others.

- *Internalizing disorders.* These are problems experienced internally; they include clinical symptoms of anxiety, withdrawal, and depression. Because these adolescents are not acting out, they are less likely to be referred for treatment. Their distress may not attract the attention of their families, schools, and communities.

- *Other behaviors.* Behaviors that do not fit the criteria for either externalizing or internalizing behavior problems may nonetheless put youth at risk of entering the mental health or juvenile justice system or incurring future psychiatric problems. Truancy, vandalism, stealing, drug use, bullying, and running away from home are just some of these problem behaviors (DiClemente, Hansen, & Ponton, 1996). For this reason, Kazdin (2003) suggested that published prevalence rates for youth behavior problems may significantly underestimate the size of the problem.

Risk and Protective Factors

The staggering breadth of the statistics described above can make it difficult to know where to begin to understand the problems faced by youth and their families. An adolescent referred to a treatment program such as FFT can be considered a "package" that includes biological, relational, family, socioeconomic, and environmental factors. This "package" also involves a range of problem behaviors, with a number of people involved. Thus, regardless of whether the behavior of the adolescent is diagnosable or whether it fits the developmental trajectory of early or late onset (Loeber, 1991), parents, other family members, peers, school, and environment are all important in understanding the adolescent and the nature of his or her problems.

The notion of risk and protective factors is a useful way to understand the "package" of problem behaviors and other difficulties that accompany adolescents and their families into the therapy room (Hawkins, Catalano, & Miller, 1992; Kumpfer

& Turner, 1990; Sale, Sambrano, Springer, & Turner, 2003). *Risk factors* are those elements that increase the likelihood that an adolescent may experience drug, mental health, and/or conduct problems. *Protective factors* are those elements that both decrease the likelihood of youth drug use and behavior problems and simultaneously mitigate the impact of risk factors. Risk and protective factors contribute independently in different ways toward understanding the severity of clients' problems. That is, risk factors are not simply the opposite of protective factors; they have to be evaluated as potentially independent contributions to outcomes. Specific aspects of family life and family relationships have strong and consistent connections to the initiation, exacerbation, and relapse of adolescent behavior problems.

A number of organizations use the risk and protective factor model to assess causes of problem behavior and to help determine which individual, family, community, and treatment model elements may stand in the way of youth getting help and being successful at behavior change. For example, the Youth Violence Prevention Council suggests that the presence of single risk factors does not cause antisocial behavior; instead, multiple risk factors combine to contribute to and shape behavior over the course of development. A confluence of risk factors and protective factors determine the likelihood of risk-taking behavior. Table 1.1 is a summary of the risk and protective factors published by the Centers for Disease Control and Prevention (1995), the National Institute for Drug Abuse (1992), and the Youth Violence Prevention Council (U.S. Public Health Service, 2001).

The risk and protective factors approach is becoming useful in the treatment of adolescent behavior problems. As will become apparent over the next chapters, the reasons why a child uses drugs, doesn't go to school, or fights are difficult to understand and may, in the end, be too complex to decipher. Approaching behavior as the outcome of risk and protective factors provides an awareness that all youths can be seen as having some risk factors inside themselves, in their family relational systems, and in their communities that may put them at risk for having serious problems, while other features may protect them from these risk factors and mitigate their impact. What is particularly appealing about this approach is that it can be directly translated to the mechanisms of treatment. These are the working parts of a treatment model that actually leads to lower probability of behavior problems in the future.

The Search for Answers: The Rise of Evidence-Based Practice

It should come as no surprise that great attention has been directed toward identifying ways to successfully help youth with a range of problems and risk factors. However, finding ways to work with adolescents in ways that engage them, help them change, and foster a continuation of that change is difficult. Most mental health and psychologically trained professionals turn to the various theory-based, client-centered, behavioral, or cognitive treatment approaches found in counseling and psychotherapy textbooks. On paper these models may seem interesting. However, a therapist who is in the room with an angry adolescent and his or her family soon

TABLE 1.1   Individual, Family, and Community Risk and Protective Factors for Youth With Serious Behavior Problems

---

Youth and Parent Individual Risk Factors

- History of violent victimization
- ADHD or learning disorders
- History of early aggressive behavior
- Involvement with drugs, alcohol, or tobacco
- Low IQ
- Poor behavior control
- Deficits in social, cognitive, or information-processing abilities
- High emotional distress
- History of treatment for emotional problems
- Antisocial beliefs and attitudes
- Exposure to violence and conflict in the family

Family Risk and Protective Factors

Risk factors

- A lack of mutual attachment and nurturing by parents
- Ineffective parenting
- A chaotic home environment
- Lack of significant relationship with a caring adult
- A caregiver who abuses drugs, commits crimes, or suffers from mental disorder

Protective factors

- A strong bond between children and family
- Parental involvement in a child's life
- Supportive parenting that meets financial, emotional, cognitive, and social needs
- Clear limits and consistent enforcement of discipline

Peer/School Risk Factors

- Association with delinquent peers
- Involvement with gangs
- Social rejection by peers
- Lack of involvement in conventional activities
- Poor academic performance
- Low commitment to school and school failure

Community Risk Factors

- Diminished economic opportunities
- High concentration of poor residents
- High level of transience
- High level of family disruption
- Low level of community participation
- Socially disorganized neighborhoods

TABLE 1.1 (*Continued*) Individual, Family, and Community Risk and Protective Factors for Youth With Serious Behavior Problems

Treatment Program Protective Factors

- Enhance family bonding and relationships through parent supportiveness of children, parent-child communication, and parental involvement
- Develop, discuss, and enforce family policies on substance abuse
- Parental monitoring and supervision focus to include rule setting; techniques for monitoring activities; praise for appropriate behavior; and moderate, consistent discipline that enforces defined family rules
- Brief family-focused interventions

realizes that these broad and at times outdated principles alone cannot help the therapist know how to handle the myriad of potentially therapeutic events that take place in that room. In response to the reality of practice, most clinicians developed, on their own, more integrative and eclectic approaches based on their clinical judgment and their own beliefs about what and who should change, and what helps the process of change. Similarly, in communities faced with rising crime rates among juveniles, county, city, and state administrators often have no idea that there are different types of psychological treatments available, that all are not the same, and that not all are intended for use with delinquent and acting-out youth.

More recently, the search for ways to help troubled youth has followed medical science, education, and other domains into the evidence-based practice (EBP) movement (Sexton et al., 2007). Anyone who works with youth and families is likely to share the central tenet of EBP: Every individual has the right to the most effective services available at the time (Schoenwald, Henggeler, Brondino, & Rowland, 2000). EBP provides the scientific evidence of effectiveness that clinicians, communities, and families need in order to choose intervention and prevention programs with reasonable confidence that positive outcomes will result.

Canada and Great Britain led the way in establishing the use of research-based evidence as a criterion for medical and clinical decision making with the aim of improving the effectiveness of treatment. Evidence-based models of prevention and treatment have arguably affected the area of adolescent behavior disorders more than any other field. While the evidence for the effectiveness of adolescent treatment programs has come from the clinical research in family psychology and prevention science, demand for that evidence has come not just from affected communities and families but also from the broader public, which is beginning to understand that adolescent behavior problems are a behavioral health epidemic. The Columbine school shootings in 1999 led the Centers for Disease Control and Prevention and the Office of Juvenile Justice and Delinquency Prevention to seek out programs with results that local communities can reliably replicate.

Even earlier, in 1996, the Center for the Study and Prevention of Violence (CSPV) had begun to evaluate programs for the first time. The CSPV convened a panel of experts who established research-based criteria for identifying effective programs. This became known as the Blueprints for Violence Prevention project (Elliott, 1998).

The original criteria for a Blueprints program were modest at best and included such questions as:

- Is the program coherent and identifiable?
- Does the program work?
- Are its effects lasting?
- Can the program be replicated in local communities?

A later, more rigorous application of these criteria identified what came to be known as Blueprints Model Programs.

By 2004, the Blueprints staff had reviewed more than 1,000 programs designed to prevent or treat adolescent behavior problems that might eventually lead to violent acting out. Only 11 (about 1%) of this huge pool of prevention and intervention programs met the Blueprints criteria. While these 11 programs vary widely in their approach, all have demonstrated results. There are seven prevention programs (Midwestern Prevention Project, Big Brothers Big Sisters of America, LifeSkills Training, Olweus Bullying Prevention Program, Promoting Alternative Thinking Strategies, The Incredible Years, and Project Towards No Drug Abuse) and four treatment-based programs (Functional Family Therapy, Nurse-Family Partnership, Multidimensional Treatment Foster Care, and Multisystemic Therapy). Two of the treatment programs are family-based counseling treatment programs (Multisystemic Therapy, FFT).

Meanwhile, in 2000, the surgeon general of the United States joined the search for answers, identifying a number of EBP programs that demonstrated successful outcomes with lasting effects in youth of a variety of ages and cultures. *Youth Violence: A Report of the Surgeon General* (2001) identified *model programs* as those that demonstrated rigorous experimental or quasi-experimental research design; significant deterrent effects on violence or serious delinquency, or deterrence of any risk factor for violence with a large effect; replication with demonstrated effects; and sustainability of effects. *Promising programs* have similar criteria, but the risk factor prevention effect is smaller, and the program need not demonstrate both replication and sustainability. Five programs for violence prevention were identified as meeting the criteria for a model program: Functional Family Therapy, Multisystemic Therapy, Multidimensional Treatment Foster Care, Prenatal and Infancy Home Visitation by Nurses, and Seattle Social Development Project. Of these five programs, three are directed at an adolescent population (FFT, Multisystemic Therapy, and Multidimensional Treatment Foster Care).

Evidence-based practices are dramatically and fundamentally transforming the treatment of adolescent behavior problems. EBP changes the way practitioners work and the way communities select programs to help families and youth. These changes impact the methods of clinical training, the accountability of program developers and interventions, and the outcomes that can be expected from such programs, creating a "virtuous cycle" of research and practice. EBP changes the focus from practitioner-centered treatment to a treatment model for clinical decision making. In the former, the therapist determines the best way to understand and intervene with the client. In the latter, it is the clinical model that sets the agenda, the treatment goals, and the mechanism of successful treatment. The advantage of a model-driven process of treatment is that clients and families can have confidence that they will get treatments that will work when done the correct way. In addition, clinical decisions are not left to the values and individual beliefs of the therapist, but instead can come from science, broad trends in the field, and shared clinical judgment.

"But where is the client?" one might ask. In fact, this question points to a common argument against evidence-based practice. Throughout this book, it will become apparent that EBP can have a very specific model focus and yet at the same time be open and responsive to the individual needs, desires, and functions of the youth and family. This is one of the seeming contradictions about EBP programs such as FFT—they are both client-responsive and clinically focused.

The Gap Between Research and Practice

While EBP is strongly supported in the profession, its emergence as a standard for care does arouse controversy as well. Some view evidence-based practice as a challenge to established, traditional treatment modalities. Others view EBPs as simple curricular approaches and refer pejoratively to "paint-by-numbers" guidelines that allegedly do not respond to client and community needs. While others may agree that EBP programs are necessary, they question the definition of "evidence-based" and the criteria for such programs. Science is still not universally accepted as a basis of human service practice decision making. In addition, the EBP movement finds itself in contention with other movements that also aim to help adolescents at risk and in trouble (the systems-of-care movement). The struggle is really over the use and place of research in clinical practice and of clinical practice within the research domain. Pinsof and Wynne (2000) noted that despite a century of systematic research, "couple and family therapy research has had little if any, impact on the practice of most couple and family therapists."

The struggle to integrate research into practice is understandable. Although practice and research share a common goal, they differ in approach and scope. Practice is a process; it involves constant decision making on very particular issues. The practitioner has to decide how to fit treatments to settings or clients, how to bring his or her own strengths and personality into the clinical work, and how to respond to the client. Thus the practitioner's primary concern is *idiographic*: applying specific interventions for an individual client in a specific situation. The researcher's focus is *nomothetic*: seeking general trends that apply to many situations. Research questions do not always have to do with practice; instead, they may relate to the latest advance in the field and the drive for future discoveries (Gurman et al., 1986). Unfortunately, these differences in focus have contributed to the gap that divides research and practice.

These important challenges to the evidence-based practice movement have been addressed in the literature. For example, in a recent paper, Westen, Novotny, and Thompson-Brenner (2004) provided a cogent review of these issues. They suggest that empirical support is not a decision made between a limited set of "lists" but instead requires many types of evidence as a way to account for the complexities of clients, therapists, and treatment settings. More recently, Kazdin (2008) argued that the field may be better served by a more complex approach to treatments and the research that is used to support them. He distinguished between evidence-based *practices*, which are broadly based on research, and evidence-based *treatments*, which are specific modes with specific outcomes and change mechanisms. Kazdin suggested that more attention needed to be paid to understanding the moderators and mediators of treatment interventions. In light of this growing debate, the American Psychological Association charged a task force to study evidence-based treatments and to develop a policy statement on evidence-based practices (APA Task Force, 2006). The task force suggested that research evidence should be part of clinical decision-making processes, in which clinicians integrate findings from research with other factors such as client characteristics, context, and clinical judgment to determine treatment decisions.

Clinical practitioners often encounter these issues in the form of the "art versus science" debate. One side of the debate sees clinical practice as an art and believes in basing clinical decision making on the practitioner's experience and intuition. The other side, which includes practitioners faced with the demand for accountability, argues for basing clinical practice on science and questions the primacy of clinical judgment (Dawes, 1994). This debate has resulted in a huge, well-documented gap between research and practice (for a more complete discussion, see Dawes, 1994; Roth & Fonagy, 1996; Sexton & Whiston, 1996).

Regardless of where one stands in the "art versus science" debate, it seems clear that the complexity of clinical problems demands the help of research to design and implement programs with the highest likelihood of success. The debate seems to have lost sight of the fact that both are necessary, and that every client deserves the best of our research and clinical skills.

In numerous publications and presentations, my colleagues and I have taken a somewhat different approach to this debate. Rather than an "either … or" view, we have taken a "both . . . and," or dialectical, view of research and practice. For us, good practice is both a clinical art and a scientific venture, each in a symbiotic and inevitable relationship with the other. As you will see in the sections of the book that follow, FFT is a science with strong foundations in research to both verify its efficacy and discover new methods of practice. The dissemination of FFT into community settings also carries this hallmark: it uses data to guide practice and promotes FFT therapists as "local scientists." As such, therapists should, as a matter of daily practice, investigate the outcomes of their clinical decisions. In addition, as model developers, we believe that research should be the place to test new hypotheses, integrate new innovations, and study different client and setting variables. In both cases, the work of research feeds back into the practice.

The challenges to EBP do point to a number of critical issues for treatment programs such as FFT. First, the dynamic and clinical nature of the treatment must be retained. FFT needs to remain a clinical intervention where the complexity and ambiguity of relationally based practice is acknowledged and supported. It can't be done as a simple model based on broad and nonspecific principles; instead, it needs to be precise and based on clearly articulated and clinically relevant change mechanisms. Those change mechanisms need to be tested and studied. It also means that FFT must be allowed to grow and evolve as new evidence and knowledge come forward from diverse areas of the profession. Finally, it means that programs like FFT must resist the temptation to become marketable and business-driven to the point where they are disseminated without the clinical complexity with which the model was developed.

What Does It Take to Help?
Lessons From the Research

Functional Family Therapy has the luxury of having come into its own within the rich research and practice context of family therapy and family psychology. The early developers of family therapy were brilliant clinicians and committed researchers. What emerged were a number of family-focused training institutes (e.g., the Philadelphia Child Guidance Clinic) and research labs and programs that sought to find the best mix of both clinical wisdom and scientific clarity. The research has evolved into a rich knowledge base involving complex and innovative research strategies for investigating change processes and clinical outcomes that broadened from simple questions of outcome (whether it works) to examinations of specific applications of marital and family therapy to specific clinical problems in specific settings (what works best in this context). The growth in complexity of outcome research has been accompanied by efforts to identify the change mechanisms that underlie positive clinical outcomes (process research). The result of the last two decades of research is a strong, scientific evidence base for the practice of family therapy in general, and FFT more specifically (Sexton, Alexander, & Mease, 2004).

The primary focus of this book is not a review of the marital and family therapy research. That can be found in a number of exceptional resources (Alexander, Pugh, Parsons, & Sexton, 2000; Sexton & Alexander, 2003, 2004). Instead, the intention is to focus on the lessons from the research that set an important stage for the emergence and the success of FFT. These lessons form the foundation of FFT. For example, we know that in order to help, we need to:

- *Work multisystemically.* Traditional approaches tend to be individually focused; the internal workings of the adolescent clients, their motivations, rational thought, and willpower are the target of change. The traditional therapist's hope is that by impacting these areas, the youths can carry changes out into the myriad of social and relational systems in which they live. The literature on risk and protective factors makes it relatively clear that focus on the youth alone is not an effective place for the primary intervention. Instead, the research literature suggests a multisystemic focus. This means that working with a troubled adolescent means working with the school, the probation and legal system, the community, the extended family, and, as noted below, the core family unit.

Unlike other types of psychological intervention, youth operate in multiple spheres, and effective help must follow suit and operate in these arenas as well.

- **Work with the family as the primary unit of assessment and treatment.** One of the core multisystemic domains in an adolescent's life is the family unit. The literature on risk and protective factors is clear in suggesting that family-based work has the quickest and longest-lasting impact on kids. Family-based interventions consider the core family unit as the best way to understand the immediate factors that contribute to acting-out behavior, the most efficient point of intervention to effect quick changes, and the source of long-term maintenance of behavior changes. Family-based interventions are quickly becoming the treatment of choice for diverse adolescents within the fields of mental health and juvenile justice for a number of reasons. First, family is often a key factor in the prosocial development of youth. Several literature reviews (Henggeler, 1989; Loeber & Dishion, 1983; Loeber & Stouthamer-Loeber, 1986; Snyder & Patterson, 1987) support the contention that family functioning provides an early and sustained impact on family bonding, conduct disorders, school bonding, choice of peers, and subsequent delinquency. Second, the basic premise of family therapy—that an individual's problems cannot be understood in isolation from his or her context—matches well to the ideology and cultural norms of many diverse groups. Third, family therapy has been identified as the intervention of choice for treating a host of adolescent behavioral problems that span racial/ethnic populations (Kazdin, 1987, 1991; Shadish et al., 1993; Weisz, Huey, & Weersing, 1998). Fourth, family therapy (frequently in conjunction with community intervention and network therapy) is often cited as the treatment of choice for the culturally mixed client (Tharp, 1991).

- **Keep troubled adolescents in their communities.** Justice- and mental-health-oriented residential treatment programs, both private and public, have exploded in popularity in the last decade. Their popularity is understandable, given the painful struggle and dismal record of traditional programs available for adolescents with behavior issues. When problems come to the point of intervention, communities and families have often lost patience with the troubled youth—everyone needs a break. Unfortunately, the research evidence suggests that most youths (upward of 75%) who go to residential treatment facilities eventually return to them. This is no surprise, given that—despite the well-intended treatment that takes place within the facilities—youths are socialized within peer groups of other youths with similar difficulties.

- **Use treatments that are both scientifically sound and clinically relevant.** Communities, parents, and treatment providers need to think carefully not only about whether their youths get help but also about what kind of help they get. The complexity of adolescents' clinical problems requires well-defined, focused, comprehensive approaches to clinical treatment, with systematic treatment plans, interventions, and theoretical principles and outcome goals that are designed to address a category of related clinical problems. To be effective, an intervention/treatment model must include a coherent conceptual framework underlying the clinical interventions; specific, core interventions must be described in detail to the extent possible.

- ***Remain open to emerging trends in research and practice.*** The cumulative body of knowledge from research in family psychology is always growing and changing. New findings may clarify practice, change its direction, or forge entirely new paths. All models, including FFT, should remain open to change based on the best emerging theoretical models and research evidence.
- ***Have a clear and clinically based role for implementing the model.*** The research increasingly shows that the treatment program itself is less critical than the way it is put into practice. Successfully translating the model into practice takes *both* the wisdom of good professional practice *and* the guidance of research on clinical intervention. Approaches to intervention must provide clear guidance to the therapist on where to go next and what interventions are the most useful ones to accomplish those goals.
- ***Work in communities,*** not just in treatment laboratories or in academic training settings. There are a lot of research-based treatments. The important question is whether they can be successfully translated to community settings. *Contextual efficacy* is the degree to which a treatment is effective in varying community contexts and with different clients (e.g., of different ethnicities or genders); it helps determine the clinical utility of a treatment program (Sexton, Alexander, & Mease, 2004).

Functional Family Therapy

FFT has incorporated the lessons described above about what it takes to provide effective help to this difficult population. Functional Family Therapy is a systematic, evidence-based, manual-driven, family-based treatment program that has proven successful in treating a wide range of problems affecting youth (including drug use and abuse, conduct disorder, mental health concerns, truancy, and related family problems) and their families in a wide range of contexts, communities, and settings.

FFT can be used with youths of different genders, ethnic backgrounds, cultures, and geographic areas (Alexander & Sexton, 2002). It works in clinical and home settings as well as in justice and mental health settings. FFT is short-term, ranging on average from 8 to 12 sessions for mild cases, with up to 30 hours of direct service for more difficult cases, spread over a 3–6 month period. Interventions target youth populations between the ages of 11 and 18, generally high-risk youths in the child welfare, juvenile justice, mental health, and/or drug treatment systems. These youths tend to have a similar array of mental health and behavioral problems. Their families are complex and reflect the pain and struggle brought on by these problems. FFT actively engages in the family relational process needed to help improve family functioning and reduce adolescent behavioral difficulties.

FFT is composed of both a set of theoretically integrated guiding principles and a clearly defined clinical "map" based on specific within-session process goals linked together in a phasic model. The guiding principles (the focus of the next chapter) provide the parameters for understanding family functioning, the etiology of clinical problems, the driving forces and motivations behind successful change, and the principles for dealing with individual families in a way that fits their unique characteristics.

In the last decade FFT has been implemented across the United States and Europe. A systematic method of training, clinical supervision, and quality assurance procedures has developed for and through this expansion. These procedures mean that FFT is more than just a good idea; it is now an implementable clinical model offering the likelihood of good outcomes where youth, parents, and communities need them most. To date FFT has been used in agencies serving clients who are Chinese American, African American, Dutch, Moroccan, Russian, Turkish, white, Vietnamese, Jamaican, Cuban, and Central American, among others. FFT is also provided consistently in eight different languages.

What Makes FFT Unique?

Today, Functional Family Therapy is among a small group of clinical models that illustrate how diverse perspectives can be accommodated in one approach. FFT is a dialectically integrated model (Sexton & Alexander, 2004, 2005; Sexton, 2009) that is at the same time clinically relevant and evidence-based in a way that speaks to a wide range of practitioners and clients. FFT has adopted both a client focus based in sound clinical experience (aligned with the practitioner's idiographic concern) while at the same time attending to the research, theory, and change mechanisms (aligned with the researcher's nomothetic focus) underlying a range of good therapeutic intervention. Today FFT represents a leading example of the manner in which science, theory, and the wisdom of clinical practice can be applied in clinically responsive ways, and transported to different contexts through systematic training, clinical supervision, and implementation protocols (Alexander & Sexton, 2004; Sexton, Alexander & Robbins, 2000).

Another thing that makes FFT unique is its seeming contradictions. Embodying the "both . . . and" principles of the dialectical approach, FFT embraces both science and practice; it is systematic, manual-based therapy that is also relational, relevant, and client centered. It is simple in its goals and objectives, yet complex in its application with people in real clinical practice.

FFT is built on the principles of good clinical practice (create a therapeutic relationship, be client-centered, etc.) and contains all of what we would today call the common factors of successful therapies. FFT also has unique, model-specific goals and objectives intended to have a clinical impact on adolescents and their families, which will become apparent in the course of this book. Functional Family Therapy uniquely takes a "true" family-based approach that focuses on the multiple domains of client experience (cognition, emotion, and behavior) across the multiple perspectives within a family system (individual, family, and contextual/multisystemic). In order to understand and intervene successfully across these domains, FFT is grounded in *relational context*, meaning that everything that happens in the therapeutic encounter (assessment, intervention, treatment planning, etc.) is done in the "space between people."

FFT is a relational model—the smallest unit of analysis is always at least a dyad, two people in relational interaction. This relational "both . . . and" approach has, I think, allowed us to embrace the dialectic tension inherent in family therapy—that is, the tension between clinical practice, foundational theory (systems, developmental psychopathology, epidemiology, the sociology of culture, etc.), and rigorous science.

Even among family therapy models, FFT is unique. It integrates theory and practice while providing specific direction to the processes that go on between therapist and client. While it has a manual, it is not about blindly following that manual. Instead, it is about a therapist with unique and differentiated strengths using clinical skills to accomplish model-specific goals and objectives. FFT is not a series of "intervention techniques." It is a systematic, theoretically based, clinical model with specific clinical and theoretical principles and a systematic clinical protocol or map that guides therapeutic case and session planning.

The FFT Clinical Model in Practice

To be clinically useful, conceptual principles need to come together to form a map to follow within the complex, emotional, interactive relationships in which FFT takes place. The principles address the questions "How does the client function?" and "What is the nature of change?" The clinical model answers the questions "What actions should I take?" and "When should I take them?" FFT consists of three specific and distinct phases of clinical intervention: engagement and motivation, behavior change, and generalization. The map details therapeutic goals and strategies for each phase of change, and specifies therapist skills that, when used competently, maximize the likelihood of successfully accomplishing these goals. Each phase also has specific and focused intervention components and desired proximal outcomes. This model is the subject of Chapter 3.

Common Factors and Model-Specific Features

From one perspective, FFT is also just good clinical practice, using the common factors or shared components of successful therapeutic work. Common factors in therapy are most often depicted through the work of Jerome Frank (Frank & Frank, 1991; Frank, 1961). He argued that all psychotherapies shared four basic components:

- An emotionally charged confiding relationship with a helping person
- A setting that is judged to be therapeutic, in which the client believes the professional can be trusted to provide help on his or her behalf
- The therapist's offering of a credible rationale or plausible theoretical scheme for understanding the patient's symptoms
- A credible ritual or procedure for addressing the symptoms

Frank and Frank (1991) also asserted that there are six elements common to the rituals and procedures of therapy:

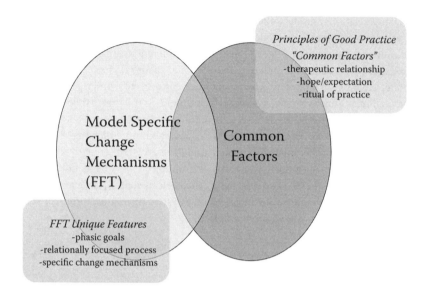

FIGURE 1.1   The relationship between common factors and Functional Family Therapy.

- The therapist combats the client's demoralization and alienation by establishing a strong relationship.
- The therapist links hope for improvement to the process of therapy, which heightens the patient's expectation.
- The therapist offers new learning experiences.
- The client's emotions are aroused and reprocessed.
- The therapist facilitates a sense of mastery or self-efficacy.
- The therapist offers opportunities for the client to practice new behaviors.

Frank believed that specific models and associated techniques were necessary both to provide a coherent structure for treatment that therapists could believe in and also to provide an experience that seemed credible to clients.

FFT provides model-specific expertise to work with at-risk adolescents and their family. The early phases of FFT develop a credible relationship with the aim of enhancing hope and expectation and reduce the negativity between family members. The middle phases provide opportunities for learning to occur as specific behavior changes are addressed. In the generalization phase the client practices the skills and develops a sense of self-efficacy. FFT provides the coherent structure to accomplish these goals.

The Art of FFT

Despite the structure, it is important to note that the FFT model can be successfully applied only when there is an emphasis on the unique therapeutic nature of the interaction between the family and the family psychologist as the primary mechanism of change. As the family tells their story, the family psychologist responds in a personal yet therapeutic way, taking every opportunity to respond purposefully, meeting the phase-based relational goals of the model and moving therapy forward. It only takes one experience in the room with a family to realize that simple models, while critically necessary, can quickly fly to the background amid the sometimes powerful relational and emotional interchanges that go on. Thus, any model that professes to have a simple approach to this complexity is probably not grounded in practice. For any intervention, including FFT, to be successful, it must be conducted in a relational way that is artful, personal, and at the same time systematic and model focused. While this is easy to say in general terms, it is very difficult to describe the particulars. All that really happens in therapy is conversation and interaction between people—clients talk and the therapist responds. But the conversation is more than just words, and it goes well beyond the simple interchanges seen on the surface. In the end it is this conversation that is the potentially powerful element clinically—the interaction between therapist as change agent and the client and family in pain and struggling with a problem they can't overcome alone.

As a conversation, therapy is an ongoing discussion in which clients describe their struggle and experience their related emotion, and that helps change their own situation. Thus, they present to the therapist their definition of the problem—the way they have come to understand, behave, and feel about the behavior(s) of other family members. This is particularly heightened and more emotional with clients involved in the juvenile justice, mental health, and/or child welfare systems. Long contact with these systems is often the reason that the family feels hopeless, very inclined to blame the troubled youth, and highly negative and caustic. They become stuck. In the therapy room, or in the client's living room, therapists encounter the outcomes of this process through the family's anger, seeming unwillingness or inability to be involved in future-oriented solutions, and negative, blaming, and ineffective behavior.

For the therapist, the task is to stay on purpose and respond thoughtfully in a way that will provide the client with the best chance to be willing to engage in family therapy. The task involves meeting the family where it is, with respect, and helping guide them along a path of change in which their values and traditions will guide who they are. The purpose of the therapy is to help them get there in alliance-based, collaborative, and sound ways. The therapist must maintain a personal level of involvement in the in-the-room process while at the same time retaining a clear view of the steps and direction of this particular change process. It is difficult to engage simultaneously in thinking and planning while also being respectfully present and systemically involved.

This is the particular value of FFT, and what makes it unique—it provides a view into understanding and working successfully within these sometimes diffuse and hard-to-understand interchanges of both overt and covert information. In the therapy process, it is the therapist who creates opportunities within the conversation to help move the family forward in small steps, first reducing negativity and blame to build a climate of alliance, involvement, and responsibility in the change process, then helping systematically change interactions within the family. This change comes about through the relational interaction of individualized plans of behavioral change and through the adoption of an empirically sound mechanism of protective factors in families: a prosocial and alliance-based relational climate, prosocial communication, effective communication and problem solving, appropriate monitoring and supervision, and attention to the peer and social systems, such as school, that surround the family.

More than just a set of goals, the FFT clinical protocol model also depicts the systematic and relational nature of therapy. Therapy takes place over time and evolves as a dynamic process. As such, the phases of FFT are based on the following assumptions:

- FFT takes place within a transaction, a set of multilevel processes between family members and the therapist.
- The change process unfolds over time. Each phase involves clinically relevant and scientifically based interventions that are organized in a coherent manner and allow clinicians to maintain focus in the context of considerable family and individual disruption.
- Each phase has specific therapeutic goals unique to that phase, specific related change mechanisms that help accomplish those goals, and specific therapist interventions most likely to activate those change mechanisms.

In the therapy room (or home), many important processes are unfolding, often simultaneously, creating a challenging and emotionally charged atmosphere. The challenge for the therapist is to be responsive to these emerging processes and the emotions they trigger, while being anchored in the FFT principles and navigating by its clinical map. One of the great strengths of FFT is that its clinical protocol is, at its core, the rudder the therapist needs to steer the discussion through the difficult waters of the negative and often blaming relational interchanges among family members in a way that increases the probability that concrete and important positive relational changes can occur.

Conclusions: Helping Troubled Youth

Working with troubled adolescents is very difficult. The clients must bring their world to a stranger in hopes of finding solutions to problems that are not always easy to identify. The therapist must deal with his or her own personal desires and hopes for the families as well as the growing and complex research on adolescent problems, evidence-based treatments, and good treatment. In the end, all of this information needs to be brought together into a relational, personal, and powerful way of working with troubled youths and their families. It takes much more than broad principles and a good heart to be successful. FFT is a model that can help—help the therapist by providing an anchor in the storm of emotion and a map to guide what to do next. For the family, FFT provides a respectful, empowering, and client-centered approach based on the best the field has to offer to help them with the unique, powerful, emotional, and important struggles they face every day.

The next chapter considers the core principles of FFT and the manner in which it uses the existing research to provide effective help to families. It speaks to why FFT works and the process of change in FFT.

2

Core Principles of FFT: Clients, Clinical Problems, and Foundations of Effective Therapeutic Change

Finding effective therapeutic solutions to adolescent behavior and mental problems has been a surprisingly difficult task. In 1990 the U.S. Surgeon General reviewed the then-current practices and concluded that nothing worked! Over the next decade the search for effective programs increasingly focused on evidence-based practice. EBP programs have demonstrated outcomes, clear theoretical approaches, and specified clinical protocols. Still, effective aid for youth with behavior problems remains quite elusive. The clients—the youths and their families—and the problems they experience are much more complex than it may seem from the outside.

The apparently simple tasks of going to school, behaving better, or getting along are embedded in powerful relational systems that make simple, "rational" solutions (such as "just say no") ineffective. So where and with whom can the therapist work to produce effective and lasting change? Finding what works becomes even more complicated given that youths (and thus any solution) exist in multisystemic social, peer, family, community, and cultural contexts that go far beyond the internal workings of the youths themselves (e.g., their criminological thinking). Is there a best technique or special intervention tools? What therapeutic approach, what clinical model is most likely to produce the desired results?

According to Kazdin and Weisz (2003), there are more than 400 different approaches to psychotherapy and hundreds of specific approaches that claim to help troubled adolescents. Clearly, these models have many similarities; however, each comes with a set of core principles, a theory, that asserts why certain therapeutic actions make sense. In some cases the assumptions that serve as the theoretical foundation are covert and not stated; in other cases they are clearly articulated. The question is whether an approach's theoretical principles and clinical tools result in positive outcomes. For youth in the juvenile justice and mental health system, positive outcomes often mean stable behavior in school, stable family relationships, or having no further contact with the police. Because there are many variables that contribute to these specific behaviors, treatment models need a theoretical foundation and core principles that are comprehensive, address known risk factors, guide systematic assessment of the client and the problems, and allow for a comprehensive treatment plan. To be successful, treatment programs need to follow the lessons learned from the research described in Chapter 1.

Functional Family Therapy is a family-based treatment system for the wide range of clinical problems that fall under the umbrella of externalizing adolescent behavior disorders (e.g., conduct problems, violence, drug abuse), along with other family problems (e.g., family conflict, communication) and any additional comorbid internalizing processes. FFT is successful in treating a wide range of problem youth and their families in a wide range of cultural and geographic contexts (Alexander & Sexton, 2002). In addition, as a prevention program, FFT is effective in diverting the trajectory of at-risk adolescents away from entering the mental health and justice systems (Alexander, Robbins, & Sexton, 2000).

FFT is not just a "tool box," a set of techniques and isolated interventions. Instead, it is a comprehensive theoretical model for understanding adolescents and families that is the foundation for systematic, phasic, and relationally focused interventions. The first chapter focused on the broad nature of the clients and a general description of Functional Family Therapy, describing the context in which FFT works and its evolutionary development and offering a brief overview of the model. This chapter focuses on the theoretical core of FFT, outlining its assumptions and theoretical constructs. These core principles serve as a lens for the therapist to look through when trying to understand the client, his or her problems, and the change process so that the youth and the family can get the help they seek now and the skills they will need later to stay out of the juvenile justice and mental health system.

Core Theoretical Principles as the Lens of Clinical Practice

I often work both with students coming into the profession of family psychology and with experienced therapists wanting to add to their clinical skills. I often hear questions such as, "When the mother yells, the youth leaves the room, and the father withdraws, putting his head in his hands, what do I do?" or "They just screamed at each other and no one would listen. What should I do?" What is the best response to these clinicians? Should I explain the theoretical back story, offer a potentially useful clinical strategy, or be honest with them and say, "That depends on the client, where you are in the change process, the events unfolding in the room at the moment, and many other things"?

The dilemma I describe is at the core of the research-versus-practice and evidence-based treatment debates in the field. Successful treatment is not easy—it requires the clinical interventionist to bring a way of comprehensively and systematically thinking about the situation, designing a specific action to take, but one that adds to what has been done before and what might come next. To take on such a complex task, clinicians need more than tools—they need a set of theoretical principles directly linked to clinical techniques. They need a structure that helps them respond in a way that is helpful in the immediate moment and at the same time lays the groundwork for the next steps in treatment. Such a structure allows them to be both creative and purposeful, and all the while client centered.

There is a metaphor that might usefully illustrate the importance of comprehensive and systematic principles in therapy. As someone with bad eyesight, I rely on glasses to help me successfully navigate the world every day. Glasses do two things for me: they bring the world around me into focus, and they help me see things that might otherwise be out of sight, helping me interpret situations, avoid disaster, and move through the world. The lenses bend light rays, redirecting them to bring what I am looking at into focus. Once my glasses are on, I usually forget they are even there and take what they do for granted. The specification of the lens diameter and the pitch and curvature of the lens are critical to my ability to see. I don't think about it, and frankly I don't much care about the research that went into creating my lenses. However, I am aware that without them, I would make different decisions and live in a very different way.

The core principles of FFT, or any model of treatment, are the lens through which the clinician looks to view the client and the situation, and thus they are the core foundation of the clinician's decision making. As a lens does, the principles focus and sharpen certain elements of the view, while letting others fade into the background. Principles help organize the nearly infinite amount of information that comes to a clinician at any given point. The FFT lens helps the clinician bridge the gap between the clinical model needed to guide the family to a better place and the powerful relational and emotional events in the therapy room. The lens shapes what a clinician sees and thus forms the foundation of how he or she works. These principles and theoretical constructs are what make therapy fit the client, the specific problem the client faces, and the clinical and relational process that is the context for treatment. It is only with the help of these principles that the therapist can systematically take advantage of the opportunities that come up within the relational conversations that constitute therapy. In a sense, that is the only way that the therapist can really meet the needs of the youth and the family.

Core Principles of Functional Family Therapy

FFT did not begin as a mature clinical model. It began as an idea based on a set of assumptions about how to think about clients, the nature of their problems, and the context in which they exist. As noted in Chapter 1, FFT evolved in a dynamic way, assimilating and adapting, growing and changing, with input from a variety of model developers. Over time the assumptions of the early FFT model (Alexander & Parsons, 1973) have been added to and elaborated through the work of Barton (Barton & Alexander, 1981), Robbins and Turner (Alexander, Waldron, Newberry, & Liddle, 1988), and finally Sexton and Alexander (Alexander, Pugh, Parsons, & Sexton, 2000, 2002; Sexton & Alexander, 2002b, 2004, 2005; Sexton, 2009). The fundamentals have not changed, but the specification and precision with which they are articulated have increased, and emerging ideas in the field have been assimilated and incorporated. This is what any good clinical model must do to remain relevant—rethink, reinvent, assimilate, and adapt to the changing context around it. The discussion presented here is based on the evolving articulations of FFT principles published over the last 35 years, as represented in the work of my colleagues and myself over the last decade in various journal articles and book chapters.

A Functional Family Systems Approach

At its core, FFT is a family systems approach to therapy. As such, the assumptions of FFT are also not totally unique to it. Family therapy and later family psychology emerged from the work of a group of mathematicians, communication specialists, anthropologists, and psychiatrists who were brilliant theorists, clinicians, and researchers, able to see outside the box—to take a view of families that focused on the space between people rather than what was inside the mind of any one individual. Originally framed as "systems theory," the work later evolved into various theoretical approaches, or core principles, in family therapy. The early pioneers' expansive view, which moved the locus of problems from inside the individual to the context, particularly the family, became a central conceptual basis for all family therapy. The early theoretical concept to describe this groundbreaking step was "family systems." This concept was made operational by examining the role of successive generations within a family or extended family as well as the role of the client's social context in the etiology, maintenance, and treatment of problems (Bowen, 1976; McGoldrick & Gerson, 1985). The family systems view revolutionized treatment approaches for mental health care by changing the focus of assessment and intervention. FFT is rooted in this heritage.

What FFT brought to the field was a series of functional constructs (from which FFT gets its name). Its focus on functionality impacts how an FFT therapist understands a client, conceptualizes how the client acts and reacts in relation to others in their family, and envisions the clinical change process that can guide families to better outcomes. FFT is a comprehensive and holistic package, representing current and past individual, biological, relational, family, socioeconomic, and environmental factors that pose risks and provide protective forces within the family. These factors pattern the way the family organizes itself and interacts around the problem behavior. In essence, it is the way they function, in multiple senses of the word. Thus, the FFT assumption is that problems are behaviors embedded within enduring patterns, rather than just isolated clinical syndromes. Seen in this way, problems serve a function for the client and family: As part of a stable pattern of behaviors, they serve to glue the family relational patterns together (Alexander & Sexton, 2002; Sexton & Alexander, 2002b).

In another sense of the word *function,* FFT's clinical model functions to help the clinician know where to go, when, and how. That is, the model can serve as a map representing the important goals and milestones in successful change and an evidence-based set of change mechanisms to help the therapist accomplish them.

Each of the FFT model developers realized that all theoretical perspectives have potential limitations, and so if a truly functional, clinically relevant treatment model was to be developed, it must go beyond its beginnings. Thus, FFT incorporates theoretical ideas from a broad range of areas into a working, organized whole. This process is like that of any dynamic system, assimilating and adapting to the context around specific choice points. Emerging ideas are not just borrowed; they are tailored to fit the unique nature of FFT and the work with adolescents and their families, further articulating and adding depth and breadth to the core principles of the model.

For example, the pages to come present theoretical principles that are rooted in the work of both structural (Minuchin, 1979) and strategic (Haley, 1976) family therapies. There is a theoretical link to the communications work done by Bateson, Watzlawick, and their colleagues at the Palo Alto Mental Research Institute (Bateson, 1972). More current ideas, such as the work of social constructivism (Gergen, 1995; Mahoney, 1991) and social influence theory (Heppner and Claiborn, 1988), also furthered the understanding of core principles of FFT. These various approaches helped explore the impact of the therapeutic relationship on clients and offer ways to understand the central role of personal meaning and the accompanying cognitive, emotional, and behavioral components. Particularly influential are the ways in which personal meaning contributed to an understanding of the problems that clients experience, and ways in which meaning might be changed in order to help achieve therapy outcomes. From this broad theoretical foundation we have come to better understand, for example, the role of meaning in emotion—the strong emotion of clients in the room is based in various meanings that have origins in each of the systems that impact the clients, and so emotion itself is a social phenomenon. This allows therapists to build treatment interventions that specifically target the meaning components. In addition, the systems view has helped FFT to go beyond the current multigenerational and historical relationships and consider the impact of external systems, however indirect, on the specific content of the client's problem and the social context in which it occurs. Thus, in its recent stages, FFT has moved beyond the notion of a case manager to include more specific and precise ways to help the family translate therapeutic change to their broader social context (Bronfenbrenner, 1986; Henggeler & Borduin, 1990). The idea is that the problem behaviors of adolescents are often maintained by problematic transactions within and across multiple systems of the child's social ecology (Huey, Henggeler, Brondino, & Pickrel, 2000).

As a model, FFT is systemic in nature, functional in orientation, and open and dynamic in its development. The multisystemic layer of the work involves specific

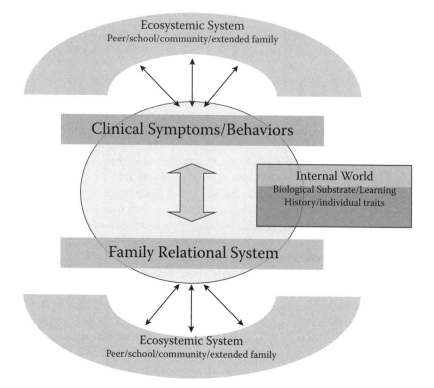

FIGURE 2.1 The multisystemic focus of Functional Family Therapy. Adapted from Alexander and Sexton (2002b).

frameworks for understanding individuals, families, communities, the environment, and prevailing cultural and social factors, and provides ways to understand the interconnectedness of these components. Note in Figure 2.1 that while multisystemic, FFT remains family focused. Families are the core from which to understand the impact of all other components of the system. Individual problems lie embedded in family relationships within the multiple layers of the family system.

Model-Specific Mechanisms

Although FFT has borrowed from other approaches, there are model-specific principles that form the core "personality" of the FFT model. The model-specific principles focus on the various ways to think about the client, the problems they face, and the change process that will help them. Section II examines how these principles work together to build a comprehensive clinical model—a clinical map to follow in the treatment of youth with behavior problems. The goals, interventions, process, and clinical examples represented in those chapters are based on the core principles presented here.

The best way to illustrate the core principles of FFT is through a clinical example. Consider the case of Regina, a 14-year-old girl who was referred to mental health treatment through the juvenile court in her area. Regina had been on probation for the last two years. By all reports, her problems first begin at the transition from elementary school. She initially showed some reluctance to attend school, an increasing incidence of teacher-reported behavior problems at school, trouble with fights and arguments with peers, and increasing conflict with her mother at home. Her mother indicated that Regina had always had trouble reading and had never been very good academically. One year earlier Regina had broken up with a boyfriend and become emotionally distraught. According to reports from her older sister and her mother, Regina seemed to "pull away" at home, becoming increasingly isolated and unresponsive. Over the course of a few months of this pattern Regina revealed to her mother that she was depressed and that she had thoughts of harming herself. Regina's mother told the probation officer and case manager, who referred her for admission to a local psychiatric facility. Regina spent three months in the facility, but immediately upon returning home her troubles began again. This time she was caught smoking marijuana. She was referred to a different juvenile psychiatric inpatient facility, this time one specializing in drug rehabilitation.

The referral came to an FFT therapist who worked at a large community multiservice mental health center. The center provided family therapy services (FFT) as well as psychiatric care, individual therapy, and group and substance abuse treatment interventions. The FFT therapists worked within an FFT treatment team that met frequently to discuss cases. Regina's case manager called the therapist, thinking that it was important for the therapist to know that the mother's former husband had abused her and the children both physically and emotionally; the girls had witnessed much of the physical conflict between their mother and her former husband. The probation officer thought it might be useful for Regina to receive individual therapy, because though she had trouble in several areas she got along with her mother very well.

What does FFT bring to an example like this? Clearly this is a case that fits the criteria for FFT—a behaviorally disordered adolescent with conduct and drug problems. FFT brings a systematic and phasically based change approach. Those steps will be described below.

For the therapist FFT is the best entry and assessment point to understand Regina's struggles. FFT also brings a "multisystemic" and clinically functional way to conceptualize a case like this (see Figure 2.1). For example, the FFT therapist might view the case in this way. The therapist is likely to recommend to the probation officer that family therapy (FFT) could be a very useful first treatment. The therapist would be aware that both Regina and her mother have individual struggles (Regina with depression, her mother with past trauma and abuse) that they bring to their relationship. As the FFT therapist sees it, the relationship they have is an interactional pattern in which Regina's symptomatic behavior is supported and maintained. The drug and conduct problems would be considered the symptoms, and their elimination is the longer-term goal of treatment. The context also presents difficult challenges in terms of Regina's relationship with extended family (including her estranged father), school, and peers. Additional school and academic help seemed warranted. The therapist would also have outcome goals. When FFT is finished, the therapist would look for Regina to attend school more regularly, work more cooperatively with her mother using more relationally focused methods, and find a way to manage her internal struggles with depression with the support and guidance of family. It may also be that following FFT, Regina might benefit from additional mental health care. For example, if psychiatric medication is needed for short-term stabilization, the therapist would work closely with the FFT therapist to integrate that into therapy.

The primary entry point for FFT therapy would be the family relationship. The therapist would work together with Regina and her mother to find a way of jointly engaging in change, developing a shared, family-focused description of the problem and reducing within-family risk factors. In a middle phase, the therapist would help them adopt specific behavioral skills, or competencies, that help the family deal with issues. Then the therapist would help Regina and her mother generalize these skills in an attempt to maintain and support change over time. The ultimate goal is to empower the family to manage problems themselves in the future. In the last phase FFT would turn attention to the interface between the family and the world, helping identify needed community and extrafamily resources that might support the family in a stable way over time.

The specific clinical interventions that might be used with this case will be discussed later. For now, consider how one would need to think about Regina and her mother to even begin to have a chance to engage them in treatment, keep them in treatment, and help them make successful changes that prepare them for their future as agents of their own change. This is a complex case with multiple risk factors; individual, family, and social/environmental problems; and a long history of unsuccessful treatment outcome. How the therapist conceptualizes the case may be as important as the techniques that are used. In fact, the most pressing question here is what lens to use to understand the case in a clinically relevant way to promote successful treatment.

Multisystemic Assessment and Intervention

One of the most apparent features of Regina's case is its complexity. There are a myriad of environmental, social, peer, family, and individual factors that influence the immediate behavioral events and choices made by Regina, her mother, and the people around them. From a distance it is probably easy to see what should happen. Regina should open up when she gets depressed and let her family know how to help. She needs to learn to manage her anger with her peers and overcome her anxiety regarding school. Regina's mother needs to find ways to help her overcome her stuck points with the right balance of structure, monitoring, support, and understanding. The school could help with a reading and academic assessment to identify what special programs might ameliorate her reading difficulties and thus help her become more successful in school. In fact, if these outcomes were to occur, Regina would make significant steps toward being more functional. While these goals seem reasonable and straightforward, they are more complex than they might seem. The difficulty is not in doing these individual tasks but in getting Regina and her mother to break the relational pattern in which they are stuck, redirecting their care and concern to different solutions in a way that is relevant, logical, and helpful to them. In other words, the difficulty is not in the tasks themselves but in the relationship in which those tasks need to be done. It is this relational view that is characteristic of FFT.

The multisystemic perspective maintains that all people are made up of multiple internal systems (physiological, hormonal, neurological, cognitive, emotional, behavioral, etc.) that interact with and form adaptive relationships with multiple external systems (family, neighborhood, school, peers, job, human service agencies, culture, etc.). The components of the systems are dynamic, interconnected, and interdependent—no system can be isolated from other systems, and no system can be reduced solely to its component parts. From this perspective, Regina is not static and isolated, but inexorably linked through complex relational patterns to her family, community, and culture. She is more than just a few behaviors—she is a complex system that extends beyond her as an individual. Regina can't be the sole focus of assessment and intervention, and the drivers, motivators, and functional assessments of her bad behavior cannot be the primary area of interest. If they are, we have fallen into the proverbial trap of missing the forest for the trees.

While Regina has some common adolescent behavior problems, those elements are embedded in a relational and social context that is unique. She is also resilient, having survived abuse, peer troubles, drug use, and depression. Her mother, with her own difficult past, has at the same time successfully provided for her daughter and continued to carry out a productive life herself. Each brings a complex history of events to the table, and for both their relationship is the place where these individual contributions impact each other and their solutions to problems. To get a whole picture of Regina's symptoms, this broader-based lens is needed.

Strength-Based and Resiliency-Driven

When adolescents get caught up in the juvenile justice or mental health system, it becomes easy to focus on the behaviors that caught the eye of police, teachers, or parents and resulted in a referral to FFT. Referral agents focus on those individual behaviors because behavior is their primary concern. However, to provide comprehensive treatment, therapists have to remember that adolescents are more than just behaviors—they're dynamic living systems with strengths and problems based upon interactions between their internal genetic/biological predispositions and their family, community, and school environments. Through research, we are uncovering more and more evidence that all aspects of environment (intrapersonal, family, peer, community, and even society) are important factors in problems that are social in nature, even severe psychiatric disorders. Contexts are important because they promote, limit, and give meaning to the behaviors occurring within them.

One core assumption of FFT is that the elements, processes, and features of the multisystemic context are complex. Each of us finds ways to adapt to and survive difficult situations and tough challenges. This is no different for the clients that come to us for help. Despite bad choices they may have made, all kids and parents have struggled, developed skills, and found ways to develop the basic resources to adapt. Thus, FFT's core belief about youth and their families is that they have an inherent strength and a natural ability to be resilient, and that despite the most difficult of situations, they do their best in the context.

There is a danger to taking a strength-based approach. Many traditional strength-based approaches are so focused on the positive that they see every behavior as good. Problem behaviors are often seen as incidents where "they didn't mean it" or "they were just trying to find their way." Those of us working with adolescents know that many times they, their parents, and the people around them do bad things. The behaviors they bring to therapy are often harmful to others and themselves. While some believe that merely discussing these bad things violates a strength-based approach, from an FFT perspective this is neither respectful, in that it doesn't acknowledge the client's problems and difficulties, nor helpful, in that it limits the way one understands and responds to clients. In FFT terms, in a strength-based approach it is important to see both the client's skills, ability, and resilience and the serious nature of the problems that have brought him or her to therapy. It is critical to focus on both the risk factors and the protective factors. And, as you will see in Section II, it is essential to talk about both the strengths and difficulties in direct and honest ways that describe them and acknowledge their existence without blame and condemnation. Thus a strength-based approach does not mean that one has to turn a blind eye to bad behavior but rather that one should embrace all behaviors in a way that is respectful, accurately descriptive, yet founded in the notion that behind all of them is a noble intention that is based in resilience.

This harks back to the old metaphor of whether the glass is half full or half empty. Many traditional mental health approaches focus on the symptoms—the diagnoses or behaviors for which the client has been referred. Such approaches have been criticized for seeing the family as half empty (examples include labels such as "single parent" and "ADHD," which are considered to be limiting factors). However, while important, a focus on symptoms and maladaptive processes can lead therapists to forget the half-full aspect, the client's strengths and resources. In FFT we work to see the glass as neither half empty nor half full; instead we simply work to see what is in the glass, even if the strengths are initially more difficult to see. Thus, the first important step in understanding problems is to keep all aspects of our clients in the foreground, rather than allowing their problematic behaviors and maladaptive family functioning to emerge as a primary focus. This is nowhere more apparent than in the customary referral process within mental health systems. Usually described are problem behaviors and sometimes associated DSM diagnoses; rarely if ever do we get referrals that also have a specific line item for individual and family strengths and protective factors.

Acknowledging What Individuals Bring to the Table

Just because FFT is a multisystemic family-based approach, it doesn't mean that individuals don't have a part in the emotional climate, the behavioral patterns, and the cognitive attributions that surround family functioning. It is abundantly clear that parents and youth alike make individual contributions to the multisystemic system (Liddle, 1995; Szapocznik et al., 1997). Every individual has a combination of pre-dispositions (e.g., level of intelligence, emotionality, physical ability) that interact with experience (learning histories, culture, role models) as well as various environmentally generated physiological and neurological processes in an emergent process involving cognitive, emotional, and behavioral domains (Sexton & Alexander, 2004). By adolescence, these domains are the cognitive and emotional basis of appraisal and reaction, which are coupled with behavioral response within relational patterns. In turn, these tendencies interact with the environment (parents, other members of the youth's microsystem) on a moment-by-moment basis in which each participant influences (constrains, reinforces, punishes, etc.) the others.

Parents, youth, and siblings, as well as extended family and others involved, bring a rich array of factors to the table. Some of these factors are biological. For example, the biological pressures and predispositions of attention deficit disorder are real and become part of whatever relational system exists in the family. Each family member also brings experience of other relationships. Parents, for example, come to their current family with experiences of growing up in their families of origin. This relational history has formed certain expectations and beliefs about what a family "should" be, how parents "should" act, and how children "should" behave. Some knowledge of these individual histories or expectations (short of a detailed family history) can help us understand the meaning that the parents attribute to events in their current families. But while these experiences are critically important, to be understood successfully they must be seen as indirect influences mediated by the current family relational systems. The therapist must be aware that parents and kids react in their unique ways to events and the behavior of others in part because of what is important to them from the past.

The role of individual contributions goes beyond just historical data. The more direct impact of individual histories, biology, and expectations is on the ways in which family relational patterns develop and are maintained. One of the biggest surprises for me as a family therapist is how an event, such as drug use by an adolescent, can have such different meanings in different families. In one family, drug use by their son or daughter is a behavior that represents a major crisis requiring immediate, massive, and intrusive help. The youth immediately finds himself or herself being assessed by a mental health professional, maybe in a hospital, and often in extensive treatment through individual, group, and/or family therapy. What is curious is that in another family, the very same event, drug use by an adolescent, can result in an entirely different reaction. Here the parents worry, talk with their child, and increase their level of monitoring and supervision. In both situations, both sets of parents acted to help their child, but the difference in the scale of the parental actions is clear. The curious question is why those sets of parents are so different.

We would suggest that what the parents are reacting to goes beyond the youth's behavior and has to do with their own values, beliefs, and standards. These values, beliefs, and standards, and the actions taken, result from what the parents bring to the table. In the example of the first family, it may be that alcohol abuse was a problem that existed in the father's life—an experience that left him particularly sensitive to and attentive to such issues. The point here is that even in a family relational and systemic intervention such as FFT, the history, biology, and environments of the individual parts of the system (e.g., parents and youth) are critical in understanding why certain things are important and others are not in the current relational functioning of the family.

Central Role of the Family

FFT is a family-centered therapeutic approach. Families play a role in how the child develops but an even more important one in the direct functioning of the family and the child every day. Families are the earliest and possibly the dominant context for childhood learning, especially for what relationships mean and how to develop and maintain them. Relational patterns that are initially developed in the family context carry over into new contexts such as schools and peer groups, and often even into adulthood. Unfortunately for many of the adolescents referred to FFT, the only interpersonal strategies supported by the systems they belong to (especially the family) are dysfunctional. Some families model and reinforce the use of drugs or violence to feel in control; others permit children and adolescents to get attention only by coercion. Some adolescents have to join a gang to get a sense of belonging. Dysfunctional patterns carried out of the home into the world end up in problem behaviors that the mental health and juvenile justice systems label according to various clinical syndromes (e.g., oppositional defiant disorder, conduct disorder, drug use and abuse).

The relational patterns, roles, expectancies, and rules (sometimes invisible) that make up a family system are very powerful factors. Minuchin (1967) described family relationship in a structural way—as subsystems with boundaries and a hierarchical relationship among them. The early internationalists (Watzlawick, Weakland, & Fisch, 1974) suggested that the patterns of relational interaction become stable and enduring and even come to define the relationship between people. The FFT lens views family patterns as stable, enduring, and functional. Relational patterns are the stage where the biological and individual contributions of the individuals mix with the more indirect expectations of culture and community. These patterns are where the history, biology, and contextual stressors are felt and noticed, and as such, they provide a point of entry for gaining a better understanding of how the family works and where in the family system to intervene.

Family relational patterns are difficult to grasp. When we look at a family, what we see are behaviors. It may be that we get a sense of the emotional context of the behaviors and a glimpse of the cognitions and beliefs that surround both the emotions and the behaviors. What we tend not to see are the unspoken connections that limit, promote, support, and encourage the behaviors and emotions we observe. The patterns are a bit like a spiderweb. Any single element of the web is connected by numerous smaller, subtle strands to other elements. Pushing on the web means that every part connected through these strands moves, adapts, and adjusts. Small and invisible as they might be, the connecting strands are strong, sticky, and serve to make a unified whole out of the individual parts. Families are much the same. While hard to see, multiple strands of connection link each member to the others in the immediate and extended family. These strands define the relationship—in a sense *are* the relationship. The implication is that moving any one part moves all the others, that if we try to pull one part out there is resistance and pullback from the other parts, and that to understand any part the whole relationship must be considered.

An Umbrella of Community and Culture

The family is embedded in the contexts provided by culture and community. Culture includes the important ceremonies, customs and folkways, beliefs, and behavior patterns that generate the values, emotions, and beliefs that manifest inside the family. For example, every culture has its rituals for important family events (e.g., birth, birthdays, marriages). The rituals of culture come with shared cultural meaning, expectations, and proscribed behaviors. The religious, ethnic, and location-specific values, norms, and behaviors that characterize the culture come to promote certain behaviors, form the basis for telling right from wrong, and indirectly influence the way that individuals and families function. Communities are surely influenced by the culture or cultures that compose them, but communities also have a location-specific culture and a social climate of their own that have an impact on youth and family functioning.

Cultural expectations contribute to patterns of interaction within the family, the ways it expresses emotion and organizes around roles, how the roles generally look and feel, and parenting style (Falicov, 1995). According to Snyder et al. (2002), attributions and assumptions regarding the cultural values and practices of the community may have an impact on participation, engagement, and specific ways of matching treatment to the client's relational system. For example, the socioeconomic composition of the community affects the kind and quality of school, community activities, and community resources to which the family has access. Furthermore, the values of different community cultures foster a climate that may be prone to violence, collaboration, cooperation, or individuality, for example. The values of peer groups in particular play an important role in the functioning of the adolescents that we deal with in FFT. This variety of influences suggests that it is important to respect and understand the potential impact of these different cultures on the clinical problems that are often more in the foreground.

In juvenile justice settings, the disproportionate representation and application of services to youth of ethnic minority status has become one of the most pressing issues facing juvenile populations. For example, although ethnic minority youth accounted for about one-third of the U.S. juvenile population in 1997, they were two-thirds of the juvenile detention and corrections population (Pope, Lovell, & Hsia, 2002; Snyder and Sickmund, 1999). In addition to overrepresentation, reviews of existing juvenile justice research literature reveal that racial and/or ethnic factors influence decision making throughout the juvenile justice process, resulting in the disparate treatment of ethnic minority youth (Pope & Feyerherm, 1991). Youth of color are arrested more, spend more time in detention, and are given longer and more punitive sentences and sanctions. Clearly both the dominant and minority cultures are important contexts in working with any youth and family.

These and other issues of cultural and racial disparity have resulted in a number of important movements in the field. The culturally sensitive treatment (CST) approach makes cultural sensitivity the central guiding principle underlying the development of therapeutic approaches (Bernal & Saéz-Santiago, 2006; Pedersen, 1997). The underlying rationale is that people from one cultural group may require a form of psychotherapy that differs from that found to be effective for another cultural group (Hall, 2001). Culturally adapted treatments (CATs) are defined as any modification to an evidence-based treatment that involves changes in the approach to service delivery, in the nature of the therapeutic relationship, or in components of the treatment itself to accommodate the cultural beliefs, attitudes, and behaviors of the target population (Whaley & Davis, 2007). These movements illustrate the importance of culture in the development, adoption, and acceptance of treatments for adolescents and their families. In addition, these approaches illustrate the work being done to try to understand what role culture should play in the development of treatment models.

Issues of disparity in the justice system and the movements advocating culturally sensitive and adaptive treatments are all part of the world in which FFT operates. We work in mental health and juvenile justice settings that by all accounts create a context that is culturally influenced. An African American youth who comes to FFT for treatment through the justice system comes from a different context than does a white youth. As a treatment program, FFT needs to have a way to understand and respond to these issues. However, the data suggest an even more important question: Is FFT culturally sensitive enough to be able to help youth from different racial and cultural backgrounds? Or, as suggested by the culturally sensitive treatment movement in psychology, do new treatments need to be developed specifically for these youth? This is a question that will remain on the cutting edge of psychological theory and practice for quite some time. Our work suggests that FFT can be adapted to different racial and cultural groups with outcomes that are the same if not better than those of youths from the majority white culture (Sexton, Gilman, & Johnson-Erickson, 2005). Our clinical experience is that FFT has been used in more than 10 different countries and is practiced in more than eight different languages on any given day. This is because FFT takes culture, race, and ethnicity as major issues in each treatment encounter. In Section II, the specific ways in which FFT addresses the issue of culture will be illustrated.

Implications for Helping Youth and Their Families

The multisystemic perspective upon which FFT is founded has a direct impact on what a therapist does when working with a family. The FFT approach considers the individual behavior of the youth as being nested within the family, which is in turn part of a broad community system (Hawkins, Catalano, & Miller, 1992; Robbins, Mayorga, & Szapocznik, 2003; Szapocznik & Kurtines, 1989). Some contextual factors exert a direct influence (e.g., an antisocial peer group), while others are indirect (e.g., poverty). The individual therapist can change some aspects of the multisystemic environment and processes, but not many others (e.g., neighborhood gangs, poverty, culture). The latter must be recognized and the therapist must work with and/or around them in ways that promote positive change in the family and diminish the impact of negative influences as obstacles to positive change. In turn, the treatment plan should prioritize processes that can be changed and systematically address them to initiate and maintain positive change in the adolescent and in the family.

The multisystem perspective also impacts some of the basic clinical decisions made by therapists hoping to help families. There are many choices of points where one might intervene. Some models, particularly those that have a more medical focus, would highlight the individuals within the system. The goal might become working on decision making, overcoming trauma, or dealing with unresolved issues of either the parents or the youth (among many other possibilities). Other models might intervene in the systems around the youth by focusing on peer groups or schools, working with people in those systems to help manage and have a positive impact on the youth. Still other interventionists might want to focus on the community level and improve the youth's environment, acting as a social change agent or intervening in community activities. Each point of intervention has as its central goal changing the youth's behavior. But the choice of where to intervene, and how, is guided by the core constructs that form the foundation of a treatment model. Thus, while there can be much spirited debate on which element of the multisystemic system is "best" to focus on for understanding and treating a youth, it is clear that the assumptions and principles must be articulated and well reasoned.

The multisystemic view illustrated in Figure 2.1 can be applied to Regina and her situation. For the therapist assigned to Regina's case, the lens from which he approaches understanding uses this contextual type of perspective. The lens directs the therapist not to forget the role of peer and school factors as a context. As noted above, both Regina and her mother bring something to the table from their past relationships. For the mother, her previous conflict with her former husband has been a factor in her attempts to avoid anger and make sure that she and Regina get along. This means that at times when she needs to stand firm, she quickly backs off if Regina's initial responses are angry. The result is that they rarely problem-solve and that Regina has few real limits for her behavior. On the other hand, Regina has almost a helpless approach to life, built on her predisposition to depression and actualized in her bimodal anger/withdrawal pattern. School and probation officers, and even other therapists, view her as uninterested, taking no responsibility, and unconcerned, and so they push her to be more responsible, when inside she is already overwhelmed. The lens would also direct the FFT therapists to see Regina's depression, school behaviors, peer issues, and other behavioral problems as symptoms that are now deeply embedded in a relational pattern that functions to keep things the same.

Clinical Problems

In addition to client-focused principles, FFT is founded on a specific set of assumptions and principles regarding the clinical problems youths and families face. Most approaches acknowledge the role that the system plays in the normal everyday functioning of youths and families and in the problems they present in therapy. School, peers, and other environmental factors create certain risk conditions that may make symptomatic behavior more likely. Despite this, most models rely on the field's diagnostic classification systems, which are based upon intrapsychic and individual etiological models of clinical problems (i.e., *Diagnostic and Statistical Manual of Mental Disorders*; American Psychiatric Association, 2000) and the International Classification of Diseases (ICD-10; World Health Organization, 1992). The diagnostic approach helps link observed behaviors with clusters and profiles of youth behaviors, allowing for a diagnostic classification or label. Unfortunately, these labels rarely are associated to the underlying family relational process, though this is necessary to identify appropriate treatment intervention programs. A multisystemic approach is more likely to recognize the complexity of the client in a way that leads to successful treatment choices and successful family-based intervention. Clinical problems of every type are mediated by the family relational systems; thus FFT focuses on the relational patterns that are represented by, and mediate, problem behaviors in adolescents. This focus increases the likelihood of being able to initiate and maintain long-term change because it targets the very patterns that represent the "active ingredients" of alterable risk and protective factors. As a result, long-term change will not depend upon continuing input from the therapist, but instead will be maintained from within the family and through positive relationships with community (i.e., multisystemic) resources.

Figure 2.2 illustrates the multisystemic organization of individual symptoms, individual contributions, risk and protective factors, and core relational patterns that are the primary target of FFT. Using the example, Regina's problems don't end with her behavior difficulties, drug use, or depression. Each must be considered in interaction with other pieces of a broader context, and each element is discussed in the sections that follow.

Risk and Protective Factors

What has emerged from the significant work aimed at understanding youth and their problems is a perspective that addresses risk factors and protective factors. The idea is that regardless of diagnosis, prevalence rates, or other defining characteristics, all youth can be seen as having some factors inside themselves, in their family relational systems, and in their communities that may put them at risk for having serious problems (risk factors), while other factors may actually protect them from these risk factors and mitigate their impact (protective factors). This concept is a useful way to understand the level of problem severity of adolescent behavior difficulties because it provides a comprehensive view of both the potential strengths and weaknesses

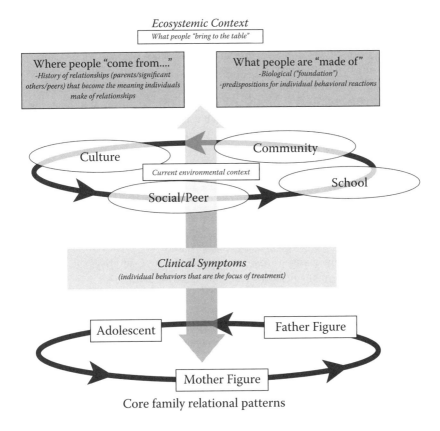

Figure content:

Ecosystemic Context
What people "bring to the table"

Where people "come from...."
-History of relationships (parents/significant others/peers) that become the meaning individuals make of relationships

What people are "made of"
-Biological ("foundation")
-predispositions for individual behavioral reactions

Culture
Community
Current environmental context
Social/Peer
School

Clinical Symptoms
(individual behaviors that are the focus of treatment)

Adolescent
Father Figure
Mother Figure
Core family relational patterns

FIGURE 2.2   Understanding problems within context. Adapted from Alexander & Sexton (2004).

of clients and their social and environmental context (Hawkins & Catalano, 1992; Kumpfer & Turner, 1990; Sale, Sambrano, Springer, & Turner, 2003). This perspective suggests that risk and protective factors exist at numerous levels of the multisystemic system of the youth (community, school, family, individual, and peer). Specific aspects of family life and family relationships have strong and consistent connections to the onset, exacerbation, and relapse of adolescent behavior problems. (See Table 1.1, page 1-8.) As noted in Chapter 1, these risk and protective factors contribute independently and in different ways toward understanding the level of problem severity experienced by clients. That is, risk factors are not simply the opposite of protective factors; they have to be evaluated as potentially independent contributions to outcomes.

What is particularly appealing about this approach is that it can be directly translated to the mechanisms of treatment. Approaching clinical problems in terms of risk and protective factors is useful because it describes patterns of behavior that can be changed rather than applying permanent labels that follow youth and family as they pass through community systems. In addition, it usefully describes probabilities rather than positing causal relationships. According to the Youth Violence Prevention Council, research suggests that the presence of single risk factors does not cause antisocial behavior; instead, multiple risk factors combine to contribute to and shape behavior over the course of development. The confluence of risk factors and protective factors determines the likelihood of risk-taking behavior. Last but not least, the risk and protective factors approach usefully suggests that the source of the family's difficulty is not one individual's problem behavior but the way it is managed within the family system.

It is important to note that risk and protective factors can't be used in a diagnostic way. Each factor may look different for different people in different situations. In addition, a risk factor for one person in one circumstance may not be a risk factor for another person in different circumstances. Risk and protective factors influence and are influenced by the youth's developmental trajectory. Over time, behaviors become more rigid with age; thus by adolescence many attitudes and behaviors are well established and not easily changed. Also, these factors can be additive; the presence of many risk factors or many protective factors can be influential.

Risk factors are typically divided into four domains: individual, family, peer/school, and community. For FFT this approach is helpful because it provides a functional way to consider each of the systems that a youth operates within (individual, family, school, community). It brings into consideration a nomothetic view based on systematic study of large groups of youths. Thus there is some reliability in the factors. At the same time, the concept allows FFT therapists to bring an idiographic perspective to bear on how these factors might function in this unique family in this specific context. These factors can then be used as part of treatment planning, allowing the therapist to go beyond the presenting concerns of the family to the factors that may have a long-term impact on their ability to function well over time and meet future challenges successfully. In each of the chapters in Section II, the specific risk factors addressed by each phase of FFT will be described.

Clinical Problems as Relational Problems

Regardless of an individual's risk and protective factor profile, he or she is not predestined to have behavior problems. The way the family manages the interaction between safeguards (protective factors) and hazards (risk factors) is more determinative. This is because family relational patterns may assimilate both types of factor into self-defeating cycles and harmful emotional reactions, which result in emotionally destructive and often volatile relationships. Many people outside the family (e.g., therapists, juvenile justice and education personnel, developmental researchers, and researchers) can generally see what changes family members should make to improve the balance of factors and solve behavior problems. However, such change, involving seemingly simple and obvious adaptations, tends to be remarkably difficult for the family, the youth, and other helpers. From the FFT perspective, the reason is that the problems of at-risk adolescents and their families are relational in nature. Addressing

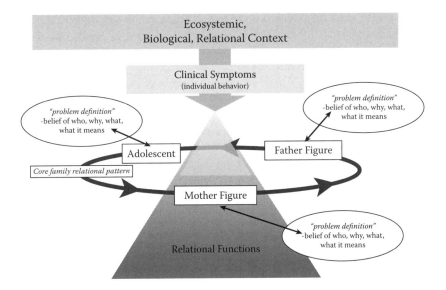

FIGURE 2.3   Context, symptoms, and relational patterns and functions. Adapted from Alexander & Sexton (2004).

the behaviors in isolation, as clinical referrals often do, is not sufficient to create lasting change. Instead, the therapist must find the meaning of individual adolescent and parent behaviors within each family relational system and target clinical interventions to the unique nature of each family.

There are three components to the relational nature of clinical problems: core relational patterns, problem definitions, and relational functions. These features define the relational playing field on which therapeutic process will take place. Figure 2.3 illustrates how these ideas go together. The core relational patterns are the main target of clinical assessment and intervention in FFT.

Central Relational Patterns

FFT adopts the traditional systems approach of a circular model of causes and effects in which the relational processes of the family are the primary unit of analysis. The goal of analysis is to derive meaning by identifying sequential behavioral patterns and the regularities within them (Barton & Alexander, 1981; Sexton & Alexander, 2004, 2005). The resulting pattern recognition is the basis for examining how individual behaviors (e.g., drug abuse, delinquency, acting-out behaviors, etc.) are inescapably tied to the relational process in which they are embedded and from which their meaning is derived.

FFT views individual problems as embedded within a core family relational pattern, which represents the way the family interacts around the problem behavior. As the concepts of systemic relational process show, these patterns become very stable, and once established, they perpetuate the problem behavior. Thus, the primary interest for the therapist is the central relational pattern, rather than each individual problem.

The FFT therapist views individual problems as manifestations of enduring family behavioral patterns. While not as easy to see as individual behaviors, family behavioral patterns are relational sequences of behaviors at the foundation of the family's identity and daily life. Some of these patterns are quite effective in accomplishing necessary tasks (e.g., parenting, communicating, supporting) and may protect the family and its members by preventing certain problem behaviors from arising. Other patterns jeopardize an individual or the family as a whole by putting them at risk for developing externalizing behavior disorders, drug use or abuse, relational conflict, and individual symptoms of mental illness. Relational patterns can be a source from which to identify critical risk/protective patterns as they are maintained and supported by the ways in which relationships function within the family and for individuals.

Stanton and Welsh (in press) provide the most coherent discussion of the role of relational systems in this regard:

> Perhaps the most crucial habit is the ability to picture the system relevant to the person(s) presenting for CFP services. Seeing the system is an abstract process that looks beyond the concrete person(s) or issue(s) to conceptualize the dynamic factors in the context around the presenting person(s) or issue(s). Seeing the system means first considering the whole system, then focusing on the constituent parts. This is important because it counters the tendency toward reductionism by many people educated in European-American arenas that look first at the parts and may miss the whole, including the interaction or connection between parts of the system. A variety of concepts are related to this habit, including the function of boundaries around subsystems and systems and the idea of self-organization in systems (i.e., systems organize and reorganize according to demands).

As noted, it is not always easy to see the relational patterns in a family. Relational patterns are usually the foundation of the descriptions of problems that family members bring to treatment, or what each family member tells the therapist when asked, "What is the problem?" These problem definitions represent each person's natural and normal attempts to understand what is causing the pain and struggle in the family. Each family member attributes causes for the problem, develops emotional reactions to those events, and demonstrates related behavioral responses, all of which are based on the problem definition. The constructed reasons for the problem also justify the emotional reaction to current events. And the behaviors that accompany these emotions and causal attributions can be perceived as fairly logical responses to the problem definition.

All behavior, whether adaptive or maladaptive, is logical and understandable in that it has a reasonable and rational context, fits within the prevailing family and cultural system, and means something specific to each member of the family. That is, behavior doesn't simply happen, nor does it emerge independently from the environment as a function of biological predisposition or conscious rational choice. The ultimate functionality of family behavioral patterns depends on context—the unique elements of the family history, individual temperaments, and environmental situations. The FFT therapist focuses on relational patterns between family members and identifies how the patterns function in the unique context of the family.

Relational Functions: The Glue

It is important to ask why family patterns persist when they are painful and seemingly dysfunctional. This question is the one that early family systems pioneers struggled with: how to account for the stability of problems within family systems. The notion of homeostasis—or the inherent tendency toward stability in all systems—was proposed by early models to account for this seeming paradox. The concept of relational functions is based on this idea but at the same time represents a departure from it. Developed by Barton and Alexander (1981), the concept represents a hypothesis for why problems endure. Relational functions embody the *outcomes* of patterned behavioral sequences, not specific behaviors per se. In other words, relational functions are the largely individual product of relational patterns within families (Sexton & Alexander, 2004). Family systems and many interpersonal theorists have identified two main dimensions of relational functions (or relational space) within the family: relational connection (or interdependency) and relationship hierarchy (Alexander & Parsons 1982; Alexander et al., 2000; Watzlawick et al., 1974; Claiborn & Lichtenberg, 1989). As such, relational functions are the glue that holds seemingly dysfunctional and painful patterns of behavior together over time.

For an individual, the relationship patterns are rarely conscious. Instead, it is the individual's experience of these stable patterns (e.g., how they feel, what they mean, the symbolic interpretation) that is in the foreground. A useful metaphor used by Sexton and Alexander (2004) to describe this is "It is only the fish who don't know it is water in which they swim." As the "fish," we don't see the relational patterns that bind us to others—but we have internal representations and experiences of these patterns that we come to expect and tend to reproduce. These become the standard by which we judge the stability of the relationship.

Relationship patterns vary in terms of interdependence (connectedness) and independence (autonomy) (Sexton & Alexander, 2004). Interdependence and independence are not the polar ends of a continuum, however; both are present to some degree in all relationships, and they are not necessarily associated with feelings of love or the lack of them (Sexton & Alexander, 2004). High degrees of interdependence are psychologically intense and can be experienced not only as a sense of connectedness but also as enmeshment. By contrast, high degrees of independence carry a much lower psychological intensity and can be experienced as autonomy or as distance. Midpointing blends interdependence and independence; this can manifest as an acceptable relational pattern (encouraging healthy development) or as a maladaptive pattern (as in borderline or ambivalent parenting).

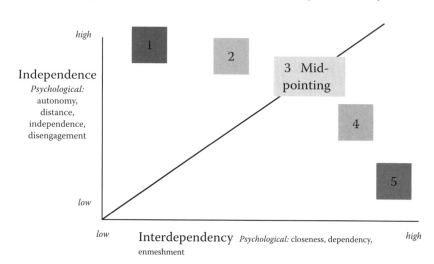

When X relates to Y,
the typical relational pattern (behavioral sequences in the relationship) is characterized by:

FIGURE 2.4   Relatedness as a relational function. Adapted from Alexander & Sexton (2004).

Figure 2.4 illustrates the range of relatedness. A 1 indicates a relational function that has a low degree of interdependence (connection) and a very high degree of independence (autonomy). A 5 indicates a relational function that has a low degree of independence and a very high degree of interdependence. These characterizations are useful in matching clinical interventions with the client's relational system.

Relational hierarchy is a different dimension of relational function. This dimension is a measure of relational control and influence based on structure and resources (Sexton & Alexander, 2004). Hierarchical influence ranges from high to low, with relational symmetry being an experience of balanced structure and shared resources in the relationship. "One-up" and "one-down" relationships ("complementary," according to Haley [1964]) are those in which one member of a relationship has influence through resources (economic, physical power, positional or role power supported by external systems) that are less available to the other member(s) in the relationship. Relational hierarchy is a simple and utilitarian approach to interpersonal relationships that has been adopted in many Western cultures. In contrast, relatedness represents a mutually enhancing approach to control in relationships—that is, people influence each other through affection and/or commitment to the relationship rather than through hierarchical power.

Identifying relational functions in a clinical setting is not easy (Sexton & Alexander, 2004). Informed by the concept of equifinality (proposed by the early communication and systemic theorists [Watzlawick et al., 1974]) and clinical experience, FFT holds that very different family relational patterns (such as constant bickering versus warmth and cooperation) can produce the same relational experience (a high degree

When X relates to Y, the relational pattern (behavioral sequences in the relationship) is characterized by:

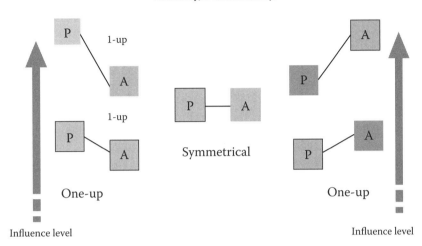

FIGURE 2.5 Hierarchy as a relational function. Adapted from Alexander & Sexton (2004).

of interconnectedness). In contrast, very similar interactional sequences (such as warm communication and intimacy behaviors) can produce entirely different relational outcomes (enhancing contact in one relationship, increasing distance in another relationship). From the FFT perspective, there is nothing wrong with any of these experiences, whether it's having a sense of control, receiving attention, or feeling a sense of belonging. Each has its strengths and its weaknesses. FFT therapists don't attempt to change the core relational functions of the family members. In fact, FFT argues that different cultures, family configurations, and learning histories produce and value a wide range of relational patterns, and each of these patterns can produce both positive and negative behavioral expressions.

Why, then, focus on relational functions? In FFT the issue is how these functions are expressed, and whether those expressions damage others. For example, parents who control their children by violence can learn to control by nurturing and guiding instead. A "one-up" pattern of parenting will be targeted for change if it involves physical and emotional abuse, but generally it will be applauded when it involves authoritative parenting, child-sensitive resource allocation, and nurturing. In other words, when parents are abusive, FFT does not try to change the relational hierarchy, only the patterns of abusive behavior that serve the relational function (one-up). Similarly, FFT does not try to force an enmeshed parent to change the relational function of connectedness; instead, FFT helps that parent replace enabling behaviors with appropriate expressions of affection and care, contingent upon the adolescent's own appropriate behavior (Sexton & Alexander, 2004).

In the sections that follow, relational functions will be illustrated as they fit into clinical treatment and assessment. For now, note that Regina's case illustrates the value of highlighting relational functions as part of a multisystemic picture of the family. In fact, adding relational functions to the protocol helps assessment become more individualized and specific to the way the family functions. One can imagine the common patterns that occur between Regina and her mother: When Regina's mother attempts to guide her, Regina responds in ways that continue the struggle ("You have to . . ." followed by "No, I don't . . .") no matter what the topic: curfew, schoolwork, or, more seriously, what to do about depression.

Over time both Regina and her mother have constructed their own problem definitions. Regina experiences her mother as standing in the way of her independence because she doesn't want to be left alone. The mother believes that Regina has a serious mental health problem that needs care that Regina can't get for herself. The definitions guide the solutions for each. Moreover, by thinking of relational functions rather than the details of what happens, the well-intended yet misguided motives of each individual emerge. For Regina the pattern is characterized by a broad feeling of relational interdependence with her mother. That means that despite the fighting, she has a connected and psychologically intense experience of her relationship with her mother. The mother experiences the pattern similarly; though the experience of "going through it again" with Regina is unpleasant, it also results in a level of interdependence that links them together. The FFT therapist does not seek to change the type of relationship Regina and her mother have (closeness and psychological interdependence) but attempts to help them change how they get there. As this example shows, relational functions can help specify treatment that "matches" the client in this way, making it easier to navigate barriers to change.

Clinical Change: Central Assumptions and Core Mechanisms

What drew me to family therapy were the magical and powerful moments that occurred between a struggling family and a master clinician who seemed to know exactly what to do. For the clinician needing to intervene in an escalating cycle of anger in the therapy room or a probation officer needing to respond to a positive drug screen, principles may not seem particularly helpful. However, in my experience training thousands of therapists in FFT, I have seen that knowing exactly what to do depends on understanding the principles behind the model. In the case of FFT, this involves understanding FFT's clinical change model.

Sexton, Ridley, and Kliner (2004) propose that therapeutic change, as defined in current models of family therapy, occurs in three arenas:

- Therapeutic processes/procedures and consequent change mechanisms inherent in the model brought to therapy by the therapist
- The change experiences of the client as he or she goes through these therapeutic procedures
- The immediate relational interactions between client and therapist through which change takes place

Kazdin (2008) argued that understanding, studying, and thinking systematically about the change mechanisms that form the effective parts of therapy are necessary to improve clinical outcomes. FFT incorporates a systematic change model that features core mechanisms, specific goals, relational outcomes, and long-term changes that result from therapy. The next chapter examines the change process in detail.

To return to our example, the principles of clinical intervention in FFT would suggest that we work with Regina and her whole family in each session. Regina and her mother would bring in their concerns, develop a trusting relationship with the therapist, and view the therapist as credible—someone who can understand both of them and who has the ability to make a difference. A therapy would emerge that followed the phases of the FFT clinical model from engagement and motivation through behavior change and generalization. Yet the content and feel of the relational process, the specific events and discussions, would match the way in which Regina and her mother are as a family.

The multisystemic assessment allows the therapist to identify the core patterns and relational functions of the relationship between Regina and her mother and pinpoint the core relational elements most accessible to change. The outcomes sought would be mutually agreed on by Regina and her mother, yet based on the principles of reducing the risk factors within the family and increasing the protective factors that may help empower the family members in the future. The therapy addresses common risk factors (peers, school, intrafamily conflict) but conceptualizes those factors through the relational pattern unique to Regina and her mother. The goal of therapy would be to enable Regina and her mother to meet challenges they are likely to encounter in the future, taking into account their particular circumstances.

Reflections on Theory and Practice

At heart, FFT is a family systems approach to clinical change. As a model, it was influenced and directed by the thinking prevalent at the time it began, which directed FFT toward a systemic, relational, and integrated way to consider clients, their problems, and clinical change. At the same time, FFT is not just a traditional family systems approach. It has a unique perspective on the role of individuals, the place of culture/ethnicity/race, and the relational and systemic nature of problems, as well as a way of thinking about clients that goes beyond the simple strength-based approach. FFT also brings "functional" principles to therapy in its way of understanding people, therapy, and the principles that make up the model. Finally, FFT is a change model represented by a number of assumptions oriented toward working with rather than working on the youth and family. It helps them solve their current problems while at the same time empowering them to be able to meet future challenges on their own.

As a change model, it possesses seeming contradictions: FFT therapy is model directed and client focused, systematic yet flexible, relationally oriented yet behaviorally specific, family focused yet multisystemic. The specific ways in which those seeming contractions go together into a cohesive, systematic, and comprehensive treatment model are the topic of the next chapter. The question that remains is, what is the change process that occurs when families move from troubled, hurt, and hopeless to empowered, effective, and confident in solving problems?

3

Clinical Change: Systematic Over Time, Relationally Focused, and Client-Centered

Doing therapy with adolescents with behavior problems is much more complicated than just following a set of steps or simply providing conditions that facilitate change in the client. It requires purposeful direction that addresses the serious problems presented and the broader risk factors unique to youth and their families. While the structure of the therapeutic process is in some sense the same for all clients, providing a temporal sequence intended to lead to lasting change for the client, therapy needs to be able to respond to the immediate, unexpected, yet important relational events that happen between family members and with the therapist. These events are the opportunities that, when dealt with correctly, can make therapy go more quickly, be more relevant, and have better outcomes. The challenge is to maintain sufficient structure that the therapist can guide the relational process of therapy process yet provide enough room for clients to express their unique needs, preferences, and struggles. Therein lies one of the paradoxes of good therapy. What makes FFT unique is that it provides a systematic plan—its clinical change model—to help the therapist use the opportunities that occur in the therapy room to help the family overcome the barriers they face in helping the adolescent. This change model is the focus of this chapter.

Systematic Clinical Change: Central Assumptions and Core Mechanisms

One of the fundamental questions in modern psychology revolves around the nature, structure, and essential conditions of therapeutic change. We are only beginning to appreciate the complexity and dynamics of change, even in the simplest of systems, and are far from knowing much about how change works in humans (Mahoney, 1991). The current evidence suggests that humans can change, but that doing so is more difficult than most models of therapy have admitted. What we do know is that change is not a simple and linear growth of small changes that lead to a clearly identified and predictable outcome. Mahoney (1991) suggests that change is "dynamic and punctuated equilibrium in which the phases and forces of change alternate and intermingle with the phases and forces of stabilization." This means that change usually takes the form of two steps forward and one step back. One of the great mysteries of therapy with most youth and families is that despite how much they want things to be different, and regardless of the degree of emotional pain involved in their problems, the change process seems to involve an ongoing tension between moving forward and keeping the dysfunctional system intact. To complicate things further, while there are common processes and mechanisms of change, individuals have unique personal systems, requiring a change process that adapts to the person. The implication is that while there may be good therapies that have widespread appeal, they need to be implemented in an individualized way.

As we've seen, FFT is a systematic change model built on the multiple domains of the therapeutic process, the client experience, and the immediate relational interchanges in the therapy room. There are five theoretically integrated principles that guide the process of change:

- Change is predicated upon alliance-based motivation.
- Behavior change first requires meaning change, primarily through techniques such as reframing.
- Behavioral change goals must be obtainable and appropriate for the family's culture, abilities, and living context.
- Intervention strategies must match the unique characteristics of the family.
- Therapy is based on purposeful, personal, and influential conversations that address the immediate needs of the client.

These principles help the therapist navigate the difficult relational interchanges among family members and cross-currents in the family behavioral patterns and find common ground from which to understand these interactions and spur lasting change.

Case Example

Seth is a 16-year-old son of a single mother, a waitress who works evenings. Seth, who has had increasing difficulties with drug use and following house rules, is often left to babysit his younger brother. Seth was recently placed on probation because he tested positive for marijuana when picked up after hours in violation of his curfew. On the day of his court hearing, his mother left him alone briefly while she went to the store and upon her return caught him using marijuana. During the first minute of the first session, Seth's mother, Anne, says, "I am done with him. I work day and night at my job to provide for him. I go to school mornings to provide us both with a better future, and he is no more thankful than his father was." She pauses for some time, then continues, "There is just too much that has happened between us. I am done. I am asking for him to be sent to detention—maybe a good strong stick will help where I have failed." Seth sits quietly and listens. Finally he just shakes his head, looks down, and says, "Maybe that's right—it isn't going to work out anyway. Why not smoke pot? I have nothing else."

The therapist knows that drug use is a serious problem and that the violence between parent and child needs to stop. She also knows that these behaviors are part of a common pattern embedded into the family through relational functions. For the therapist, it is easy to see that, with some help, Seth and his mother could communicate better and move beyond their hurt feelings so they could face their current challenges. Seth could use his mother's guidance, and she could use his help with the daily routine.

On the other hand, the emotions in the room say otherwise. The therapist is keenly aware of the resignation that fills the room. She realizes that the depth of this hopelessness and helplessness is probably matched by the strength of the emotion with which they fight. She knows she must intervene quickly or Seth and his mother may drop out of treatment or move quickly to the option of residential care.

Therapeutic Change Is the Result of Alliance-Based Motivation

Deciding what to do and in what order is the first goal of the therapist. This is where the core principles of clinical change and the specific phase goals of FFT prove invaluable.

The importance of the therapeutic relationship is one of the most well-known and well-accepted principles of therapeutic practice. Despite its central role, the therapeutic relationship has many different meanings. For Rogers, the therapeutic relationship was support and validation of the client (1957). Henry and Strup (1994) proposed alliance as an active ingredient, providing corrective emotional experience that counters the client's expected relational patterns. Yet others view the relationship as a personal bond, an empathy that provides the necessary conditions for the client to change. Thus the relationship is a complex construct that, to be clinically useful, requires further definition and specification (Sexton & Whiston, 1998).

One of the most useful ways to consider the therapeutic relationship is captured by the construct of alliance. Alliance, also a common construct in psychotherapy literature, is usually defined as therapist and client agreement on the tasks and goals within the context of an emotional bond (Horvath, 2001). The value of alliance in individual, couple, and family therapy is well established; it predicts retention, client satisfaction, and outcome (Pinsof & Catherall, 1984; Quinn, Dotson, & Jordon, 1997). Yet understanding how alliance works in family therapy is difficult, given multiple clients and thus multiple perspectives. For example, Heatherington and Friedlander

(1990) found alliance with the therapist was higher when the therapist was more in charge; therapist directives were interpreted as competency and authority.

As used in FFT, alliance is similar to the notion described by Bordin (1979). This view suggests that alliance is a personal connection with another that is characterized by feelings of being understood and trusting the other. For the alliance to be therapeutic, it also needs to include an agreement on the tasks and goals of the therapeutic work (Bordin, 1967). A therapeutic alliance is more than personal trust. It must also include the experience that, in some way, client and therapist agree on the goals and tasks of working together. To family members, this means that they feel they can trust one another's feelings and struggles and feel as if theirs are equally understood. In addition, they feel that they are all "on the same page" and that the path to change makes sense to each family member. In a therapeutic context, alliance is the relational base for working together (Sexton & Whiston, 1994).

Regardless of the specific issue that is presented, it is not uncommon for the struggle in families to center on goals, the tasks required to accomplish the goals, and the climate or bond between family members. In a working family alliance, the family members agree, at least tacitly, on the problem at hand and the best ways to address it. Alliance is demonstrated by family members working together to the same end, with mutual respect. Those of us who have worked with adolescents and their families know these conditions of alliance are a lot to ask, given the emotion-filled, behaviorally complex interchanges that go on in families. For FFT, this type of alliance is a goal of the early stages.

For therapy to work, another important form of alliance must be present: family-to-therapist alliance. Similar in form to what happens between family members, this type of alliance is demonstrated by mutual understanding, agreement on the goals and task of therapy, and a personal bond based on trust and understanding. This type of alliance occurs when the family and therapist have developed a common view of the problem and developed, again at least tacitly, agreement on how to get to the solutions. In the early stages of FFT, much of this involves perception by the individual family members that the therapist understands their position and what is important to them and possesses the credibility to move the entire family toward common goals. Credibility, or the belief of the family members that therapist has the skills, abilities, and knowledge to help them, is a critical element for therapist-to-family alliance.

If alliance can be developed within the family and between the family and the therapist, one of the outcomes is an elusive yet critical element—motivation. One of the goals of all therapies is to find a way to help the clients help themselves, to take new action, to try new solutions. Webster's dictionary defines *motivation* as "incentive to action." In our work with adolescents, often everyone seems motivated, even in the first session. Listening carefully, however, we frequently find that each person is motivated to a different end—which usually involves having the therapist help them accomplish with their parent or child what they have been unable to do themselves. Clients are often not as motivated to adopt and follow the new directions and suggestions provided by the therapist. Therein lies the difficulty: Incentive or therapeutic motivation is necessary for change—many therapeutic approaches require client motivation as a necessary condition for therapy to begin—yet clients rarely, if ever, come to therapy with that type of incentive. In addition, many perspectives view motivation as a static construct characteristic of the client—a condition that exists within that client. For example, Prochaska (1999) suggests that the focus of early assessment should be assessing the client's readiness or stage of change; this often leads community practitioners to choose or at least prefer clients who they feel are ready for change. It is not uncommon for clients who struggle with motivation to be seen as resistant to change.

When working in community practice, it is more common than not for families referred to FFT to contain one or more members who are not motivated to change; in fact, many initially present as unwilling to even answer the phone or make an appointment. FFT takes a different perspective on the role of motivation: Motivation is the goal of the early stages of therapy rather than a preexisting and necessary condition of therapy. In FFT motivation is an outcome of a set of interchanges in the therapy process in the course of which each family member develops a growing sense of personal responsibility, a shared view of the problem, and a feeling of direction and alliance to solve the current problems and any future problems they will experience. Because motivation is so central to FFT, the science and clinical work of the model developers have produced a number of strategies and techniques to help the motivation to change, leading to high success rates even in populations characterized as "unmotivated." Motivation is then an outcome of good alliance between therapy and the family, and between the family members themselves.

One of the implications of this view of motivation is that FFT therapists don't see clients as resistant to change. Instead we expect them to be wary, hopeless, blaming, and negative in their interactions within the family. By the time they reach us, many painful, hurtful, and difficult things have happened, many of their attempts to change have been unsuccessful, and the problem has persisted and is having a significantly negative impact on their daily life. If successful, FFT embraces the clients' lack of motivation and provides concrete actions that demonstrate that things can be different when an alliance is present. Successful motivation (for positive action) occurs when the therapist helps family members to view the presenting concern as one to which all members contribute but for which none are to be blamed.

Behavior Change Is Based on Meaning Change

For kids who come to FFT there is a very direct need for some specific behavior outcomes; these commonly include reducing violence, stopping drug use or abuse, avoiding police contact, and not hurting others. As a result, the discussion in therapy needs to focus on the specific reasons for referral and has, as a part of the desired long-term outcome, a focus on these specific behaviors. To get there, however, the more immediate focus is on the family relational system, which is also the central focus of therapy—the place where change can happen that will ultimately have an impact on the youth's behavior and on the family's ability to manage daily challenges.

Understanding the mechanisms of successful behavior change is another of the elusive goals of all applied psychology for decades. In pursuit of the core mechanism of behavior change, the field has tried a variety of behavioral approaches, including reinforcement contingencies, psychological awareness, and rational choice. The difficulty is not in finding a solution; after all, the solutions are fairly evident—good parenting happens when parents try something new, good communication skills resolve conflicts. The hard part lies in overcoming the relational struggles between family members that make these simple solutions seem so difficult to implement. A history of blame, negativity, and conflict accompanies the family into the therapy room. For FFT, the focus is on these relationally based aspects of the presenting problem.

One clue to the mystery of why change is so difficult is the personal meanings, strong emotions, and powerful behavioral patterns that have come to surround behavioral problems. Mahoney (1991) suggested that significant psychological changes involve changes in personal meaning, represented in our behavior, cognitions, and emotions. That is, the heart of any type of behavior problem is embedded in our personal theories about the problem, the people involved, and the motives and intentions behind what happened (Mahoney, 1991). Personal theories are forms constructed as meaning is attributed to events (e.g., what it means that your son ran away, what it means when someone yells, what anger means). An important implication of this view is that the meaning of the event does not lie in either the behavior or in the event (the stimulus or the physical behavior) but in the context and personal theories that color and shape the meaning of each individual event in ongoing daily experience. These meanings are not always easily accessible; often they are hidden behind the overt behavior. The meanings form the background to events and can easily be overshadowed by the events themselves.

Over time the meanings of single events coalesce into a common theme, which then is quickly applied to new events. This phenomenon, whereby people tend to distort current experience in order to make it fit memories, expectations, and beliefs about similar events in the past, is called *confirmatory bias* and is well documented in the social psychology literature, yet it has not often been applied to family therapy. Mahoney (1991) quotes a centuries-old explanation of this phenomenon by Francis Bacon:

> The human understanding when it has once adopted an opinion . . . draws on all things else to support and agree with it. And though there be a greater number and weight of instances to be found on the other side, yet these it either neglects or deceives or else, by some distractions sets aside and rejects in order that the authority of its former conclusions may remain inviolate. (p. 97)

So the idea that solutions for individual behavior problems could be found if the client just had the requisite level of motivation is an illusion; there is much more involved. Behavior change must involve changing the meaning around the events that are at issue in therapy. Each person in the family is an active participant in the construction of meaning. Thus the therapist focuses on the meaning ascribed by the individual to an event, rather than the event itself. In FFT this focus is achieved through directly intervening in the initial problem definitions offered by each family member, reattributing the personal theories that comprise the emotion and behavior surrounding the problem.

The Role of Cognition, Emotion, and Behavior

One difficulty in changing behavior and the personal theories and meaning behind it is the inexorable connection between different domains of function (e.g., behavioral, emotional, and cognitive) that characterize the client's problems in therapy. That is, every meaning system involves some degree of attribution (who did it and why), an emotional reaction (how and why this is important to the individual), and a corresponding set of behaviors that are a logical follow-up to the attribution and emotion. In FFT three primary mechanisms help translate the goals of the model into the relational process of therapy: cognitive restructuring, emotional regulation through meaning change, and dissonance.

There is an emotional basis, just as there is a cognitive basis, for the personal realities that are the central components of behavior. Emotions serve as the engine driving the behaviors seen by teachers, other family members, or therapists. Knowing, feeling, and action are inseparable expressions of the same system (Mahoney, 1991). And anyone who has been in a family therapy session knows the powerful emotions that can arise in discussion among family members about issues they must resolve.

As such, emotions play an important role in the change process. The cumulative process research in family therapy has consistently suggested that there are three clusters of intrapersonal processes that are important for success in therapy and that may be facilitated by the development of positive emotions: (1) emotional experiencing, including feeling validated by other family members, a feeling of hope, and a sense of safety; (2) cognitive change, insight, and awareness; and (3) a strong connection with a therapist who is caring, competent, active, and attuned to the family's presenting concerns (Heatherington, Friedlander, & Greenberg, 2005). As is evident from this list, the therapeutic role of positive emotions involves significantly more than just creating a list of inherently "good" emotions to evoke in therapy. In fact, we would suggest that the mere existence of positive emotions is not necessarily therapeutic.

Cognitive Restructuring

FFT did not invent cognitive restructuring; it is one of the common factors of psychotherapy. As applied in FFT, the goal of cognitive restructuring is to change the personal meanings and explanations that each family member comes in with. Until each person stops blaming and focusing the problem on one individual and starts seeing that everybody plays a part and that any solution will require the whole family to work together, they are stuck. Getting them unstuck usually means redefining or expanding each person's definition of the presenting problems. Changing the premise of willful and malicious motivation for behavior to a premise of understandable and benign motivation changes the problem definition. This change elicits from parents more constructive attributions in the future. Consequently, targeting the problem definition and the negative attributions that supported it can both improve family functioning and also facilitate greater engagement in therapy.

Friedlander and Heatherington (1998) did an extensive study of reattribution/cognitive restructuring and found it to be an essential mechanism from many theoretical perspectives. But what is most pertinent here is their discovery of the critical steps that lead to changes in attribution (Coulehan, Friedlander, & Heatherington, 1998). This sequence consists of eliciting individuals' views and attributions about the problem, identifying interpersonal contributions, acknowledging differences of opinion, acknowledging positive attribution in the child, linking problem behaviors with family stressors, and identifying strengths.

In FFT similar steps are taken to systematically reframe the meaning attributed to difficult events, thereby reducing negativity and blame, engaging the family in treatment, and helping them adopt and maintain new behaviors. The new, more family-focused frame, based on a sense of shared responsibility, helps them regulate their emotions and introduces changes in behavioral patterns. Reframing represents a relationally based way of changing the cognitive and perceptual basis for negative interaction, painful emotions, and unsuccessful change strategies. (The next chapter examines reframing in greater depth.)

Behavioral Change Goals Are Obtainable and Appropriate to the Family

Therapists often ask a lot of their clients—rational thought amid powerful relational patterns, for example, or stable and calm emotions and stable patterns of behavior in midprocess. Some therapists try to mold families into someone's version of "healthy," or to reconstruct the "personality" of the family or individuals to fit their models. However noble and desirable the goals, they often relate more to what the therapist thinks is good rather than what is functional and necessary for the family to gain in order to be empowered to meet their current needs and future challenges. By contrast, a core principle of FFT is the pursuit of obtainable outcomes that fit the values, capability, and style of the family and offer significant yet obtainable behavioral changes that will have a lasting impact on the family.

Therapy seems to work best when the content of the specific behavior change is targeted in this way. The specific and obtainable behavior changes we attain in this manner have a major impact on family functioning because they are targeted to alter the underlying risk and protective patterns that support and maintain other problematic behaviors. Thus, what can seem to be small behavior changes in family process (e.g., positive monitoring, providing affirmation of prosocial steps rather than emotionally abusive criticisms) are ones that last because they enhance the relevant protective factors and decrease the important risk factors for the family in treatment. The changes that occur with this approach not only have an immediate effect of changing a specific problem behavior but also have the additional impact of empowering a family to continue applying changes to future circumstances. What currently seems like a small change becomes, over time, a significant and lasting alteration in the functioning of the family that is reflected in major behavioral outcomes such as cessation of drug use and of violence within the family.

Intervention Strategies Match and Respect the Unique Characteristics of the Family

This principle complements the one just discussed. FFT intervention strategies are matched along three dimensions: to phase of therapy, to client, and to sample. The concept of matching represents a way to negotiate the dialectic between the theoretical and clinical goals of a model and the individual differences of a specific client (Sexton & Alexander, 2004).

The FFT change model (discussed in greater depth later in this chapter) is phasic; that is, it has a temporal sequence of phases, each with specific change mechanisms focused on specific outcomes. The principle of *matching to phase* means that the therapist considers the phase of intervention he or she is in with the family, adheres to the goals of that phase, and decides how to respond in the room and where to focus intervention or assessment activities in alignment with those goals.

Matching to client means accomplishing the phase goals in a way that fits with the clients' relational needs, their problem definition, and the family's abilities. It also means respecting and working with the important cultural, racial, religious, and gender-based values of the client.

Matching to sample means that the therapist targets outcomes that fit this particular client and family in this particular situation. The principle of matching to sample reminds therapists to avoid imposing their own value system, social agenda, and interpersonal needs.

The principle of matching to phase, to client, and to sample encourages therapists to view resistance as a situation that occurs when an activity, intervention, or new belief offered in therapy does not feel to one or more family members as if it will be in their best interest.

What allows FFT to match therapy and outcomes to the client is a fundamental attitude of respect. Respect is a central component of therapy in various ways. First, as with all therapies, those doing FFT bring an attitude of respect into the room. Good FFT therapists show clients that they understand, are supportive, and have empathy and regard for each person in the family. Second, FFT views specific presenting clinical problems (clinical syndromes) as relational problems—as specific behaviors embedded within enduring patterns of behaviors that are the foundation for stable and enduring relational functions within family relationships (Alexander & Sexton, 2002; Sexton & Alexander, 2002). Thus, there is no blame for the problem, only a functionally based hypothesis about how the family works. The focus on functions allows FFT to be respectfully supportive yet behaviorally specific. It allows the "problem child" to feel supported—and everyone else as well. It creates a process where the clients feel that they are okay even though the way they previously sought to solve the problem may not have helped. They feel that there is more to do, but that it can be achieved only if they work together; everyone is part of the problem and the solution.

Therapy Is Based on Purposeful Conversations That Address Immediate Needs

Therapy occurs in conversation between the family, the adolescent, and the therapist. Somewhere in this conversation, something happens that changes the meaning of past, current, and future events. Something happens that changes the probability that each member of the family will act differently when problems arise in the future. The question is how conversation can make those changes in the cognitions, behaviors, and emotions of participants happen.

According to Martin (1997), "Psychological therapy is a unique form of conversation that attempts to alter the personal theories about themselves, others, and their own life circumstances that clients have acquired through their participation in other (previous and ongoing) intimate, social and cultural experiences" (p. 3). It is the social interaction—the conversation—between adolescents, family members, and the therapist during the process of therapy that is the source of the change process. To have an impact ultimately on future behavior, this conversation has to leverage interpersonal influence (Jackson & Messick, 1961; Kiesler, 1982; Strong & Claiborn, 1982), be purposeful, and be based in mutual collaboration and respect. FFT fulfills all these criteria.

Through this multilevel conversation, the members of the family and the therapist work hard to change the meaning attached to events, memories, and the behaviors of others. The clients go into sessions with ideas, worries, thoughts, and expectations, all of which need to be acknowledged and responded to by the therapist. FFT therapists go into session with a plan—not for what needs to happen, but for what process goals provide the best help in moving the family to change. The result, over time, is that what were blaming and negative interactions become more alliance focused.

Some narrative-based models of psychotherapy view this reliance on a plan as contradictory to being client-centered. The criticism is that the clients know themselves, know what they need, and likely have the resources with which they can accomplish those goals—that is, the client is the expert. Seen through the FFT lens of respect and collaboration, the notion of who is the expert is a bit more complex. Certainly the client is the expert on his or her life, values, hopes, and dreams. As mentioned earlier, FFT is willing to let people live in the way they wish, without imposing cultural and historical templates of "health" on their lifestyle choices. On the other hand, we are also willing to acknowledge, with no less respect, that clients are not particularly good at getting themselves out of the situations in which they are stuck. In fact, they may be the least able to find unique solutions to problems (Bateson, 1972). Instead, we view the role of the therapist as contributing expertise about how to change the family system. The therapist brings a set of theoretically and scientifically reliable processes and interventions to the family to help guide them out of difficult times. In this way, the therapist is also an expert—a change expert. The respect inherent in the FFT model means that we are willing to respect the clients' struggle, their need for help, and the therapist's role. For FFT, every therapy has two experts that have to collaborate to construct a way of working that fits each, yet follows the most reliable and efficient pathway to positive outcomes.

Case Example

There are a number of fairly straightforward changes that could help Seth and his mother. Changes in communication and problem solving, for example, could strengthen her method of monitoring and supervision and better match it with his desire for independence. However, acquiring those skills is not the first and most pressing challenge facing Seth and his mother—it is motivation. If they don't have sufficiently strong motivation to engage in therapy and work on their own parts of the problem in the belief that it might be successful and help them get through difficult times, there isn't much hope that they will be able to try new behavioral skills.

Thus in the early phases of treatment, the development of alliance-based motivation is the initial goal of FFT treatment and the primary principle shaping therapists' interventions with families. The interactions, conversations, and experiences between the family and the therapist all serve as pathways to enhanced alliance and motivation. The FFT therapist knew that Seth and his mother both needed to feel supported, yet challenged to think again about their problems. Consequently, the FFT therapist did not ask for a detailed history about either the problem or the family relationships, or work immediately to promote problem solving and communication between Seth and his mother. Instead, the therapist looked for risk and possible protective factors, relational patterns, and relational functions in the course of a discussion aimed at alliance building. During this conversation the therapist talked about specific events between Seth and his mother in ways that promote, support, and motivate an alliance between mother and son. Nor would the FFT therapist be likely to refer either person to other services (e.g., drug treatment); rather, the therapist would see the behaviors as embedded in relational patterns and functions.

The issues of meaning were equally important to both Seth and his mother. On a close view, the earliest conversations with the family revealed that there were multiple times when Seth did not seem to hear his mother's intent. From his perspective, his mother was overly controlling, interfered in his social life, and felt overly guilty and consequently tried too hard to change things she didn't need to change. For Seth, his mother was hiding in her schoolwork and abandoning him because he was just "too much trouble to deal with." Because he carried such a negative definition of the intent behind his mother's behavior, it was not surprising that he was quick to react to her by pulling back, becoming defensive, and disagreeing. Why not? For him there was nothing to gain by doing otherwise. Anne had an equally negative view of the intention and meaning of her son's behavior. For her, he was selfish and just "hasn't learned how hard life is." His drug use was an excuse not to take responsibility for his behavior, and his struggle with her indicated that he wanted to be on his own. She thought that if he had to experience how hard things are, he might come to appreciate her efforts. When he misbehaved, it was an opportunity to "teach him a lesson" so that "he will take responsibility for his own actions."

In this example both Seth and Anne were struggling with the meaning part of what goes on in relationship interactions. For each of them, their behavior was consistent with their belief as to who was responsible, the intentions of the other, and what actions were necessary to fix the problem. FFT is particularly well suited to address the issues that Seth and Anne were experiencing. Meaning change is the mechanism through which longer-term behaviors change. As a result, meaning change is also a goal of the initial phase of FFT.

Determining what changes are obtainable, potentially lasting, and relevant is no easy task. The therapist has to consider what specifically to change and how much change to expect in what areas. In Seth's case, the desired changes in peer, school, social, and family domains had to be translated by the FFT therapist into specific relational interchanges between Seth and his mother so that the therapist could have an impact on them. One part of their struggle, drug use, was an area where there could be immediate and yet relevant changes. It might also be an area for them to develop behavioral skills and a way of interacting that would be the basis of how they face problems in the future. Thus, the goals have to be simultaneously powerful and relevant to the family. The challenge for the therapist is to identify a small enough part of one aspect of family interactions to serve as the direct target of FFT in the early phases. If change here is successful, it makes therapeutic change obtainable and at the same time generalizable at a later point in therapy—increasing motivation and engagement.

Matching the treatment to the style, patterns, and individual preferences of the family members helps engender further engagement and motivation. In talking with Seth and his mother, the FFT therapist had a number of clues about how to match short-term and longer-term elements of treatment to them. The therapist adopted a somber tone to acknowledge the heavy nature of the discussion and the hopelessness felt by both. In early portions of the first session, the FFT therapist noticed that whenever details were discussed, the conversation escalated into increasing levels of anger for both. The therapist used this assessment to guide his questions and statements to a more thematic level. The potential outcomes discussed by the therapist also matched the hopelessness both mother and son felt. Rather than paint a rosy picture, the therapist talked about therapy as being very possible but difficult and challenging. In this way the therapist wanted to acknowledge their limited expectations. Each of these small changes helps match the therapy to the client.

In the first FFT session Seth was particularly quiet. He often looked down and away, and he seemed unengaged. The FFT therapist resisted the temptation to respond by finding ways to get to know Seth so that they could later talk about difficult issues. Instead, the therapist repeatedly redirected Seth's attention to the process goals of alliance and meaning change. It is a hallmark of FFT that in the early sessions the discussion tends to be very personal, family focused, direct, and at the same time purposeful. In fact, only by being clear about the goals of the session was the therapist able to focus so specifically on promoting the changes needed early in therapy. Each time Seth ignored the therapist, the clinician reframed Seth's quietness and included him in the discussion. Each time Anne blamed Seth, the therapist focused on ways to use that statement to build a sense of understanding between them. Yet at the same time the therapist solicited and encouraged discussion regarding their experiences of the problem between them. The strong emotion and struggle that emerged during the discussion became opportunities for the therapist to further build alliance.

The Clinical Process of FFT

When family therapy works in the room, it looks and feels like magic. Something occurs that breaks the "spell" afflicting the client or family. But as we have seen, it takes hard, systematic work, based on core principles, to produce this change. The therapist has to find a way through many quandaries: What type of treatment plan to make? What type of session goals to set? What kind of progress is being made? The answers to these questions are contained in the change model followed by the therapist. Diamond, Reis, Diamond, Siqueland, and Isaacs (2002) suggested that treatment models be conceptualized as consisting of "multiple, distinct, yet interrelated tasks" (p. 44). By their definition, treatment is not an event but a multitask, multimechanism process during which the components interact, overlap, and intermingle.

A change model offers therapists answers to the two big questions of practice: what to do and how to do it. The *what* describes the steps that, when taken, will increase the likelihood that youth and their families can make important and lasting changes, empowering them to take on future challenges. Change models are built on a set of principles that are temporally sequenced to be efficient while producing good outcomes, when done well. This change model can be studied and evaluated. But the *how*—putting that model into place—is a different task. Here the therapist translates the principles and process of the model into the relationship he or she develops with the youth and family, taking on the intertwined tasks of ongoing assessment (of the problem, the family, the context) and intervening (accomplishing the phase goals) in a way that matches the client. The therapist takes a therapeutic stance toward that relationship, embodying the model's core principles (respect, alliance, curiosity, and active participation) and exerting relational influence that develops from the credibility gained through performance, not mere promises.

The FFT Change Model

As we've seen, FFT has three phases of clinical intervention, and each phase has specific proximal goals and intervention strategies specifically designed to address these goals. When used by the therapist, it is like a map for change (engagement/ motivation, behavior change, and generalization) that guides the family psychologist through the intense, emotional, and conflicted interactions presented by the family (Sexton & Alexander, 2004). When followed by the family, it is experienced as a seamless process, a conversation that is highly personal, very specific, relevant to the issues of most concern, and something that engages all family members. Each of the three phases of FFT sets distinct goals and therapist skills that, when used competently, maximize the likelihood of successful accomplishment of these goals. Figure 3.1 illustrates the FFT change model.

The engagement and motivation phase has three primary goals:

1. Alliance building
2. Reduction of both negativity and blame
3. Developing a shared family focus to the presenting problems

Engagement and motivation begin with the first contact between the family psychologist and the family, as the psychologist attempts to involve the family in the immediate activities (the session or the initial phone call) such that they become interested in taking part in and accepting of therapy. FFT therapists immediately focus on the process goals of the phase, namely, reducing negativity and blame between family members, while trying to develop a family focus on the problems presented by actively reframing and creating a sense of balanced alliance. The desired outcome of these early interactions is that the family develops motivation by experiencing a sense of support, hopefulness about the possibility of change, and belief that the family psychologist and therapy can help promote those changes. When negativity and blaming are reduced, more positive interactions among family members foster hope. This allows the family psychologist to demonstrate that he or she is competent, capable of guiding the family toward change. An alliance develops where each family member believes that the family psychologist supports and understands his or her position, beliefs, and values.

The primary goal of the *behavior change phase* is to target and change individuals' and families' specific risk behaviors. Changing risk behaviors involves increasing family members' ability to competently perform the myriad of tasks (e.g., communication, parenting, supervision, problem solving, conflict management) that contribute to successful family functioning. Risk factors are reduced as family members develop more protective behaviors for use in these common family tasks. This phase is not curriculum-based, as in many other approaches; rather, the family applies new skills to issues particularly salient to them. The behavior change phase achieves this goal of changing individual and family risk patterns through activities both within and outside the therapy session. These are carefully chosen to match the unique relational functions of the family and to be consistent with what is obtainable by this family in this context.

In the *generalization phase*, the focus of attention turns from extending the changes accomplished around the specific areas targeted in the second phase to other areas of family relationships. In this phase the primary attention is on the family's interface with the external world. Once again, the therapist accomplishes the phase goals by engaging in discussion of issues salient to the family rather than with a

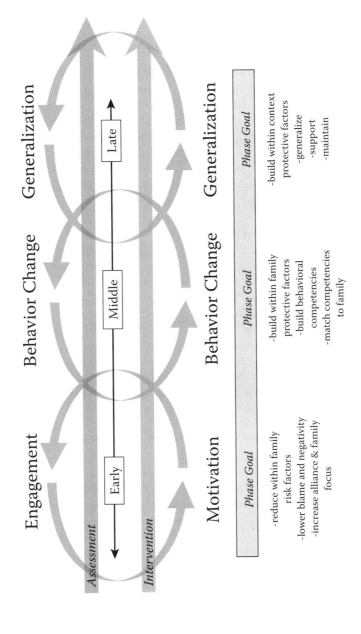

FIGURE 3.1 Phases of FFT. Adapted from Alexander and Sexton (2002); Sexton and Alexander (2002).

predetermined curriculum. Focused and specific relapse prevention strategies are implemented to help preserve the changes that have already been accomplished, and those changes are supported and extended through the incorporation of relevant community resources into treatment.

Assessment, Intervention, and the Family

Much of what the therapist does in FFT is captured by the dual tasks of assessment (understanding the individual, family, and context) and intervention (taking purposeful action to change the relational, emotional, cognitive, or behavioral actions of the family). As we've noted, both of these activities occur within the conversation that is therapy. Throughout the process, the focus of both change and assessment centers on what Mahoney (1991) called the three P's—problem, pattern, and process. Problems are the felt discrepancies between the way things are and the way one wants them to be. Patterns are regularities or recurrent themes in the problems. The clinical process addresses both.

Assessment and intervention are inexorably intertwined. Every action that the therapist takes in each phase has to have therapeutic potential. Similarly, assessment takes place in each phase of the model; it is only the focus of assessment that changes across the phases. The FFT change model simplifies, to the extent possible, the simultaneous tasks of assessing and being respectfully present and systemically directive. In FFT these functions are braided together with the unique nature of the family in a dynamic process of therapeutic interaction.

Unlike other forms of family therapy (e.g., structural family therapy), the FFT clinical model does not have a separate enactment or assessment phase. Instead, assessment is an ongoing process based on clinical observation. The therapist forms hypotheses about how the family's behavior pattern functions and what holds it together, and creates a mental model of the family relational system; as he or she gains more information, he or she revises and adds on to the model. The therapist systematically intervenes in this ongoing process to change it (e.g., by reframing) while simultaneously listening for and observing the family's risk and protective factors.

Clinical observation, when guided by a comprehensive conceptual model, is capable of making a trustworthy and valid assessment of what needs to happen in therapy. From the beginning, as each family member describes how the presenting problem affects him or her, the therapist can identify attributions, emotions, and blaming interactions. These will help the therapist target interventions. The therapist's understanding of how a family functions around problems comes through observing interchanges among family members as they talk about the reasons for their referral, the problems they experience, and the difficulties they have with one another. The therapist develops hypotheses about what each member of the family brings to the table in terms of relational histories, environmental context, and biological substrates (see Chapter 2) and begins to guess the order of events within their history together and the sequence of relational interchanges.

This is not to say that this type of clinical assessment is foolproof. As we saw in Chapter 2, making a valid assessment requires a thorough understanding of behavior, developmental psychopathology, and risk and protective factors. However, the FFT change model directs clinical observations toward those features of the process that allow the therapist to make a valid assessment. By adherence to the FFT model, then, the therapist develops a family-based meaning for behaviors—it is idiographic rather than norm-based and nomothetic. In this way, the practitioner can accomplish the vital goals of engagement and motivation in the early stages of therapy, while also building a comprehensive understanding of individual and family functioning.

Case Example

For Seth and his mother, the early phases of FFT were the most difficult. The level of hurt, pain, and accumulated negativity and blame that had grown over the past 18 months made it very difficult for them to get unstuck from their fairly rigid definitions of each other's intentions and motives. They seemed unable to prevent the pattern of anger from overtaking them. Near the end of the engagement and motivation phase, both Seth and his mother acknowledged that their biggest struggle was to let go of the past and take each problem as it came. Anne needed to come to believe that both she and Seth were part of the problem and the solution. Seth came to see what he had previously experienced as his mother's "giving up" on him as her way of protecting him from future problems by preparing him for life, and as her way of protecting herself by "doing something."

The behavior change and generalization phase also progressed following the model. The therapist worked with Seth and Anne to problem-solve in ways that were behaviorally specific and anticipated problems in carrying out the plan. Through discussion about school problems and future drug use, the therapist found opportunities to make changes consistent with the model. The therapist tried to match each interaction in the therapy room to the way the family worked, what connected them, and what was in line with their resources and values. The result was that Anne was able to keep focused on problem solving in a fairly consistent manner, Seth found a way to follow, and both decreased both their negativity and blame. They were able to use problem solving for a number of different issues (school and drug use) and demonstrated the ability to keep it up in daily life. Seth had two additional encounters with the juvenile justice system during the period of therapy; both were for curfew violations, and he worked with the probation officer to follow through with the additional sanctions he received. Anne never again told Seth he needed to leave. In fact, she helped him get a job at her place of work. Seth began paying a modest amount of rent to his mother each month; that contribution eased his mother's financial difficulties and allowed her to work a little less each week. Seth and Anne worked with the FFT therapist for five months and had 14 conjoint sessions.

Scientific Foundations: Support for This Way of Working

FFT has produced demonstrated positive outcomes in many settings and with thousands of diverse clients. Specifically, these outcomes have centered around three critical issues in the treatment of adolescents and families:

1. The range of behaviors associated with externalizing behavior disorders (e.g., violence, drug use and abuse, and conduct disorders)
2. Effectiveness in engaging youth with difficult problems in therapy and in reducing dropout rates
3. Cost-effectiveness

The research includes both traditional clinical trial and matched control group designs as well as community-based effectiveness studies that overcome many of the criticisms of traditional clinical research by investigating how the therapy works with youths who come from a variety of ethnic and socioeconomic backgrounds and who have multiple problems. It investigates the therapy as it is performed in the home and in community settings by practicing professional therapists with diverse training backgrounds. These studies led the Center for Substance Abuse Prevention and the Office of Juvenile Justice and Delinquency Prevention to identify FFT as a model program for both substance abuse and delinquency prevention (Alvarado, Kendall, Beesley, & Lee-Cavaness, 2000). Similarly, the Center for the Study and Prevention of Violence designated FFT as one of eleven Blueprints programs (Elliott, 1998). And the U.S. Surgeon General's Office identified FFT as one of four intervention programs that deal successfully with violent, acting-out youth. Below we briefly review the scientific evidence for FFT in three areas: dropout rates, behavioral outcomes, and changes in family functioning.

Studies that investigate the dropout rates of FFT as compared to other treatments suggest that FFT is successful in engaging between 78% and 89% of youths in settings where FFT was delivered in community contexts with community-based therapists (Sexton, Ostrom, Bonomo, & Alexander, 2000). By contrast, Kazdin (1997) suggested that only between 25% and 50% of youth who receive other clinical intervention services continue to completion of therapy. In this project, 91.7% of the youth who came to a first appointment completed FFT. Given the historical difficulty in engaging this category of youth, these are certainly impressive outcomes. We consider engagement and retention in therapy as a necessary but not sufficient condition of treatment success, a view held by most in the clinical practice community. Greater engagement leads to greater behavior change.

Specific youth behavioral change via FFT is also well established. The initial study of this method (Alexander & Parsons, 1973; Parsons & Alexander, 1973) followed court-referred delinquent adolescents, 13 to 16 years old. The youth and their families were randomly assigned to FFT, no treatment, or one of two ongoing alternative treatment conditions (client-centered family group therapy or eclectic psychodynamic family therapy). At 6-to-18-month follow-up, the group of 99 youths treated with FFT had a reoffense rate of 26%, compared to 50% for no treatment, 47% for family group therapy, and 73% for psychodynamic family therapy. The study also established that FFT had an impact on communication patterns and frequency of interaction. Particularly notable was that communication for clarification and feedback increased, and negativity and blaming decreased. What was dramatic about this study at the time was its demonstration of the positive effect that family therapy might have on recidivism, a compelling and valuable outcome to achieve with this population of youth.

A later study (Klein, Alexander, & Parsons, 1997) looked at rearrest rates for the siblings of these youth in an attempt to assess the systemic effect of a family therapy model such as FFT. This 2–3-year follow-up study found that siblings in the families that received FFT had only a 20% post-FFT court referral rate, while siblings of adolescents in the other treatment groups had significantly higher recidivism (no treatment, 40%; client-centered family group therapy, 59%; eclectic psychodynamic family therapy, 63%). These dramatic findings demonstrated that FFT had a significantly greater relative (as compared to a reasonable alternative treatment) and absolute (as compared to no treatment) effect on siblings that were not even the primary focus of attention in treatment. They also found that the FFT families had improved their family interactions compared to those who received other treatments. Finally, these researchers made an even more clinically relevant discovery: Improved family processes differentiated families who ultimately experienced a sibling referral from those who did not. This means that therapists can focus on the proximal clinical goal of improved family interaction patterns and be confident that they will have an effect on longer-term behaviors.

Barton, Alexander, Waldron, Turner, and Warburton (1985) conducted a series of three small studies of youth delinquency of different severities. In the first study, FFT was delivered by undergraduate paraprofessionals to a group of "status offenders." These were youth with offenses typically considered lower-level (e g., running away, possession of alcohol, promiscuity, and ungovernableness). The youth were not randomly assigned but instead were referred directly by probation officers. The undergraduate students trained in FFT produced significant reductions in one-year recidivism rates (26% for those in the FFT group as compared to 51% in the juvenile justice jurisdiction as a whole). These results were equivalent to those obtained by senior/graduate-level therapists in earlier studies, giving some insight into the level of training that might be required to successfully reproduce FFT. Once again, changes in the family processes, most notably decreases in family defensiveness, were seen with this sample, just as they were with more senior therapists.

The second study examined reductions in out-of-home placements for neglect, disruptive behavior, or family conflict, a serious problem for child welfare systems. Comparison rates of placement for workers trained in FFT skills found significant decrease in out-of-home placement rates (48% versus 11%). As another comparison, those case workers not trained in FFT retained the initial high rates of placement (49%). While small and preliminary, the study suggests that FFT skills can be used by case managers to prevent costly and emotionally traumatic events such as out-of-home placement of youths in trouble. By itself, preventing such placements makes a positive impact on the developmental trajectory of the youth.

The final study in this series investigated the effectiveness of FFT with serious youth offenders. The researchers worked with a group of youth with multiple felonies, substance use, and considerable within-family violence who had been incarcerated in a state facility for serious offenses. Some of these youth had as many as 20 prior adjudicated offenses. Averaging 30 hours of therapy, the FFT group had a 60% recidivism rate at 16-month follow-up, compared to 93% of comparison youth released to alternative reentry programs (primarily group homes) and an 89% average annual institutional base rate. When the FFT youth did reoffend, on the whole they did so for crimes significantly less serious than the reoffenders in other groups.

Don Gordon and his students in Ohio were the first independent lab to study the outcomes of FFT. In two studies (Gordon, Arbuthnot, Gustafson, & McGreen, 1988; Gordon, 1995) they established that FFT could be replicated outside the Utah setting. The youth were referred to FFT by the court system because of their risk for out-of-home placement. The families in these two studies tended to be of lower socioeconomic status than those in a previous study, which was conducted in a more rural environment. Using a model of FFT that emphasized problem solving and specific behavior change skills, they found FFT to produce much lower rearrest rates both 2 and 5 years after treatment. Compared to juveniles who received regular probation services (n = 27, 67% recidivism rate), clients in the FFT group had significantly reduced recidivism (n = 27, 11% recidivism rate) at 2-year follow-up. In any given 12-month period, the FFT group committed 1.29 offenses and the treatment-as-usual group committed 10.29 offenses. At 5-year follow-up, the same subjects were compared for rates of adult convictions. The group that received FFT had a 9% recidivism rate as adults, while the control group's rate was 41%. These studies not only reaffirmed FFT's robust outcomes but established that it remains effective for a considerable follow-up period. This means that youth can be helped to make a successful transition during the difficult time between late teenage years and youthful adulthood. It also means that therapists and community practice settings can have confidence that FFT will produce lasting results.

In the mid-1990s Hansson (1998) began a series of studies of FFT in Sweden. Youths who had been arrested for a serious offense were randomly assigned to either FFT or a combined treatment involving case managers and individual counseling. In Sweden, juveniles can be arrested and moved into the criminal justice system only after multiple interventions have already been attempted, and so changes in arrest rates are of great interest. At 2-year follow-up, the FFT group had significantly lower rates of recidivism (48% versus 82%). Mothers of the FFT-treated youth showed improvements in a variety of individual symptoms, including depression, anxiety, and somatization. Notably, this was the first study in which FFT was replicated by someone other than the initial model developer, and it was done in another country with a different system of care. The results demonstrate that FFT has a community-based applicability and that the positive outcomes can even occur in other cultural contexts.

Some of the most recent research on FFT (Waldron, Slesnick, Turner, Brody, & Peterson, 2001) involves drug-using youth. The study evaluated competing therapies (CBT, psychoeducational groups, and family therapy) for their overall and cumulative effects for drug use among adolescents. Adolescents receiving FFT or combined showed significant reductions in the percentage of days using marijuana from pretreatment to 4 months following initiation of treatment. These results provide support for the immediate benefit of family therapy for substance-abusing youth and are generally consistent with the family therapy outcome literature for adolescent substance abuse. Adolescent marijuana use in the psychoeducational group therapy condition was not significantly lower than baseline at the 4-month assessment, but it was significantly lower at the 7-month mark. The CBT group showed no significant differences from baseline at any of the follow-up measurement conditions ($t <$ 1.0). These findings provide tentative evidence that family therapy may produce more rapid changes than group therapy (i.e., at 4 months) but that group therapy may provide long-term benefits in reducing substance abuse.

The Washington State FFT Study investigated FFT within the complexities of real clinical settings. Three questions guided the study: Does FFT work in a real clinical setting? What role does therapist adherence to the model play in clinical outcomes? What family risk factors moderate the clinical outcomes of FFT? The study is particularly informative because it identifies the effectiveness of FFT around three important outcomes (recidivism, engagement and dropout, and cost savings to the community) and also tests the training protocol. The project results have been reported by Barnoski (2002b), Sexton and Alexander (2004), and Sexton and Turner (in press) in varying forms and with different subsets of participants.

The project is impressive in its size (38 therapists and 917 families in 14 counties) and in its systemic approach to standardizing treatment (the therapists were trained to use the principles and intervention model according to a common manualized clinical protocol). Therapists and families were diverse and the clinical settings were different.

The youth in the study had serious problems before entering FFT. Of the adolescents in the data set, 85.4% were involved with drugs, and many reported alcohol use or abuse (80.47%) and other mental health or behavioral problems (27%). Most of the participants had committed felony crimes (56.2%), and many had committed misdemeanors (41.5%). Of these, 10.4% had adjudicated weapons crimes, 16.1% had gang involvement, 10.5% had out-of-home placements, 14.1% had run away from home, and 46.3% had dropped out of school. Of these adolescents, 13.1% began their crime history before age 12, 63% did so between the ages of 12 and 14, and 23% started between the ages of 14 and 17. To assess treatment outcomes, total recidivism, felony recidivism, and violent recidivism rates for the families treated by adherent and highly adherent therapists were compared to the control condition recidivism rates.

Figure 3.2 illustrates the outcomes of FFT in this large-scale community project. Holding critical variables constant (e.g., having prior criminal history, age, and family risk as covariates), the findings show that youth with hard-core criminal activity (felonies) receiving FFT had a 31% reduction in criminal behavior (13.2% versus 19.2% recidivism rates). In addition, those in FFT experienced a 43% reduction in violent recidivism (2.5% vs. 4.4%). These differences were also statistically significant $[b = -.51, p < .033]$.

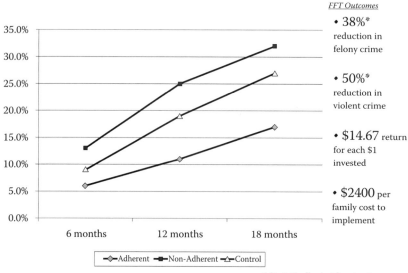

FFT Outcomes

• 38%* reduction in felony crime

• 50%* reduction in violent crime

• $14.67 return for each $1 invested

• $2400 per family cost to implement

* *Statistically significant outcome*

FIGURE 3.2   The outcomes of FFT and the role of therapy-model-specific adherence.

However, these studies also show that the positive effect of FFT is not universal. Those therapists who delivered FFT with high fidelity to the model as it was designed had the outcomes noted above. However, those who did not deliver the model with high fidelity had outcomes that were worse than those of youth who received no therapy at all but instead were merely supervised by their probation officer. This finding has dramatic implications: models of intervention can be successful, but the likelihood of success is strongly affected by the way in which the model is practiced. This would suggest that quality assurance and implementation plans are a critical feature in successful community implementation.

Finally, these outcomes also translate into important cost savings. Table 3.1 illustrates a range of cost benefits of FFT. These data support the cost findings of the Washington Study. As reported by Sexton and Alexander (2004), the total cost of FFT per family was $2,500, a remarkably low figure. Using the algorithm developed by Aos and Barnoski (1997), we found that FFT saved the Washington State system $16,250 per youth in court costs and crime victim costs, not to mention the incalculable emotional pain suffered by family members. This added up to $1,121,250 saved in the first year of the project. Thus for every $1 invested in delivering FFT, more than $14.67 is saved.

Conclusions: Challenges and Opportunities of Systematic, Model-Based Practice

Evidence-based models have great potential to provide therapists with ways of working that will improve outcomes for youth and families. They provide a structure to

TABLE 3.1 Costs and Benefits of FFT Compared to Other Adolescent Treatment Programs

Intervention Program	Percentage Change in Felonies (if Program Implemented)	Cost of the Program	Criminal Justice Costs Avoided	Crime Victim Costs Avoided	Net Gain (Loss), Taxpayer and Crime Victim Costs Avoided	Years Before Cost Is Paid Back
Functional Family Therapy	–27%	$1,900	$7,168	$8,640	$13,908	1
Multisystemic Therapy	–44%	$4,500	$12,381	$13,982	$21,863	2
Juvenile Boot Camp	+16%	N/A	$4,426	+4,998	(–$7,910)	Doesn't pay back
Intensive Supervision (Ohio)	–13%	$5,959	$1,955	$4,159	$2,204	Doesn't pay back
Intensive Supervision (Orange County, CA)	–22%	$4,446	$6,164	$6,961	$8,569	4
Adolescent Diversion Project (Michigan)	–34%	$1,028	$6,055	$7,299	$12,326	1
Treatment Foster Care (Oregon)	–37%	$3,941	$9,757	$11,760	$17,575	2

guide practice that ensures therapists address the relevant risk factors and promote the most useful protective functions while at the same time creating a pathway for change that acknowledges the unique ways individuals and families function in the world every day. This is a level of structure that allows room for—in fact, demands that that therapist bring—a focused, personal, and respectful creativity to understanding and helping families change.

There are also great challenges. It is easy for any model to lose its clinical core and unwittingly become a curriculum-like, check-the-boxes approach. But FFT has clinical and theoretical specificity that allows the therapist to creatively apply the basic structure to a particular family's dynamic relational system. This increases the likelihood of making helpful clinical choices in efficient and client-centered ways. This is not to say that the FFT model never succumbs to the dangers of reductionism that face all models. It can and does get applied in a paint-by-numbers manner where the steps are followed blindly.

FFT also works because it has been allowed to change and adapt over time. Each new articulation feeds back to the previous ones and adds another layer of theoretic and conceptual sophistication to the model. What is exciting is that a number of model developers are working both independently and in collaboration to continue this evolutionary process.

The next section gives close attention to the use and clinical specificity of the FFT model in clinical application. It is intended as a clinically based illustration of how FFT unfolds in real practice settings with clients typical of those for whom FFT is intended. The clinical practice is where the theoretical ideas of the model get translated to the family and put into a unique way of working that fits them. Each of the next three chapters examines one of the phases of FFT. Each chapter describes the phase, its goals and outcomes, and the therapist skills necessary to accomplish those goals. Case examples are used to illustrate the phased nature of FFT.

II

The Practice of FFT

I N EVERYDAY PRACTICE, CLINICIANS DON'T work directly from theoretical models. Instead, they bring their beliefs, knowledge, and therapeutic skills as the basis of clinical decision making and case planning. Every day they are faced with the practical realities of clients who come in angry, emotional, seemingly unmotivated, and negative toward one another, who often lack the resources they need to get unstuck and move forward. Often, what gets said and done in family therapy seems to have a clear content but actually contains so many relational messages as subtext that it is difficult to find common ground, work together, and solve problems. As a therapist, I want to know how to respond to these challenges. I want clinically useful guidance on specific session goals, strategies for managing the conversation to accomplish those goals, and examples of how to do so in a way that matches the family. What I don't get from broad theoretical approaches is a clinical protocol that integrates short-term process goals (such as alliance, emotional regulation, and motivation) and the longer-term behavioral outcomes (improved school behavior, fewer contacts with legal authorities, reduction in behavioral problems). What helps me is a systematic way to plan the process of therapy and to know how to take advantage of immediate opportunities in the therapy room, all of which promote lasting impact.

Many clinicians use a toolbox approach—the idea that they have a wide variety of interventions that they can choose from to fix clients' problems. This approach encourages therapists to gather as many potentially useful strategies as possible, just as a carpenter might collect power tools. These interventions might include a particular way of presenting directives (i.e., paradox), "homework assignments," cognitive techniques that help clients confront various types of irrational beliefs, or specialized interventions such as EMDR (reprogramming the brain to help overcome trauma) or parent education/training (teaching skills through curriculum-based approaches). While intuitively appealing, the toolbox model does not really equip therapists with the therapeutic competencies needed to engage the change process with families, especially those at greatest risk. The toolbox approach is limited by the lack of a comprehensive theory to guide the use of the tools. It leaves the clinician without guidance on how, when, or in what order to use those tools. Tools are for building, but the toolbox approach ignores the need to have tools *and* skill training *and* a construction plan that puts the tools to use in a way that maximizes one's impact and gets the job done effectively.

The FFT clinical change model fills this gap. It brings to the clinician a comprehensive, systematic approach to helping families that is temporal (phase-based), relational (occurring in the within-session relational processes), goal-directed (specific phase-based treatment goals), and client-focused (matching the client's relational system). The change model is an integration of theory and research (reviewed in Chapters 1 and 2) and clinical practice (discussed in the chapters in this section). The principles by which the model is implemented are relational, family focused, and alliance based.

Instead of being a toolbox of discrete techniques and interventions, FFT is an architectural plan for directing change in complex human structures. It reflects a higher-level organization of sound principles of human behavior and family relational systems research. Similarly, the core principles of FFT extend beyond clinicians to clinical supervisors who direct FFT services, administrators who create service delivery systems in which FFT must operate, and evaluators who track quality assurance. Clinically relevant protocols allow all of these other participants to approach FFT in the same systematic yet dynamic way—following the plan with a high degree of adherence while understanding that no task is static and each new, unanticipated event requires a response based on principles that respect the particular situation of the client.

Clinically FFT integrates the simultaneous task of clinical assessment and intervention into phases of change. The relationship between clinical assessment and intervention, the family, and time is that they are all strands of a braid. Individually a strand represents a single thread with its own strengths and weaknesses. When braided together each thread gains strength. In FFT the braid of assessment and intervention is made even stronger by adding the thread that represents the unique needs and patterns that is the family over time. Assessment and intervention intermingled systematically with the family strand creates a strong core to the clinical work of FFT.

The next four chapters are devoted to application of the clinical model in practice. Chapters 4, 5, 6 examine the three phases of FFT, one by one, in a clinically focused and specific way, using examples from different clinical cases. The examples are intended to illustrate the phase-specific constructs and therapist skills being discussed. Chapter 7 looks at the total process of FFT in regard to treatment planning and session planning, as the therapist translates the FFT model into action.

In this section the focus is on the clinical realities of being "in the room" and trying to understand and at the same time therapeutically engage and motivate the many different members of families that FFT works with. I use the term "in the room" to mean the clinical "dance" that goes on between FFT therapist and family each time they meet. The moment by moment transactions between therapist and family are the "stage" on which FFT happens. The main story contained within these chapters is to take the "theoretical" and integrate it with the clinical reality so as to provide a clear pathway to follow such that you know what goals to pursue, what outcomes to look for, and what relationally based interventions to use to increase the likelihood that you can help the family reach these goals. This section is intended to illustrate FFT's clinical power: the personal and direct engagement of the family amid the intertwined threads of assessment of client and situation, and systematic intervention in the best opportunity of the moment to accomplish the goals of the phase in a way that is relevant and helpful to the needs of the family.

At the outset, a point of clarification is required. The section that follows attempts to describe a relational and clinical process. The goals and desired outcomes of each phase are straightforward. The manner in which the goals are obtained is far less than linear. In every way possible, I tried to describe the phase, as it would be experienced by the therapists in real time as they work with a family. That means that concepts are occasionally repeated—just as the family patterns are to the clinician as they come around and around. As described by Sexton & Alexander (2004), this is how therapy should be when you are in the room with a family. In FFT things are often said more than once; the process must, however, be focused and evolving, not just repetitive. Examples always help, but they can never be detailed enough. Thus the intention of this section: to be "purposefully descriptive."

4

Engaging
Individuals
and Motivating
Families

When working with adolescents with behavior problems and their families, getting started with the seemingly simple goals of all therapies—creating an alliance, developing shared goals, and understanding and assessing the problem—is more difficult than one might imagine. Families and the interactions they bring into the room feel chaotic, emotionally powerful, and relationally complex. It often feels as if the therapist is working against the family—needing to pull them along. This really isn't a surprise if you consider what the youth and their families have gone through as they struggled with the challenges in their daily lives. As noted in earlier chapters, they bring with them a complex history of struggles, attempts at solutions, and at times feelings of hopelessness about the system, other family members, and even themselves. Some are forced to the therapy room by mandates from judges, probation officers, other mental health workers, or child welfare agencies. In these cases the family often brings with them anger and concern over the referral itself in addition to all else. Looking beyond the specific problems or referrals, however, it becomes evident that all families enter therapy in a similar way—bringing powerful emotional experiences right into the room. From an FFT perspective these powerful experiences both provide the keys to understanding the family and lay the pathways to helping the family change.

One of the things that makes FFT different is its immediacy. There is no orientation, assessment, or beginning phase; instead the therapist jumps into the center of these experiences, responding to the events in the room in the most helpful way possible. The therapist is faced with the need to simultaneously make an assessment (what the problem is, how the clients work, what systems are involved) and intervene, acting on the opportunities that immediately present themselves as the family tells their story. To take advantage of these crucial early events, the therapist has to be active and engaging, focusing on the process goals of the engagement and motivation phase:

- Reducing negativity and blame between family members
- Developing a family focus for the problems presented by the family
- Helping the family experience a sense of support and hope that the problem can change
- Establishing that the therapist and therapy can help promote those changes

What I have always found most interesting is that an observer of this early process would see nothing more than a conversation between a struggling adolescent, a struggling family, and someone who is a stranger to them. The conversation would likely look as if the family is reporting what has happened and what they want done. But what is actually involved is a round-and-round of interchanges among these strangers—the therapist looking to find a way to understand the complex, multilayered communications and interactions unfolding in the room, and the family looking to be understood, to get help, and to find relief from their pain and discomfort.

From an FFT perspective, these early conversations hold a series of opportunities to understand how the family functions and to achieve some of the relationally focused goals of the early phases of change. On the assessment side, the therapist must put together a multisystemic picture of this family's unique organization, with a view of how the presenting problem functions within their relational system as well as the extent and nature of each member's contribution to the problem. At the same time the therapist must intervene in a way that shows rather than tells the family that he or she is credible, supportive, and focused on the family, yet simultaneously responsive to the each family member's specific perspectives.

These tasks are not simple. The clinical reality is that the therapist is pulled by each family member, by his or her own values, and by the expectations of referral agents and other outside systems that therapy can "make a difference" and "change the youth's behavior." Yet therapists know that making these changes in the family takes more than just problem solving, negotiating, and mediating differences. They know they need to focus on the present and take the opportunities provided to achieve some of the relationally focused goals of the phase.

Early Change Goals: Building Engagement and Motivation

In FFT, the goals and desired outcomes are clear-cut and straightforward. The therapeutic creativity lies in how to achieve those goals by working within the family. This is difficult because there is no script, no checklist—only a set of core principles that provide the foundation for how to understand what is happening together with a clinical map that guides the clinical decisions, session goals, and outcomes that the therapist will use to judge progress. The challenge is that multiple goals all need to be accomplished at the same time, but that progress can't be forced; rather, it must come from what is going on in the room—the immediate context, what clients bring to the problem, and the nature

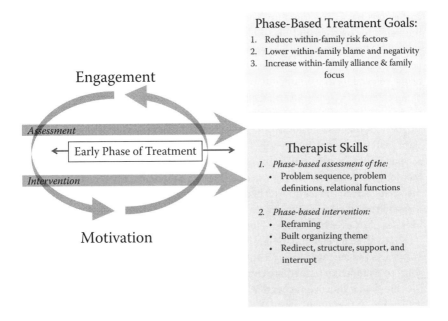

Phase-Based Treatment Goals:
1. Reduce within-family risk factors
2. Lower within-family blame and negativity
3. Increase within-family alliance & family focus

Engagement

Assessment

Early Phase of Treatment

Intervention

Motivation

Therapist Skills
1. *Phase-based assessment of the:*
   - Problem sequence, problem definitions, relational functions

2. *Phase-based intervention:*
   - Reframing
   - Built organizing theme
   - Redirect, structure, support, and interrupt

FIGURE 4.1 Treatment goals and therapist skills in engagement/motivation phase.

of the problem. The therapist has to see these immediate events, understand them, and at the same time use them to achieve the goals of this early phase of therapy. In the room, however, each family member pushes from his or her own set of needs, wanting the therapist to take action that supports them and their individual agendas. The events that occur in the therapy room are often problems and crises that seem to cry out for immediate problem solving or intervention. It is not that the immediate needs are not important; they are. But the therapist must respond to them not as problems to solve but as opportunities to pursue a set of relationally based goals that are the first steps in the change process that will ultimately help the clients achieve their long-term goals.

Figure 4.1 illustrates the assessment and intervention goals that guide the therapist's activities in this phase of FFT. The goals and outcomes represented in this figure are the map for the early sessions. The discussion that follows provides the clinical, theoretical, and research-based support for these goals.

Case Example

Peter is 13 years old. Peter's mother is Indonesian and his father is Dutch. He lives with his mother and his stepfather. He has a pair of twin brothers who are 5 years younger. The first FFT session occurred in their home. According to the referral, Peter had "fired" three different therapists in the last year. Each time he found the sessions "boring" and spent most of the time talking to his mother. The referral gave a characterization of Peter's mother, Anja, as "motivated to do anything to help." There was no mention of the stepfather, who had not attended earlier meetings. The therapist knew her first step needed to focus on engaging Peter, his mother, and his stepfather so that they felt motivated to take new steps. Finally, the therapist knew that Peter had been referred because of "mental health concerns" and his inability to follow rules and stay in school. The last line of the referral form contained a message from the case: "This might be the last chance Peter has to take advantage of the treatments we are offering. If this referral doesn't work out, placement should be reassessed as a viable option."

Early in the first session it was clear that the family would demonstrate the same patterns. Peter began the session bored and uninterested, his mother seemed willing to help, and his stepfather was not there; he had to work. It didn't take long for Peter and his mother to get into it. She quietly said to Peter, "Just tell me what I can do." Peter quickly became disgusted and replied, "Leave me alone! Move to the other side of the Earth!" After that he withdrew, pulled the hood of his sweatshirt over his head, and looked down. His mother began to cry.

Given all that Peter and his family brought to therapy, what would help most? What was the best way to enter into their system of interactions and relationships so as to make immediate changes and, at the same time, set the stage for the things that must come next? What would it take for Peter and his family to get started in therapy in a way that was most likely to produce both short-term and long-term changes in Peter, in his parents, and in the relational system that supported their current feeling of being stuck? At the same time, the therapist needed to consider the best way for her to take the expert role in terms of how change occurs while the family assumed the role of expert on their own lives.

Four things would help Peter and his family overcome their struggles: becoming involved in the therapy process, developing the motivation to take different action, a family-focused definition of the problem, and acceptance of the therapist as a credible helper.

Involvement in the Therapy Process

Engagement occurs when each member of the family becomes involved in the immediate activities of the session. Engagement reflects that the activities in the early session are relevant to family members, that therapy is perceived as a potentially useful way of helping, and that they are more and more willing to move forward in a different way than they have in the past to solve their problems. Engagement is not a given—it is not a preexisting condition of the client or something the clients "should" do if they "really want to change." Rather, it is an outcome of what the therapist does in the initial conversation with the family. Engagement comes from using humor, asking interested questions, working relentlessly to understand and respect family members, and from the therapist's presence in the room. It comes from talking about the "problems" the family experiences in an alliance-based, nonblaming, and strength-based way. Engagement is both a goal (what the therapist tries to accomplish) and an outcome (what the family demonstrates), and it can be measured by the level of family-specific involvement in the session.

An Incentive to Try Something New

At a glance, one might think that Peter and his mother were motivated. Peter had a strong incentive to get her to let him handle the issues at school himself, while Anja had an incentive to get Peter home on time, have him act more respectfully, and end his drug use. Each was motivated to get the therapist's help to do what they had been unable to accomplish with the other on their own. Each was motivated to find solutions based on his or her own beliefs about the cause of the problem and the motives of the other person. While this type of motivation is certainly an incentive to action, it does not help either side do something new, take different action, or work in a different way with one another. Instead, it simply motivated both Peter and his parents to do more of the same—maybe just a bit louder, more frequently, and with greater force. To be clinically useful, motivation needs to be therapeutic in the sense that it is an incentive to pursue solutions differently than has been done in the past. Therapeutic motivation is an outcome of a successful FFT session—a state in which family members come to hope that the problem can change, believe that the therapist and therapy can help promote those changes, that things can be different, and that they, along with other members of the family, are willing to undertake change.

A Family-Focused Problem Definition

Peter's family came to FFT as they come to each incident they face in this phase of their life: with a view that the troubles they encounter are someone else's fault. For Peter it was his parents' fault; for his parents the problem clearly lay with Peter. Given those beliefs and what they imply regarding the intentions and motivation of others, it is easy to see why both sides continued to respond to each seemingly new and different problem with the same strategies. It is also easy to see why it was so hard for them to adopt fairly simple solutions that to succeed only require that they work together.

Peter and his parents had strong emotional reactions toward one another, and had developed patterns of acting on their attributions and emotions that supported and constantly reinforced them. Imagine how different the relationship and the actions taken by both Peter and his parents would be if each thought that they all had a part in the problem (that is, they took some degree of personal responsibility), that it would take all of them to change, and that any success required all of them to work together. This would be a family that looked and functioned in very different ways.

Perceiving a Credible Helper

It is in the early phases of therapy that therapists must establish themselves as a credible helper. Frank (1969) and others suggested that the "helper" role comes with the socially defined role of "therapist," "psychologist," or other professional label associated with a body of knowledge and expertise, but when working with adolescents, this basis for credibility is not particularly relevant. Similarly, if the parents and other family members have been involved in the system for some time, they have seen and worked with many "helpers." For such families, credence is not something that the therapist promises (e.g., "Later in the therapy we will . . ."). In FFT, the therapist's credibility comes from what he or she does in the early sessions in reaction to the events in the room. The therapist has to demonstrate that even the first session can be different, engaging, and motivating.

Engagement, alliance-based motivation, a family-focused problem, and the acceptance of the therapist as a credible helper are all goals of the early phases of therapy. Each of these goals comes about because of how the therapist responds to events that happen in the room. When these goals are achieved through the interactions in the therapy room, the youth changes, the parents change, and the whole family system changes. Events and behaviors come to mean something different, and the escalating spirals of strong emotion and the behaviors that accompany them are interrupted and changed. Change comes not in the form of new solutions but in the form of a willingness to work together, a different understanding of what is behind the sometimes irritating and anger-producing behaviors of someone else, and a softening of the emotions between family members. Thus, when successful, the engagement and motivation phase of FFT is not just the foundation of the skills of the next phase, but an important and powerful change-producing phase in and of itself.

Case Example

The initial goals that guide the therapist are the same at the start of each FFT case. Even before arriving at the home for the first session, the therapist began to prepare. The therapist had two competing interests—to gain a better understanding of Peter and his family, and to make an assessment of their level of blame and negativity toward one another. The goals for the session were to reduce blame and negativity between them, create a family focus to the problems they face, and acknowledge their individual struggles and contributions. But the therapist was faced with another reality: This was the one opportunity she had to make a lasting impression on Peter and his family, to engage them in a relevant yet supportive conversation about the issues that faced them. The real question was how to stay focused on the goals while using the opportunities and experiences between the family members.

It is the interactions between the family members that are the focus of immediate clinical assessment and intervention. The therapist needed to better understand Peter's school difficulties, what went on in the family, what was behind his strong emotion. The therapist had a sense that Anja had been through a lot and carried some resentment of her current husband for not helping more. She clearly believed that Peter needed additional mental health care and that medication, along with a strong dose of responsibility, would put him on the right track. She was also terrified of the fighting and didn't want to lose Peter. The therapist knew that if she did not attend to the immediate issues of engagement, motivation, and finding a common problem definition, she might never be able to help with the pressing issues of school and conflict. She felt that she had to balance understanding with acting immediately, even without totally understanding how this family worked.

Integrating Assessment and Intervention Into a Therapeutic Conversation in the Early Stages of FFT

When the family enters the therapy room, they bring with them a complex and multilevel relational system in which the problem is embedded. There are individual factors that everyone brings to the table; there is a context of peers, school, and community that has a strong impact on the behaviors and actions of the family; and there are the powerful core relational patterns that surround the problem. To be successful and address the critical risk factors, to have a quick impact, the therapist has to assess the client's current situation and intervene in the events that appear during the session. These events are, as noted earlier, opportunities to learn how the family works and to change that way of working in the immediate moment. The events are useful because they represent powerful expressions of the family struggle and thus provide relevant points of understanding and impact. One of the unique aspects of the FFT clinical model is that assessment and intervention are woven throughout each phase. This means that the therapist must see each encounter as both a therapeutic opportunity and a piece of data from which to understand how the family functions so as to match therapy to the family's unique needs, style, values, and resources.

An observer watching FFT from behind a one-way mirror would see what Hoffman (1981) describes as bringing out what is "hiding in the bushes." How the dynamic commingling of assessment and intervention in a client-centered, model-focused, and client-responsive process occurs is difficult to communicate on the printed page. What the observer would see is not a series of static statements and pronouncements by the therapist but instead a circular process of hypothesis testing in which the therapist finds a way to understand and intervene in this unique family system. The therapist makes guesses that are to be corrected or added to by the family. There would be surprises, as FFT therapists often act well before they have all the information they need. Instead they make a judgment to try something; based on its impact, they will fine-tune the next question, statement, or intervention. Over time you would see the therapist's guessing, listening, and adding result in a layered portrait of this family and how they work. As noted in Chapter 3, FFT specifies areas to look for and specialized goals to pursue that guide the therapist through this maze.

What to Look For: Clinical Assessment

Assessment is really just a process of understanding. There are two primary areas of understanding in the engagement and motivation phase: understanding how the problem functions within the family relational system, and assessing the level of blame, the level of negativity, and the problem definitions that the family bring into the room. In FFT assessment, however, these are done in an inside-out manner. The therapist begins with the immediate problem presented by the family and the meaning that the problem holds for the family members. In FFT, unlike other therapies, the therapist does not take a psychosocial history or make a formal assessment of the problem. Instead, it is through the stories that the family members tell about how they see and experience the problem that the therapist begins to understand the nature and the extent of the behavior, how these specific behaviors fit into the predominant relational patterns in the family, and the risk and protective factors involved. To develop a multisystemic understanding of the individuals, family, and relational context, the therapist looks for the problem sequences that underlie the family's relational system. Assessing the underlying issues helps the therapist understand how the family works well enough to match to them and begin to plan for the behavior change phase. Anyone observing an FFT session would not see assessment happening, except in the form of statements of what the therapist understands. Thought of in this way, assessment happens inside the therapist, based on what the family says and how they react.

Assessment of the Presenting Problem

There are a number of factors that are important to understand in regard to the specific problem. First, the nature of the referral and the specific behavior contained within it provide useful information about what the family faces. Whether it is drug use, violent and disruptive behavior, curfew violations, school problems, or conflict among family members, the description of the problem is what's important. It is crucial to remember that the referral represents only one form of a problem definition. Problem definitions are attributions by individuals that describe who, why, and what caused the problematic experience; they contextualize the problem and give it meaning. As noted in Chapter 3, problem definition is the cognitive, emotional, and behavioral representation of the perspective of one person.

In FFT, assessment involves creating hypotheses about what is behind the expression of emotions, the behaviors of each individual, and the struggles between family members. The task of assessment is to understand what organizes individual, contextual, and family-related factors into a particular way of functioning. As a result, assessment feels more like building a model of the family rather than discovering the causes of behaviors. It is important to keep in mind that the definitions from the various family members' perspectives are not necessarily "real" or even based in the facts of the case. The problem that is perceived by family members instead represents meaning placed on the events by the family and helps identify the relational mechanisms that promote the behaviors and responses of the individuals involved. Problem definitions are to be observed, understood, and intervened upon—not to be mined by the therapist for "reasons."

Understanding Individual Problem Definitions and Creating Family-Focused Themes

What is important to remember, and sometimes difficult to see, is that Peter and his family come into the therapy room having struggled with the current problem for some time. It is only natural, and maybe uniquely human, that we all try to make sense of what has happened and is happening to us (Mahoney, 1991). In a therapeutic context, the connection between perceived and experienced problems and potential solutions was first identified by the early Mental Research Institute systemic therapy models (Watzlawick, Weakland, & Fisch, 1974). Their research suggests that our experience of problems both forms and limits the solutions we can see. Family members' problem definitions may be phrased in terms of emotion ("It hurts and I am angry"), behavior ("Stay away from me"; "You don't deserve a break"), or cognition ("You are just trying to hurt me"; "Why does he intentionally do this?"). These individual problem definitions are cognitive sets that contribute to the emotionally intense negative interchanges often seen between family members. By contrast, a family-focused problem definition is one in which every member of the family contributes some part of the problem and thus bears some responsibility. However, no family member is to blame for the family's situation. The therapist has the difficult task of reducing blame while helping the clients take and retain personal responsibility for their actions.

The idea of problem definition is important in another way as well. We have all had the experience that our solutions are directed at what we think is the problem. Imagine being at home alone one night. As you fall asleep you hear a noise. If your first thought is "Someone is outside," your emotional fight-or-flight response prepares you to protect yourself. That is the most natural, appropriate, and automatic response. On the other hand, if you remember that the neighbors have a pesky cat that is out at all hours and makes a lot of noise, rolling over and going back to sleep might be a more appropriate response.

One of the biggest challenges in family therapy is that there are as many definitions and meanings for the problem as there are family members. In fact, much of the negativity and blame that fuel the troubled interactions between family members comes from each member feeling the clash of conflicting problem definitions and solutions. Because the whole family is in the room, there are powerful relational struggles going on that do not lend themselves to the simpler cognitive restructuring approaches commonly used in psychotherapy. Instead, it takes a more immediate, relationally focused approach to successfully redirect what each family member experiences as the problem and, thus, what each is willing to do about it. Much of the family's struggle comes from the powerful emotions that accompany behavioral problems.

To create a family-focused problem definition, each member of the family has to reattribute perceived motives, intentions, and behaviors. This is the principle of behavior change as a result of meaning change, discussed in detail in Chapter 3. Reattribution requires the cognitive restructuring—shifting, redefining, and expanding—of family members' definitions of the presenting problem, with the therapist eliciting more constructive attributions of motivation, emotions, and behaviors. This restructuring can focus on the meaning of each other's behavior, beliefs about the intentions and motivations behind those behaviors, and the definition of the emotional expressions that family members see. For example, Peter's "disrespectful" behavior is actually a way of distancing himself from the anger that he feels unable to channel in productive ways. His parents' strong focus on rules is, in another sense, an attempt to protect Peter.

Identifying the Problem Sequence

One of the fundamental principles of FFT is that problems are embedded within core relational patterns (see Chapter 3). The core patterns are the "what comes before" and "what come after" context for the specific behavior that is identified as problematic. While intervening to reduce negativity and blame and create a family focus, the therapist is also observing and piecing together a hypothesis about how this core pattern works. These core patterns are referred to in FFT as "problem sequences," or the patterns of behavior that surround the problem behavior, maintain it, and even promote it. These patterns are the sequential behavioral patterns and the regularities in those patterns (Barton & Alexander, 1981; Sexton & Alexander 2004, 2005). To identify the meaning of individual behaviors (e.g., drug abuse, delinquency, acting-out behaviors etc.), the therapist observes, over time, the ways that problematic behaviors are inexorably tied to the relational process in which they are embedded. As the concepts of systemic relational process suggest, these core patterns can become very stable and ultimately serve to maintain the problem behavior. While not as easy to see as individual behavior patterns, family behavior patterns are relational sequences of behavior at the core of the family "character"; they form the basis of the family's daily life. Some of these patterns effectively accomplish necessary tasks (e. g. parenting, communicating, supporting) and may protect the family and its members by preventing certain behavior problems.

Identifying Risk and Protective Factors

Beyond the current presenting problem lie a number of more indirect features of the individuals, family, community, and context that increase the probability that the family will struggle. These risk factors aren't directly visible in the reports of the family members, but emerge in the therapist's clinical assessment. The assessment is done co-mingled with direct intervention strategies. As discussed in Chapters 2 and 3, risk and protective factors are those characteristics within a person, family, and context that make it more likely that families will struggle and have difficulty, or features of each that serve to protect and buffer the family from the pressures and influence of history, the current context, or the person. Certain risk and protective factors are specifically addressed in the early stages of therapy. For example, from Table 1.1 you can see that high emotional distress and exposure to conflict and risk are individual factors and make it more difficult for the family to find a different way of working. The chaotic, coercive, and difficult blaming relationships that often accompany clients into the room are a family risk. Developing a strong bond, parental involvement, and support all serve as buffering and protective features. Both risk and protective factors are important to address in early stages of therapy. It helps further the creation of a working "team" of parents and kids who can tackle further problems. It is also important to note that treatment programs that enhance family bonding are critical in reducing dropout rates and, ultimately, helping the adolescent. Individual, family, and treatment program features are all addressed through systematic assessment and intervention in the engagement and motivation phase of FFT.

Monitoring the Ongoing Progress of Therapy

Assessment is often thought of as a process of finding the problem and assessing the client. In FFT, assessment also means watching and assessing the ongoing progress in each stage of therapy. This is a different type of assessment, focused not on diagnosis but on monitoring how important certain features are in the current context and the progress that is being made. This is critical because it is the basis for the therapist's decision whether to move ahead, continue and do more, or even change phases. This type of assessment generally centers on the specific goals of the phase. In the early phase of engagement and motivation, for example, the assessment focuses on levels of negativity, blame, and the degree to which the family is adopting and expressing personal responsibility and a family focus to the problem. Monitoring the ongoing process of therapy means that the therapist is constantly asking the clients, "Did that work?" "How can I add to that to make it more personal or have greater impact?" "What is the level of negativity and blame—higher, lower?" This type of assessment is a critical feature of clinical decision making.

Case Example

Let's consider how this might happen with the FFT therapist working with Peter and his family. The therapist started the session with goals for the session that were common for all first FFT cases. Even before arriving at Peter's home, the FFT therapist began to prepare by anticipating how the family might work, even with the little information that was available to her. As noted above, the first session was characterized by high levels of negativity and blame between Peter and Anja. Knowing the immediate need was to jump into the conversation between them, trying to reduce negativity and blame and finding common ground between them, the therapist learned, as much through observation and inference as through direct questioning, how both Peter and Anja attributed the problem, some ways in which it was personally important to them, and how their actions were logical attempts to solve the problem as they perceived it. For Peter, as we've seen, the problem was his mother's fault. While he had some struggles, he was very proud of the way he had managed school and how he had managed to deal with the style of the stepfather. From Peter's perspective, Anja just needed to "get over it" and leave him alone. If she wasn't such a nag, he would be okay. And Anja thought Peter had serious emotional problems for which she was incapable of doing anything except finding help for him. For the therapist the problem definition became the target of intervention.

The problem sequence became clearer as more parts of the story emerged. Figure 4.2 illustrates a core pattern or problem sequence that the therapist gleaned from the early conversations. The exact point of initiation is less important than getting an idea about how the pattern works and who is involved. In

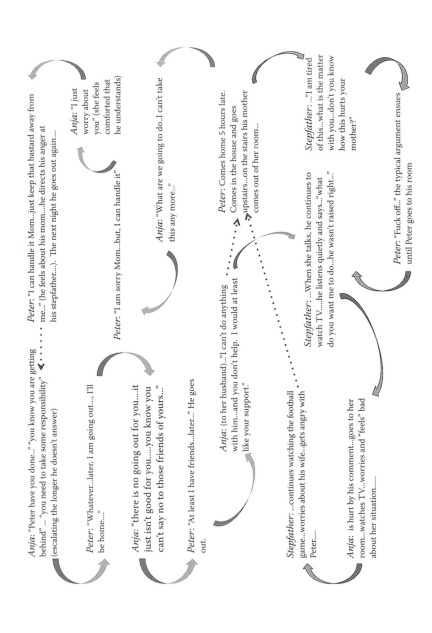

FIGURE 4.2   Relational sequence: Peter and Anja.

the case of Peter, there are actually two interlocking sequences. The first goes between Peter and Anja. It often begins as a request, worry, or monitoring question addressed to Peter. It is his reaction that she responds to, becoming angry. Peter leaves; Anja sits. At some point she goes to her husband and complains, eventually asking him directly for help. His reluctance is the trigger for her response. He is dissatisfied at the state of affairs. Later, when Peter comes home, Anja and occasionally his stepfather continue a sequence with him that involves the escalation of violence. With Anja, Peter feels some relief at reassuring her that he is okay. She never changes her behavior but is happy things are back to normal while still angry at the lack of real progress.

Even early on in this case, some of the risk factors were clear. The therapist quickly suspected that Peter might have an attentional problem that contributed to his school difficulties. In addition, she saw that Peter might have difficulty fitting into a regular school, given his long absence and the streetwise ways he has developed. Peers and other contextual factors did not seem to be a risk. However, the within-family struggles between Peter and his stepfather were of concern. The therapist also began to wonder if Peter's mother felt out of control because she did not know what her limits should be in monitoring and supervising Peter's activities. At times she seemed more like a friend than a mother.

What to Do: Intervening to Build Engagement and Motivation

Knowing what to do is built around specific phase goals (what the therapist tries to accomplish) and an awareness of the desired outcomes of this phase of FFT therapy (see Figure 4.2). In a sense, these are the same. Goals represent the aspiration and the direction, while outcomes represent a state that, if reached, means the therapist and family can move on to the next phase. Both goals and desired outcomes are accomplished through responding to the naturally occurring opportunities or events that happen as the family interacts. During these interactions, the therapist looks for things such as reports of information, negative interchanges, or instances of telling the story in a way that attributes the problem to just one individual or seeing malicious intention in the motives of others. The desired outcomes for the early phase includes increased alliances between family members, the reduction of negative and blaming interactions between them, and the development of a shared family focus to the presenting problems (see Figure 4.1).

While the goals are easy to learn and remember, applying them in the therapy room is another task altogether. Families seldom come in asking for help with reducing blame or negativity or seeking to create a family focus to their problems. Instead, they act in ways that reflect what their problems have come to mean to them—they may be angry, accusing, quiet, or seemingly uninvolved. The parents may focus on the youth's drug use, violent behavior, or other symptoms, while the youth focuses on what is seen as overinvolvement, excessive control, or a lack of understanding on the part of the parents. The therapist's challenge is to focus less on the content of the specific presenting problems or diagnostic categories and more on the family processes underlying these specific behaviors, looking for the same relational processes (e.g., blame, negativity, a lack of family focus, etc.) regardless of the specific problem behavior. In each case, the therapist focuses attention on the family's unique ways of expressing these processes. This highlights both the goals common to the engagement and motivation phase of all FFT therapy sessions and the unique behaviors and relationships of each individual and family. It has the same goals and desired outcome, and yet it is individual and unique to each family.

Become a Credible Helper

Therapists are helpful to families not only because of the expertise they bring to therapy but also because of how they bring it. It is no surprise that the therapist can only be helpful if the family perceives him or her to be credible. Credibility just means that the therapist's suggestions, direction, advice, and guidance are viewed as reliable and potentially helpful. In Chapter 3 the discussion focused on the well-established models for establishing therapeutic credibility as an outcome of a social influence process (Strong, 1988; Strong & Claiborn, 1989). According to this idea, the therapist shows that he/she is trustworthy by being active, directing the session, and attending to the important overt and covert issues in the room. Therapists show expertise by demonstrating that they can both listen and direct; by overcoming the seeming barriers created by high emotion, anger, and the history each family member brings, they show that they are capable of helping the family. They are attractive in that they are involved, engaged, and honestly part of the conversation. These three features (expertness, trustworthiness, and attractiveness) combine with the family's felt need that something must change to give the therapist a degree of influence. It is not the kind of influence that results in the therapist telling the family what to do but the kind that allows the therapist to have an impact, to be heard, and to change the family. It is important to remember that from an FFT perspective this type of credibility is not about controlling the session; instead it is about the therapist showing that he or she can be trusted to meet the family where they are, embrace the struggle they feel and the emotions they express, and at the same time guide the family to a new place.

Bring an Attitude of Respect and Collaboration

One of the most important interventions in this phase is not a technique but an attitude. The FFT attitude is represented by a belief in the relational patterns, belief in the noble intentions of people, curiosity about how they work, and an openness to experiencing how they work and how their family is structured. The attitude needed to be successful in FFT is based in the core principles of FFT described in Chapters 1 and 2. It is an attitude of respect, understanding, and belief in the resiliency and strength of each member of the family.

This attitude is not really something that can be taught. It comes from the therapist taking what was described earlier as an inside-out approach in which the job is to do what many of the early models of psychotherapy called "putting yourself in the shoes of the client." As described by Greenberg and Safrin (1990), this is a type of empathy based not on agreeing with the family but on understanding the functioning of the family as if the therapist were embedded in the same relationship system and context. For many therapists, getting this far inside the family system triggers a struggle with the therapist's own values and beliefs.

Engage the Family

Engagement is not an idea that is new to FFT—client engagement has been part, although indirectly, of many of the traditional theoretical approaches to mental heath care. In fact, with growing evidence that dropout rates from traditional therapies are as high as 75% (Kazdin, 2003) for adolescents with behavior problems, most approaches have recently developed engagement "modules" or "interventions" as adjuncts to the therapy. Many approaches view engagement as the foundation upon which the core change mechanisms occur. Traditionally, a client is viewed as engaged if he or she talks, leans forward, looks interested, and shares problems and feelings. Many times engagement is seen as synonymous with the clients' "telling their story." These approaches lead therapists to look for and solicit a certain predetermined set of behaviors from the clients.

From an FFT perspective, the involvement that comes with being engaged can take many forms depending on the family and the situation. In FFT the hope is that the family can openly share their struggles, but whether this is done verbally or non-verbally, loudly or quietly, and so on all depends on the individuals' and family's unique style. For example, I don't find it uncommon to work with adolescents who don't look at me, exhibit behaviors that some would find disrespectful (rolling their eyes, talking under their breath, etc.), and even pull the hood of their sweatshirt up to hide their face. Yet they do listen, and their reactions, despite not being particularly nice, show that they are listening and participating in their way.

The therapist's job is to engage them by providing a relational environment that is supportive yet direct in its discussion of each family member's struggles. Some parents present in a way that is powerful, blaming, and demanding of immediate change. The therapist must provide a relational context in which that behavior can be shaped and understood as contributing part of the way forward. In FFT we would rarely build engagement in the traditional way by saying, "Let's get to know each other" or "Tell me about yourself." Instead, we would be direct in talking about the immediate and reported behaviors, the emotions that might lie behind these behaviors, and the attribution and meanings that form the foundation of both. From our perspective it is not *whether* we talk about these issues but *how* we talk about them that produces an engaging relational environment. Thus, engagement comes out of the discussion of the important issues facing the family as a result of the purposeful responses of the therapist. In the upcoming sections of the chapter the clinical "how" of creating engagement will be the focus.

Reduce Negativity and Blame, Build Personal Responsibility

One of the major intrafamily risk factors is the coercive, emotionally negative conflict that arises as the family confronts daily life and its problems. It is not at all uncommon for families to bring this negativity and blame into the FFT discussion. It can usually be felt as the family members each describe their problem definitions. Negativity is both the emotional expression around these descriptions and the overall climate within the family. Blame is the attribution of problems to a particular source. As noted earlier in the book, attribution is the common human way of reflecting on, understanding, and acting on the world around them. There are a number of research studies that suggest that just by reducing and reframing blame, the risk level within the family goes down, allowing alliance and more effective problem solving to emerge.

In a study of family negativity, Nitza (2002) discovered that, with all other things held constant, the families most likely to continue and finish FFT were ones where negativity was evident initially, rose in the middle third of the session to a high level, and in the final third of the session fell below the point at which it started. Families that dropped out were more likely to be ones in which the negativity also was apparent at the start of a session and grew to a high point in the middle third but did not drop in the final part of the session, instead growing even higher. Negativity is important at the beginning of a session because it brings urgency and relevance to the discussion; during the session, the family expresses their felt negativity, but before the session is over, it is important for negativity to recede into the background. If therapists use reframing, redirecting, interrupting, and process pointing through the session, you can hope to see blame and negativity reduced before the session ends.

There is also an important inverse relationship between blaming and personal responsibility: The more family members blame, the less they take personal responsibility for the problem they experience. Given that blame is an attribution of cause placed with another, this makes perfect sense. If you find no part that is yours in the causes or changes of the situation, there is less likelihood that you will be motivated to try something that requests the initiation and persistence of a new behavior. The flip side of this relationship is that as personal responsibility goes up, blame goes down. In FFT the therapist usually uses reframing to respond to a family member in a way that acknowledges his or her part in the problem without blaming.

Build Therapeutic Motivation Through Balanced Alliance

Alliance is a critical mechanism of change in all therapies. As suggested in Chapter 3, alliance is built around agreement on the goals, the tasks needed to achieve those goals, and methods of accomplishing those tasks. In FFT, therapeutic motivation is a result of three different mechanisms of change—alliance, a shared family-focused definition of the problem, and a perception by the family that the therapist has the ability to provide something different, can help, and can make a difference. This alliance-based motivation is based in a relational incentive—one that comes from wanting the relationship between the therapist and each family member and between family members themselves to improve or continue (Sexton & Alexander, 2004).

It is the experiences of working together, being understood, and being helped in the earliest encounters in FFT that provide the powerful relational incentive for family members to take a different action toward change. Alliance-based motivation may not have the immediate power of a fear-based approach and it likely will not work as quickly as making deals about rewards, but once it is established and experienced by family members, it has a staying power that will carry the family through tough discussions of the problems between them. In addition, unlike the situational impact of punishments, promises, and rewards, relational and alliance-based motivation can serve as the foundation of other behavior changes and problem solutions. What is important to remember is that alliance-based motivation does not simply exist in the client because they want to change—it is the result of what happens in the early session of FFT. Thus, it is critical that alliance and its motivational outcome be addressed early, through each opportunity that may present itself. The next sections of this chapter outline the specific in-the-room strategies for creating motivation.

Balanced alliance is a particularly important outcome of this phase. While it may seem on the surface as though high alliance would be the desired goal early in the intervention, creating high alliance with everyone is not always easy. It is also fascinating to note that in FFT high alliance may not be the most effective type. Robbins et al. (2002) studied the role of alliance in early dropout from therapy. The researchers expected to find that high alliance was associated with successful FFT cases, but they were surprised to discover that it was alliance discrepancy, rather than total amount, that predicted family dropout. What that means is that when both parents and youth felt roughly the same *degree* of alliance with the therapist, the likelihood of dropout was low, even when overall alliance was low.

Case Example

In the earliest parts of the first session, the therapist took a very active role. She quickly intervened in the escalations between Peter and his mother, refocusing the discussion to what they shared, how each had a role in the escalation, and how there were opportunities for a difference in the future. In the first 20 minutes the therapist spoke more than 70% of the time. Each time Anja blamed Peter through either direct or indirect attribution, the therapist redirected the conversation to Anja's role. When Peter blamed his mother, the therapist reversed the process. Each time the therapist responded she built alliance by acknowledging the client's concern and built engagement through active curiosity. Over time, negativity and blame became less and discussion of each one's personal responsibility went up. They seemed to find a shared part of the problem that engaged both in wanting a different kind of change.

How to Do It: Interventions in Engagement and Motivation

Relational Reframing

Reframing is a relationally based way of enhancing family engagement and motivation by changing the cognitive and perceptual basis for negative interaction, painful emotions, and unsuccessful change strategies. Made popular by the early communication theorists (Watzlawick, Weakland, & Fische, 1974) and strategic therapies (Selvini-Palazoli, 1979), reframing is used almost universally across all family therapies. Over the years reframing has taken many different names, including *positive connotation, finding positive intent*, and *interpretation*; regardless, reframing is often classified as a technique in which the therapist gives the client an alternative frame of reference in hopes that the client will accept the new interpretation and use it to reduce feelings of negativity and blame. We don't find the traditional definitions of reframing to be enough to help address the powerful relational interchanges that occur when working with troubled adolescents and their families because they are too general, are not personal enough, and lack therapeutic power to make a difference.

In FFT, reframing is a relational and therapeutic process. It involves a series of ongoing interchanges between therapist and clients over the course of therapy that, when successful, create alternative perspectives for clients that help redefine the meaning they attribute to events, thus reducing negativity and redirecting the emotionality surrounding the events. Reframing challenges clients (tacitly at first, then explicitly later) to find new possibilities for the future, and it links family members together in such a way that each individual shares in the responsibility for the family's struggles. This understanding of reframing has roots in the attributional and information processing constructs of cognitive psychology (Jones & Nisbett, 1972; Kelley, 1973; Taylor & Fiske, 1978), the social influence process of social psychology (Heppner & Claiborn, 1989), and the more recent systemic (Claiborn & Lichtenberg, 1989) and social constructionist ideas regarding the meaning basis of problem definitions (Gergen, 1995; Friedlander & Heatherington, 1998; Sexton & Griffin, 1997).

The first question involves what to reframe. In FFT the goal is, as noted in Chapters 2 and 3, ultimately to change behavior by changing the assumptions an individual makes about a given relationship or relationships in general, the standards the person holds for how a relationship should function, and the attributions the person makes to explain the events that occur. For the therapist, this means that reframing will target both specific events (a reported incident, a struggle within the room) and the relationship in general (assumptions about the motives of the other). Throughout, the therapist must stay focused on the reframing process, taking each new event and adding it into the circular reframing process.

FFT's version of relational reframing (Alexander, Pugh, Parsons, & Sexton, 2000; Alexander & Sexton, 2002; Sexton & Alexander, 2004; Sexton, 2009) has three components or stages:

- Acknowledging
- Reattributing
- Assessing the impact of the reframing in order to build on it and create organizing themes

Figure 4.3 illustrates the dynamic nature of these components.

Acknowledgment

Reframing begins with the therapist *acknowledging* the speaker's position, statement, emotion, or primary meaning. Acknowledgment may come in the form of describing

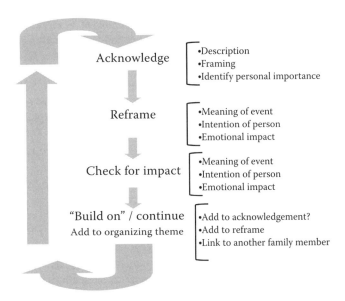

FIGURE 4.3   Relational reframing. Adapted from Sexton and Alexander (2003).

the event ("when you got angry," "when you yelled," "when this occurred"). By acknowledging the event, its personal importance to the client, and the emotion expressed, the therapist supports and engages the client. The acknowledgment shows that the therapist understands what was said, it supports the importance but not the content of the statement, and it shows respect for the client's position and feelings. A successful acknowledgment avoids broad generalizations ("all parents feel this way"); instead it is personal, individual, and insightful, so that the client can believe the therapist is working hard to understand his or her perspective. Thus, successful acknowledgment requires the therapist to speak directly and be willing to talk about the difficult yet significant issues between family members. If it is not direct and specific, there is nothing to reattribute.

Reattribution

Following the acknowledgment, the therapist makes a *reattribution statement* that presents an alternative theme targeting the attributional scheme embedded in what the client presents (see Figure 4.2). The reattribution statement can take many forms, but three general possibilities stand out: The reattribution statement may offer an alternative explanation for the cause of the problem behavior, may provide a metaphor that implies an alternative construction of the problem, or may even use humor to imply that not everything is what it seems. The clients must find the alternative meaning or theme plausible and feel that it fits them.

Meaning change helps reattribute an emotion, a behavior, or another person's intention to a more benign cause. For example, the therapist may reframe one person's anger as the pain that individual feels in response to the family struggle; in this reattribution, the angry person is seen as "willing to feel the pain and be the emotional barometer for the whole family." The reattribution is helpful because it redefines the anger as the person's internal state rather than something that is directed outward toward others. Thus, the blame inherent in anger is now redefined as hurt, even sacrifice, which reduces negative emotions in the family while retaining behavioral responsibility for the person who is angry. Reframing can also link family members together and develop a joint family definition of the struggle (see Figure 4.3). Arriving at a joint or family-focused definition of the presenting problem is essential in the early phases of FFT. As noted earlier, the family comes in with well-defined explanations for the problems they experience, and may express these in emotional, behavioral, or cognitive terms. The salient fact, though, is that each explanation is unique to the individual.

When reframing is effective, it changes the meaning of what was acknowledged in the first step of the reframing process. This has two important implications. First, to successfully change the meaning, the acknowledgment must have been of a specific and clearly identified behavior, event, emotion, or intention presented by a family member. Vague or nonspecific validations are more like empathy and don't provide an opportunity for a meaning change through reattribution. Second, to reattribute meaning, the therapist must add something to the conversation. The therapist is not merely reflecting on what has been said but must put something new into the conversation. Adding something to the conversation is done by relying on what we call themes (discussed in a later section).

There are times when reframing doesn't work. In general, this is related to issues of content, or to the timing and context of the reframing. Therapists often fail to adequately acknowledge the problematic aspect of the behavior being reframed, thereby seeming to minimize and excuse it. It is not unusual for therapists to shy away from negativity by going directly to the reattribution part of a reframing without first acknowledging that the behavior or event is problematic (painful to others, dangerous, etc.). If the family feels the therapist is merely "making nice" and not understanding how frustrating or painful the problem behaviors are to other family members, this evasion reduces the therapist's credibility.

It may seem to the family that a therapist who suggests a noble but misguided intention is just normalizing or excusing the problem behavior ("He meant to go to school but he overslept. That is natural when someone is that tired"). Reframing does not excuse problem behaviors or describe them as "normal" or "accidental." Reframing includes the concept of responsibility—the behavior was intended, but the underlying motivation was not necessarily malevolent. It can also happen that the therapist unintentionally demeans or implies blame for someone in the family ("He was just trying to let you know he wished you hadn't gone to work," implying the parent "caused" the problem by going to work). Before offering the reframing, the therapist should have assessed how the parent feels (e.g., in terms of guilt/defensiveness) about going to work.

Reframing doesn't work well when it is rushed or it oversimplifies complex behavior. Problems with the timing of a reframing can occur in two ways. A therapist may rush the reframing by jumping in, sometimes even interrupting the speaker, to provide "relief" and to "help" rather than waiting and accepting the sometimes painful emotion being expressed. While well intended, such quick intervention interrupts the very experience that provides the emotional power needed to generate change. That disrespects the person, robbing the family member of the opportunity to engage in and discuss the salient and important issues within his or her experience, and in a sense dismissing his or her experience. It also disrespects the therapeutic process. On the other hand, the therapist can be too late in reframing, waiting until everybody has expressed their emotions. As noted above, honest and open communication is not always helpful when it consists of negativity and blame. If the therapist waits too long in an attempt to help everyone be heard, it may actually promote the very negativity the therapist hopes to decrease by providing too much room for the negative relational patterns between family members to establish themselves. This too is a matter of disrespect—in this case, disrespect for the family's ability to change. Thus, timing is a crucial element in reframing. There must be enough engagement of the experience to provide the energy for change, while not so much as to perpetuate the core problem sequence. Reframing is an ongoing contextual and relational process, not an isolated statement on a particular behavior.

Assessing the Impact and Building an Organizing Theme

Reframing does not end with an intervention. Instead, the therapist follows up on the acknowledgment and reframing with an assessment of the "fit"; the therapist listens to the client's response and incorporates changes or alternative ideas into the next validation and reframing statement. In this way, reframing becomes a continuous loop of therapist–client interactions that build toward the therapeutic goal. It is a process whereby the therapist and client actually construct a mutually agreed-upon and jointly acceptable alternative explanation for an emotional set of events or series of behaviors. This makes the explanation real and relevant to both the therapist and the client. Over time small individual instances of reframing become a theme as they link up to involve many family members, a series of events, and a complex alternative explanation for the problem. The constructed, family-focused problem definition helps shape the therapy; it becomes the major theme that explains the family's problems and thus organizes behavior change efforts. Without going through this iterative process of redefinition to include all family members, it is almost impossible to get everyone in the family involved in the behavior change phase.

Reframing ... Again: Building on the Last Reframing

Because reframing is a circular process rather than a single event, what the therapist hears in the client's reaction to the reframing guides him or her in what to add and what to eliminate to make the next reframing more personal and comprehensive.

A metaphor may help describe the process of reframing and its outcome. Those of you who live in cold climates may have experience with building snowmen. My experience is that while they all look the same in many ways, each snowman is different and has unique characteristics and features. The outcome of reframing is like this—it is similar for each family but it also has unique features. The process that leads to the snowman outcome begins with a small snowball you form in your hands. Once it is packed together, you lay the ball on the ground and roll. At each turn the ball collects a fresh layer of snow. The direction of the rolling process determines the outcome. If you want a fat snowman, you roll a large round ball, changing directions frequently to create a sphere. To make a different shape, you roll it in such a way as to layer the new snow differently. Other people can take turns or help you roll the ball. Regardless, each time the snowball is rolled, it picks up a new layer. This is like the process of relational reframing—the therapist is constantly adding to the last statement by incorporating what the client says until the desired shape is obtained. The look of a snowman depends partly on what the builder wants it to look like and partly what's available to work with. The constructive process of reframing is much like this. There is always a general outcome in mind—less blaming, less negativity, and a constructed story that includes everyone. But it too takes its specific features and components from what is available in the moment—what the family brings to the room. It is here that the details, the important features, and the parts to be emphasized come together.

Interrupting/Diverting to Structure Sessions

Many times reframing is not possible. In those cases it may be useful to interrupt the escalating and self-defeating patterns that develop between family members and divert their attention and energy in a different direction. Interrupting and diverting can take the form of questions ("I know you are really angry. May I ask how it is that this has come about and what you are struggling with?") or merely refocusing the direction for the conversation ("There is an important thing that I need to know to understand what is going on. Could you tell me about how things work in school?"). While not as elegant or complete a therapeutic intervention as reframing, interrupting or diverting the sequence of escalation between the family members does immediately reduce the tension in the room. The most direct and therapeutic element of diverting and interrupting is an immediate shift in levels of negativity and blame—a goal of the phase.

Process Comments

A specific form of diverting and interrupting that deserves special note takes the form of making process comments or pointing to an event or interaction in the room. This intervention is a bit like shining a spotlight on a particular part of the common relational pattern between family members. The therapist may say, for example, "Is this the kind of thing that typically happens when you try to talk about school?" or "Look at what happens: When your mom says that you need to be respectful, you are quick to react and turn the conversation back to her, which only escalates the discussion." The particular value of process comments is that they have the effect of interrupting the pattern while at the same time providing the family with an example of how things work between them. This knowledge has the potential to be helpful in the later phases of FFT when the therapist tries specifically to add social skills to the relational pattern. In addition, process comments help the therapist understand the pattern and verify it with family members.

It is also important to remember that relational reframing is not imposed but constructed by the therapist and the family through a relational process of suggesting, responding, and adding details, features, and elements. This means that the therapist is not just reflecting back to the family what is there but actually adding something new to the discussion—something that the family did not previously know or think about. Just as a snowman is built up of layers, there are layers to reframing that help it be direct, personal, and focused on the specific family in treatment.

Building Organizing Themes

One of the major outcomes of the reframing process in engagement and motivation is what we have called *organizing themes*. Organizing themes describe problematic behavior patterns and/or relationships in a way that suggests that they may be motivated by positive (but very misguided) intentions. Themes help inform reattributions made during the reframing process. While there is no definitive list of themes and no formula for creating them, there are criteria for successful themes that promote the goals of the engagement and motivation phase.

In the clinical work of FFT, themes become descriptions of the family, their problems, and their experiences that are nonblaming alternative explanations for bad behavior. The suggested alternative refocuses responsibility from the person or event being discussed onto an understandable and nonmalevolent aspect of the person in question, thus reducing negative behavioral interchanges. It is important to remember that themes are useful only when they are mutually developed by therapist and family (alliance-based) and when the theme includes a specific understanding of what is important to each person and a family-based description that is not negative.

Some possible themes that meet these criteria are among those described by Alexander, Pugh, Parsons, and Sexton (2000):

- Anger implies hurt
- Anger implies loss
- Defensive behavior implies emotional links
- Nagging equals importance
- Pain interferes with listening
- Frightened by differences
- Need to feel okay about self in context of problems
- Protection
- Giving up so much power to someone else

Organizing themes speak to the concerns of both the individuals (the parents and the adolescent) and the family as a whole. In this way themes are like a braid; they weave the individual views together into an explanation of the problem that involves everyone in the origin of the difficulty, yet blames no one. An organizing theme serves as the basis of the behavior change and generalization phases to come. The real challenge is to make sure that the organizing theme is mutually developed and specific in a way that engages the family, feels relevant and potentially helpful, and is personal enough to feel supportive.

One valuable way for the therapist to think about organizing themes is that they help clients see the big picture rather than get lost in the small details. These small details are the very points that get the family stuck and create many of the escalating patterns that are represented by "Yes, you do!" "No, I don't!" Thinking about the family in a thematic way brings up a broad, multisystemic picture of the family. Thematic thinking helps everybody stay out of the unsolvable details and focus on moving forward and linking individual family members in a nonblaming way.

Case Example

Given the high level of initial negativity and blame between Peter and his mother, reframing was a particularly useful tool. Sitting in the room with the family, the therapist first focused on the attributions behind the statements of each. When Peter angrily dismissed Anja, the therapist responded, "This is exactly the point [*acknowledgment*] . . . this is the important issue [*framing*] . . . this is the part that gets lost between you [*reframing*] when you talk like this." Sensing Anja's stronger emotional reaction, the therapist responded differently: Each time Anja attributed the whole of the family's difficulties to Peter's "problem," the therapist looked at Anja and said, "Now I think I understand. This isn't about you and getting your way, this is about you wanting so badly to help him [*acknowledgment*] . . . it is more about protecting him [*reframing*]."

While these themes were just guesses by the therapist based on things Peter and Anja had said, the themes of loss and protection quickly seemed to link Anja and Peter together and help them overcome the emotional struggle each felt in almost every interaction. Over the course of the session, the themes were elaborated and more events were fitted under them.

Near the end of the session, the therapist said to Anja: "I think this sums it up—what you just said, that it was never about controlling him, it was only about helping. You know this is important because it is among your most cherished values. Yet, clearly, you quickly find yourself irritated and waiting for Peter to just leave. Yet at the same time you know, somewhere, that Peter is much less disturbed and actually more impendent than it may seem. His anger is often hurt and a feeling of great loss, loss of his mother. . . . You know that the biggest issue now is not him but finding a way to become more thick-skinned and able to look beyond moments of tension without being derailed."

And, in response to a strong dismissive reaction by Peter to his mother, the therapist said to Peter: "I think I understand . . . maybe now I am getting a better idea. I must say that I have been sitting here all this time trying to figure out how to respond to this type of response you sometimes make to Anja. At first I thought maybe she was right, that you were just disrespectful, but then I listened more carefully. What I actually hear, although it is done with a tone that makes it difficult to hear the real message . . . but I think you mean to protect her and at the same time retain your sense of control over your own life. Unfortunately, it seems that your anger is so quick that it is easy to miss the lessons she is trying to help you with . . . it is probably even harder to find her good intent . . . that seems to be how it works in anger. Do you know what I mean?"

It took an entire session of intense listening and active relating for the therapist to help Anja and Peter move from negative and blaming interactions to ones where they felt some relief.

Outcomes of the Engagement/Motivation Phase

The engagement and motivation phase is successful when the family members begin to believe that while everyone in the family makes a different and unique contribution to the "problem," everyone also shares in the ongoing emotional struggle. The family comes to trust the therapist, believe that the therapist understands their unique positions (even if the family members don't agree with each other's positions), and believe that the therapist has the ability to help. Each person comes to know that no matter what he or she may have done, the therapist will extend equal protection and help to all; the therapist is not there to take sides or make one person change. The family members become engaged in the process, come to believe that it will benefit each of them personally and the family as a whole, and realize that the solution will require changes from each of them. They will have more hope that a solution is possible and feel motivated to try new behaviors and techniques in search of this solution. Initial themes and reframing become organizing themes, the outcome of which is a new, jointly constructed problem definition that reduces negativity and blame and increases family (rather than individual) focus.

The major interventions of FFT in the engagement and motivation phase are probably not new to any reader. These techniques are part of many different approaches to family therapy. When they are part of FFT, however, they show some important differences. For example, in FFT reframing is specific, meaning that the acknowledgment portion of the process shines a light on an event and links it directly to something relevant to the family; it is not simply relabeling or focusing on strengths. Reframing doesn't make the problematic behavior go away, but rather engages it, acknowledges it, and identifies it as bad. This specificity gives FFT relational reframing the power to make a difference.

Similarly, the use of themes is not uncommon. In FFT themes are specific, multilayered, systemic stories from each family member that are ultimately braided together into a family story. The goal of these stories is not to interpret but to mutually construct a different perspective through a process of conversation.

Diverting and interrupting are also not unique to FFT, but here these techniques are not used to control the session. Instead they are used to refocus a sequence of behavior in the immediate moment. In FFT what follows a diversion or interruption is a reframing that redirects the family to something new. In all of these activities, the goal is to be direct, personal, and immediate.

Changed Family Relationship

One problem with labeling the initial phase of FFT *engagement and motivation* is that it might lead people to believe that the outcome of the phase is just a foundation, a beginning, not real change. In fact, in a successful engagement and motivation phase, families change—they change very much. The attributional and emotional changes that occur and the alliance that develops create changes in behavior as well as feelings of motivation. When negativity is reduced and blame is lowered, family members act differently toward one another. These behavior changes are not specifically prescribed or suggested by the therapist, nor are they even the major topic of the conversation. Even so, families report that things are better as a result of this early phase of therapy. The changes in the family as a result of engagement and motivation are powerful and meaningful and have a major impact on the culture of the family and the interactions between its members. In this way engagement and motivation reduce many of the intrafamily risk factors that get in the way of productive changes in how families confront and changes problems they face.

Clients Ready for More

A final outcome is that the families are ready for more. The experience is like that of reading a good book: The early chapters set the stage and entice the reader into the story, but they also create a desire for more. After good engagement and motivation, the family is ready for what is to come. In fact, in the most successful FFT engagement and motivation phases, the family comes to a point where what happens is incorporated into their worldview, and they begin to respond by saying, "Okay, of course—now what?" It is as though the family members begin to sit up in their chairs and lean forward, awaiting the next step.

Alliance-Based Therapeutic Relationship

Alliance is often seen by therapists as a fleeting and momentary thing, always needing attention. This is true—the alliance needs constant monitoring. When the alliance fades, it is important to bring it back to life in the session. On the other hand, when an alliance-based relationship like the one central to FFT gets developed, it is fairly stable and enduring. What this means is that one really valuable outcome of this phase is a strong foundation that allows both the therapist and family members to be more open, more free, and more direct. It means that the therapist can be a bit bolder and the clients will understand his or her good intentions; conversely, the family can take risks without worrying that the therapist will not understand. This type of enduring alliance is critical as the family moves through future phases because it allows both therapist and client to focus on other issues. It is as if the alliance remains but moves more into the background, becoming a foundation for and backdrop to the work to come. This type of alliance is not uncommon in other therapy models; however, in FFT it is more an outcome of the assessment and intervention activities than a goal in and of itself.

Case Example

After four sessions in the engagement and motivation phase of FFT, Anja and Peter's struggles were far from over, but they were committed not only to therapy but also to trying new things themselves. They had the feeling that while things might not be right just yet, they had the potential to be better. Peter knew his mom was protecting him, in her own way; Anja knew Peter was being independent. These realities didn't sting so much or derail their every move, as had happened earlier. Mother and son were ready for more and trusted that the therapist could do the job.

Challenges of the Engagement/Motivation Phase

There are a number of significant challenges for the therapist in implementing this phase of FFT, notably the need for courage. Working in engagement and motivation requires therapists to be direct and active; sometimes they need to act before they have the whole story. Therapists who struggle with this phase often are timid, fearful, and unwilling to deal with their own reactions to difficult (even at times nasty or abusive) adolescents and family members. Successful FFT therapists are not frustrated by the different manifestations of resistance that they encounter, and they don't ask families to become almost symptom free (e.g., no longer abusing drugs, no longer interacting hatefully with each other, no longer experiencing suicidal ideation) before treating them. Instead these therapists accept the family members on their terms, even when their terms include behavior patterns that traditionally have been seen as treatment resistant. The model, goals, and specific interventions of the engagement and motivation phase are intended to give therapists the support they need to be fearless. However, to be successful, therapists have to be able to join with the intensity, not try to shut it down with medication, rules and structure, or threats of consequences should the family members not accept the therapist's rules. FFT therapists do not run from intensity and the honest expression of all the pain that family members often bring. Instead they accept and join with the family to face these difficult challenges.

In this phase one of the most difficult challenges is to use what happens in the room to move forward. Traditional psychodynamic models require a fair amount of time to develop a therapeutic alliance that can then be leveraged in intervention techniques such as interpretation. The outcome data suggest this approach is simply not effective with the populations FFT deals with; also, with the high risk these adolescents have of acting out, we often simply do not have the time required to use these types of techniques. Traditional cognitive reattribution interventions (e.g., challenging and refuting irrational beliefs) are faster but run the risk of creating reactance, which may require institutionalization or create high dropout rates. In a way, cognitive reattribution inventions are like karate—a set of strategic moves designed to overpower an opponent, and in which success depends on how much power the karate master brings to bear on the target. A better metaphor might be judo, in which the judo master's power comes from his opponent. When approached, the judo master instinctively moves with the opponent and gathers momentum and strength from the very force that is coming at him, then "turns" the opponent with a move that changes the course of the power. FFT's way of relational reframing is like this, using the power of the client's experience to generate the energy needed to make clinical changes. Successful FFT therapists acknowledge the specific experiences of family members who have been negatively impacted by a bad behavior, then use that energy to immediately reattribute the possible underlying motivation of that experience in order to create powerful changes in how members of the family experience behaviors, events, and each other in the interpersonal relationships of the family.

With Peter and his family, the conversation was not a linear one. It was not as though Peter presented his story and Anja hers. Instead, they came to almost every discussion filled with anger. Each time they talked, the air filled with not just information but anger. The therapist met these expressions with acknowledgment and then reframed them—anger became the hurt that an individual feels in response to trouble in the family, and adolescent rebelliousness became independence and even an attempt to "protect" the parent by reducing the burden on the parent of having a dependent child. She attended to their feelings of hopelessness by challenging the family in a way that made alternative solutions, still ahead in the behavior change phase, seem like a natural next step for the family.

Conclusions: The Early Stages

Today many therapy models recognize the need to engage and motivate clients. In FFT, we have always believed that engagement and motivation are not characteristics of the client but goals of the early stages of therapy. We also know that this demands a lot of the therapist. But when therapists approach engagement and motivation as discussed in this chapter, they find that the initial phase of therapy generates critical, powerful, and important therapeutic changes in and of itself.

One benefit of having specific phase goals is that the therapist is able to judge the progress of sessions, using both direct observation and family reports to assess the reduction in negativity and blame, the development of a family focus, and alliance building. As these changes occur, it is time to think about moving to the next phase of FFT and reorienting toward the family in a way that refocuses discussion on a different set of goals—the goals of behavior change.

5

Behavior Change Phase: Enhancing the Relationships of Adolescents and Families Through the Development of Social and Behavioral Competencies

One of the things that FFT has done well is to incorporate both the relational focus of traditional family therapy and the behavioral focus of other types of approaches. Specifically addressing the behaviorally based skills that result in competencies used by family members in their interactions among themselves and with those around them was always an important feature of FFT. In fact, in the first edition of the *Handbook of Family Therapy* (Gurman & Kniskern, 1981), FFT was labeled a behavioral therapy approach to working with families. This was due in part to the significant body of research literature that found skills building to be related to successful outcomes in therapy and the existence of prosocial behavioral skills to be important in family functioning. But FFT was unique in that it promoted both the specific skills needed by the adolescents and families and the relationally focused "how" that is needed to facilitate this type of change.

Like every part of the FFT model, the role of behavioral skill development also evolved. In the early FFT models there were essentially two phases of treatment:

a therapy phase and an education phase. The therapy phase was the first attempt at describing what is now called the engagement/motivation phase. The education phase was just as its name would suggest—a time to teach the family how to act with different behavioral skills that might result in a reduction in delinquency and other behavior problems. In fact, there was some suggestion in the early days of FFT that the therapy phase (engagement/motivation) was to be done by a therapist who was skilled in the work of relational interacting, while the education phase was to be done more by a technician who was skilled in teaching behavioral models and instructing people in specific behavioral skills. The early focus on behavior change as a technically focused, skill-based teaching process was also a sign of the times. The work of Gerald Patterson (1982) and others emphasized the role of parent education as a focus of therapy, and improvement in parenting ability as the primary change mechanism in helping adolescents with the myriad of mental health and behavioral problems seen in clinics and practices of community practitioners. This work took a strong hold on the field as parent education became a primary way of working within families, and it also had a big impact on the early development of FFT. The early focus was on parenting strategies, including monitoring and supervision of adolescents by their parents. For many models, past and current, it is only important that supervision happens, not how it is done. But over time it has become clear that the key is, in fact, not what is done but how it is done, and this is now a central part of what contributes to the success that families experience as the result of going through FFT. Also, in FFT it was always clear that *both* the ideas of the emerging family therapy—ideas that focused on relational functioning and interaction in the room—and the use of specifically focused behavioral skills were important in successfully intervening to help adolescents with their problems.

For me, the initial appeal of FFT was its focus on engagement and motivation. I focused more on the initial phases—reframing, meaning change, and alliance building—and to some extent thought that the communication, problem solving, and other prosocial skills that the families were to be taught were only technical in nature. However, after logging many hours of work directly with families, while I still find engagement and motivation to be exciting and powerful, I have also found a similar relational focus to introducing, implementing and helping families start and maintain new behavioral skills that I now find to go well beyond the technical and very much into relational, therapeutic, dynamic and exciting realms. The nature of the behavior change phase in FFT has evolved significantly since the early days. It has moved from being a technical activity to a therapeutic one—from a teaching task to a clinically based intervention done with families as an integral part of the therapy process.

The primary goal of the behavior change phase is to target and change specific behavioral skills of family members, thereby increasing their ability to perform more competently the myriad of tasks (e.g., communication, parenting, supervision, problem solving) that contribute to successful family functioning. Successful behavior change is accomplished by identifying the risk factors that contribute to the specific problem behavior and helping change these in a way that matches the family. This phase emphasizes building protective family skills that will mitigate the factors that

put the family and adolescent at risk. Desired outcomes of this phase are competent performance of the primary activities associated with risk factors—including
parenting, the use of rewards and punishments, communication between adolescent
and parent, negotiation of limits and rules, and problem solving and conflict management—in a developmentally appropriate way, matching the relational capabilities
and the culture of the family. Thus, the goal might be to increase competent performance of communication, but the task will be approached in a way that matches the
relational functions of that particular parent and adolescent

The purpose of this chapter is to identify the types of skills and, more importantly,
how to clinically implement these skills so as to fit the unique ways in which families
work and thus lead to lasting change in the family relational system. In practice, the
task is to find a way to take those skills that fall into the domain of protective factors, link them to the problems the family faces, and implement them in a way that
matches the family's current and past experience, their family structure, and their
unique cultural, racial, and religious background.

Middle Phase Change Goals: Building Within-Family Protective Factors

Successful behavior change is a process of helping the family add core relational skills
that will help them solve their current most pressing concerns and at the same time
function as family-based protective behaviors buffering the family from future or
current risk factors within and outside the family. For the therapist two questions
emerge when in the middle phases of FFT: which skills does the family need, and
how should they be implemented, given the unique ways that the family functions?
The therapist's clinical task is to determine how to act on the very specific content of
behaviors, emotions, and problems that the family brings into the room while at the
same time purposefully building new and specific behavioral skills (including cognitive and emotional levels of behavior) that will serve as solutions to those very problems. To accomplish this difficult task, the therapist needs an individualized change
plan that addresses the specific, immediate behavioral problems and sets goals that
are obtainable by the family, while matching the unique relational functions of each
family member.

The process goals and therapist skills for the behavior change phase are described
in Figure 5.1.

Case Example

Simone, age 14, lives with her father and older brother. Her father obtained
custody of Simone more than seven years ago, when her mother left. Simone's
father, Bernard, is a construction worker who works long hours during the construction season and has long layoffs during the off season. Simone is a good
student, regularly attends school, and helps around the house. She was put on
house arrest for her part in a street fight with another group of girls. This is not

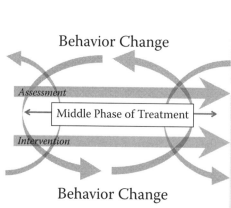

Phase-Based Treatment Goals

1. Build behavioral competencies that fit the family
2. Target the most relevant, obtainable, and maintainable competencies
3. Match competencies to relational functions

Therapist Skills

1. *Phase-based assessment of:*
   - *Additional information regarding the problems sequence*
   - *Assess relational functions*
   - *Prioritize BC target with sequence*

2. *Phase-based intervention*
   - *Reframing*
   - Teaching, coaching, supporting, adapting skills/to fit the family

FIGURE 5.1   Phase goals and therapist skills in behavior change.

the first time Simone's behavior has resulted in police interference. Earlier in the school year Simone was made fun of and bullied at school. By her report she was very passive for weeks until one day she "snapped" and repeatedly hit the other girl (the bully) until a teacher broke up the fight. When Simone's case came before the judge he put her on house arrest with GPS monitoring. This meant that her every move was watched electronically and that if she left the house, her violation would be registered at the juvenile court office and she would be held in violation of her probation. According to Bernard, things went well with house arrest until Simone became angry with her older brother. During the fight she cut off her GPS monitor and left the house, returning two hours later. She was sent to detention for 14 days for this violation. She has now been home for more than two weeks. Simone says things are going well. Her father is equally happy with things since she "learned her lesson."

Simone, her father, and her older brother attended six FFT sessions before beginning the behavior change phase. In each session the family brought in a new area of concern (a bad report from friends, an argument between them, etc.). The therapist reframed the event, looking for the common link (a family focus). After a number of difficult and angry discussions, the theme that had developed suggested that Simone was a passionate and assertive young woman, and that while this level of passion was a strength, she had not yet developed the ability to carefully consider the consequences of her actions. That is a lesson her father, given his long history of fighting and alcohol use as a younger man, had come to learn the hard way—through experience. His irritation, desperation, and nagging were a reflection of his attempt to teach her these lessons. The theme and accompanying reframing significantly reduced their angry interactions. In the last session Simone had said, "This is getting a little boring . . . didn't you say that before? Come on, I get it. He is trying his best—he just doesn't know how."

The primary goal for Simone and her family in the behavior change phase is to add specific yet relevant protective behaviors to the new climate between them in order to provide the family with a long-lasting way out of their problematic relational behavior patterns (and cognitions and emotional reactions) while decreasing the existing within-family risk factors. Therapy aims to add prosocial relationship skills, building on the work of the earlier phase of FFT, and match these skills to the way Simone and her family currently operate; the hope is that it will help buffer the many unchangeable risk factors they face now and will face in the future. When embedded within the core relational patterns of the family, new behavioral skills mediate the impact of risk factors, current problems, and current challenges. The change mechanism behind this goal is that if family risk behaviors decrease, the adolescent's problematic behavior no longer has a functional role in the family relational system. As the family protective factors increase, the family becomes empowered and builds their ability to manage the inevitable new challenges of the future. If the therapist succeeds, Simone and her family can use these new skills to replace the negative behavioral risk factors within the family relational system. Without building up the within-family strengths and protective factors, it is likely that, despite the positive effects of reducing negativity and blame in the engagement and motivation phase, they will have a very difficult time dealing successfully with the powerful negative community factors that will so often be part of their future.

To achieve these goals Simone and her family needed some additional help from FFT to build on what happened in the earlier sessions. The therapist's job was to help the family find new ways to act, integrate new behaviors into everyday life, reach obtainable yet lasting change, and address the bigger issues.

Find New Ways to Act

Small, obtainable changes may be simple for the therapist to identify but often are difficult for the family to implement. Despite the lessening of blame and negativity and the strengthening of interpersonal alliances that come from the reframing, relational focus, and multiple positive alliances developed during the engagement and motivation phase, family members still face significant challenges in learning how to identify and to implement seemingly straightforward changes. FFT therapists must listen to the unique content of the family struggle and translate it into the clash between core risk and protective factors evident in the family relational processes.

For Simone and her father, this means turning to behaviors they don't currently have or do not use in their interaction with one another. These may be small changes that promote effective communication or problem solving. What they don't need is to fundamentally reconstruct the functioning, functions, and core structure of their relationship. Instead, they add new skills that change the problems' sequence.

Integrate New Behaviors Into Everyday Life

It is not likely that Simone and her family will make major changes to the core patterns of how the family functions. The task for them will be to add skills in ways that fit their family but not their existing patterns of interaction. To help Simone's behavior, her father needs to find a way to monitor and supervise her activities—but in a way that will work. Most of their current interactions are marked by high degrees of conflict, poor basic communication skills, and inability to successfully negotiate or solve problems that face them. It is almost as if they lack the requisite individual and family interpersonal competencies in the areas of communication, problem solving, parenting (including supervision and monitoring), and conflict management to overcome what start as fairly normal daily hassles.

Here's the major question: What do Simone and her family need that is developmentally appropriate for all family members, and possible for this family with these abilities in this context? Currently, four behavioral areas constitute the protective factors within the family available as a foundation for the behavior change phase: communication, problem solving/negotiation, conflict management, and parenting. While these behavior targets are likely familiar and clear-cut, it is the application of them in a clinical and relational context that is the key to success. It is also important to note that an FFT approach does not view behavioral skills as discrete units that stand alone. They are small slices of behaviorally specific actions that fit within a larger relational pattern of behaviors (See Chapter 3). Thus, communication is always part of problem solving; conflict management is likely a feature of negotiation in a family where certain topics are emotionally charged.

Implementing behavior change in FFT is more than teaching, telling, or giving homework. Instead, these specific targets must be understood and implemented in an integrated way.

Reach Obtainable Yet Lasting Change

Simone and her family need something they can do that has a chance of succeeding and fits with their values and their context. One of the unique features of FFT is that the therapist is able to find ways to address the empirically grounded targets for change while at the same time making these changes meaningful for the family. A core principle of FFT is its focus on small, significant, yet obtainable behavioral changes that will have a lasting impact on the family. The outcomes sought and the targets along the way must fit the family's values, capability, and style rather than attempt to mold them into someone else's version of "health" or reconstruct their "personality."

What may seem to be small behavior changes in family process (positive monitoring, affirmation of prosocial steps rather than emotionally abusive criticisms) are ones that last because they enhance the relevant protective factors and decrease the important risk factors. When changes are obtained in this way, they have an immediate effect on a specific problem and the additional impact of empowering a family to continue applying changes to future circumstances. Thus what starts as a small change becomes, over time, a significant and lasting alteration in the functioning of the family that is reflected in major changes in behavioral outcomes, such as cessation of drug use and within-family violence.

Address the Bigger Problems

The therapist must help the family with two major tasks. The first is to work on the immediate issue at hand. This might be the reason for the referral or it might be an element of the problem sequences that gets in the way of successful resolution. The second task is a longer-term one: addressing the more indirect risk and protective factors and providing a causal link that ties these seemingly indirect and contextual features to the specific behavior of the adolescent. Oftentimes risk factors such as socioeconomic status and the parents' problems (criminal behavior, alcohol and drug use, etc.) are important yet indirect in their immediate impact on the daily functioning of the family. One of the great values of a family-therapy-based approach that is aimed at the relational interactions of family members is that it allows for a change in or a buffering of these factors because they are actually mediated by the family process (Sampson & Laub, 1993). In addition, the risk and protective factors literature can serve as the initial basis for identifying specific targets of the behavior change phase. In the earlier engagement and motivation phase, the target was reducing within-family risk. In this phase the goal is to build within-family protective factors.

These findings suggest that a therapeutic approach to helping with adolescent behavior problems should systematically target parental monitoring and supervision; parent–adolescent communication, problem solving, and negotiation; consistency in providing developmentally appropriate consequences; and methods to reduce conflict. In fact, many have found that adding specific behavioral skills aimed at improving these within-family factors helps buffer the adolescent from other peer, school, and community risk factors. This work also supports the idea that the "how" is as important as the "what." In other words, how parents supervise the adolescent is important, and how behavior management is implemented in the relational context between adolescents and parents is critical. These are the specific targets of FFT behavior change. FFT brings to the table a relational and therapeutic approach to inserting these risk and protective factors into the core functioning patterns of the family, thereby meeting both the what and the how.

Integrating Assessment and Intervention in the Behavior Change Phase

In FFT the task of helping families use more effective behavioral skills as a change mechanism has a unique look and feel. FFT is a relational approach, and one of the core features is its focus on the patterns of interaction between parents and adolescents. Unlike other approaches, FFT views each of the skills described here as two-sided activity, involving both an attempt at a different behavior and a response that adds to and completes the skill. A single interaction like this is also embedded in a broader relational pattern among all the family members, with specific and individually oriented relational outcomes. For example, communication requires a good, clear message from one party and active responses by the other. Problem solving works only when both parties engage and take part. Conflict management is successful when one party tries and there is an appropriate response from the other. Thus, the lowest common denominator in the process is the relational unit. To be successful, all parties must work together in alliance to acquire the skill. Thus, despite the more behavioral focus of this phase, FFT remains multisystemic, relational, and focused on alliance as a core mechanism of change.

What to Look For: Clinical Assessment

The ultimate goals of assessment in the behavior change period are the following:

- Identify the targets of change (risk and protective factors)
- Identify barriers to change
- Determine a uniquely appropriate way to implement a behavior change strategy
- Determine the manner in which behavior change interventions can match the relational functions of the problem behavior

To reach these goals, the therapist must identify a specific target or skill for the desired change; know how, where, and when that skill is used; and understand how that behavior functions within the family's common behavioral sequence. Assessment of these elements should have been going on throughout the therapist's contact with the family, so the therapist should already have some ideas about what types of protection to add and where to intervene in the problem sequence. But, as in the earlier phase, assessment is ongoing and occurs at the same time as the therapist models, suggests, and helps build family competencies. In actual clinical practice, however, there is more to consider: relevant risk and protective factors, specific problem sequences, relational functions, and the unique structure and functioning of the family. These features are the context that allows behavior change to be successful.

Identifying Relevant and Specific Risk and Protective Factors

Risk and protective factors assessment is conducted largely through clinical observation. These are the within-family protective skills that will help the family solve the current problem and function more effectively as future problems arise. But families are unique, and not every family needs every protective factor. This means that in clinical practice, risk and protective factors are useful only when they are highly specific and clearly relevant to the current situation, context, and functioning of the family. For example, in Simone's family parental supervision seems a particularly relevant skill. For other families, problem-solving or communication skills may be the highest priority and the most relevant for the issues at hand. Sometimes both supervision and an emphasis on communication change might be most helpful. Specificity also applies to the type, manner, and use of supervision in a family. For example, with Simone's father, supervision is a task that can be done in a fairly general way, based on discussion and negotiation done consistently so they don't get off track. In a different family, supervision might need to be more specific and detailed, involving a written contract and strong consequences. Thus, therapists must go beyond the general (communication skills, parental supervision, etc.) to a specific description of exactly what the needed skills might look like in the specific family. Understanding the problem sequence helps identify both which protective skill is relevant and which specific features of that skill will help most. This is one of the unique features of FFT—a focus on what family-specific skill to identify and what it takes in the therapy room to help the family change in enduring ways and meet their future.

There are a number of common risk and protective factors. Some suggest that parental discipline, supervision, and attachment are the primary mediators of problem behaviors (Sampson & Laub, 1993). Within the relational patterns of the family, parental rejection, indifference or hostility, and the use of harsh and erratic punishment or ineffective supervision are major risk factors associated with subsequent delinquent behavior by the child. In a study of the family environment of offenders, Kogan (1990) found that the lack of family togetherness and the existence of high conflict along with ineffective family management practices were among the most important family risk factors. Additional studies of risk factors (Kazdin, 2001; Kumpfer, 1999; Patterson & Stouthamer-Loeber, 1984) suggest that conduct disorder in adolescents is directly related to harsh and inconsistent punishments, poor supervision and monitoring, a lack of parental acceptance of the child, and poor parent-child communication. Patterson and his colleagues found that twice the variance in delinquent behavior could be accounted for by poor monitoring by the parent (Patterson & Stouthamer-Loeber, 1984). In addition, increasing communication and problem-solving skills were found to result in fewer juvenile arrests and convictions (Klein et al., 1997; Clark & Shields, 1997). These features seem to cross age groups and cultures (Griffin, Botvin, Scheier, Diaz, & Miller, 2000). Mulford and Redding (2008) also found parenting to be a critical issue in the conduct problems of delinquent adolescents. This work is supported by that of Dodge et al. (2008), who found that inconsistent parenting predicts social and cognitive deficits, which in turn predict conduct problems (Pettit, Bates, & Dodge, 1997). In probably the most complete work in this area, Dishion and colleagues identified lack of monitoring of children's whereabouts, failure to supervise behavior and time allocation, and lack of engagement with the adolescent's schooling as associated with antisocial outcomes in adolescence (Dishion & McMahon, 1998).

Further Assessment of the Problem Sequence

Understanding the problem sequence and its role are critical. As we've seen, the problem sequence is the core relational pattern that surrounds the specific behavior for which the referral is made. As a relational pattern, the problem sequence involves the behaviors of all family members in the time leading up to and following the so-called presenting problem. FFT suggests that this problem sequence is the lowest common denominator, or the smallest unit to which the problem can be reduced.

As another example, consider for a moment a couple that you or your significant other might know, people that you often spend time with. Over time, you have probably noticed certain patterned behaviors in their arguments. Perhaps one partner makes a statement and the other takes offense, or one partner dominates the conversation and the other partner withdraws. Regardless of the content of the argument—their children, one partner's long work days, the other's financial decisions—when you observe the relational dimension of the argument, you notice the same patterns recurring. It is no different with families of adolescents who have externalizing behavior disorders. The content of the problems varies—curfew, friends, following rules, showing respect—but the family follows very similar patterns each time one of these problems arises. This recognition, basic to family systems theory, has led us to place the problem sequence at the center of assessment in the behavior change phase.

Careful inspection of the sequence reveals two important therapeutic elements: the specific target (what has to change) and the specific role that target might need to play in the current functioning of the family. In each of the examples in this section, understanding the problem sequence allows the therapist to think in a clinically specific and precise way about where and when to intervene. In some families it might be best to stop the escalation in the sequence by intervening early, through a communication exercise. In other cases, it might work best if done later, after the sequence occurs and there is a strong-felt need to do something different. Once the therapist identifies the specific behavior target and the location of that target, the question is how to intervene in this sequence to implement a different set of behavioral skills in a way that builds on the earlier work of the engagement/motivation phase.

It is up to the therapist to make a clinical judgment about which specific point and which specific skill best fit this sequence. The problem sequence is only a tool to help specify the where, what, and when of behavior change.

Assessment of Relational Functions

Identifying a family's relational functions helps the therapist determine the relational strategies through which changes in the targeted risk factors will occur during the behavior change phase. The theoretical side of relational functions is discussed in Chapter 3. For clinical purposes, the main question is, "When person X relates to person Y, what characterizes the typical pattern of relatedness?" In FFT, relational functions are the drivers, the ultimate motivational energy, and the desired outcome of behavior patterns. Identifying the problem sequence makes relational functions easier to see. Relational functions can be conceived of as the state of the relationship over time and across situations. For the purpose of FFT, relational functions are a stable state to be assessed and matched to help the family adopt new skills that have the same outcomes as the negative and problematic behaviors they replace.

Case Example

Over the course of the first six sessions, it became clear that two particular protective behavioral skills, problem solving and negotiating, would help Simone and Bernard become effective in working together to solve the fairly big issue of Simone's anger. Problem solving and conflict management would help deescalate the anger between them when it happened; finding a different way of solving problems could help prevent anger. At the same time, the organizing theme the therapist had developed in the early sessions had become a consistent new explanation between the therapist and family to describe the myriad of situations that came up. The organizing theme helped bring together the small momentary reframings into a more global response that worked to reduce blame, reduce negativity, and develop a family-focused understanding of the problem. To move ahead, the therapist had used the last session to talk about the challenges that the family faced. In particular, what began as normal, simple requests or problems escalated into situations in which anger was an outcome of a pattern of behavior between Bernard and Simone. This helped clearly identify problem solving and negotiating as different ways to accomplish their mutual goals.

Relational interdependence refers to a characteristic pattern in which high rates of emotional exposure are necessary to maintain the relationship. Based on the problem sequence, the therapist came to see Simone as relationally interdependent (noted by a 4 and 5 on Figure 2.4) relative to her father. This meant that the typical pattern between Simone and Bernard was marked by a sense of interconnectedness, psychological intensity, and a strong desire for frequent contact on Simone's part. For Bernard, however, the pattern was typically marked by *relational independence*—a pattern characterized by seeking or maintaining self-direction, distance, and a low degree of psychological intensity (represented by a 1 or a 2 on Figure 2.4), and low desire for prolonged contact. The therapist saw Bernard as having a one-up relationship with Simone—the relational hierarchy was marked by an experience of feeling that Bernard had a great deal of influence over Simone in the relationship.

The goal in this case was to have problem solving happen between them in a way in which Simone retained her feeling of interconnectedness while Bernard retained his feeling of independence. As behavior change interventions started, the therapist made the problem-solving events relatively short yet frequent, matching the relational functions to both Bernard (short discussions) and Simone (frequent discussions). She tried to make problem solving about the facts and not the feelings.

What to Do: Intervening to Build Protective Behavioral Skills

In many ways the "doing" part of this phase of treatment is not unlike the intervening part of the earlier engagement and motivation phase—the focus is on making immediate changes in the events going on in the room. In the earlier phase, problems brought into the room by the family were met with reframing responses that were intended to refocus their attention onto reattributing problem definitions, reducing negativity and blame, and building alliance *before* responding to the family's requests for behavior change suggestions. In the behavior change phase, the therapist takes the events and issues that arise from the family and focuses them toward behavior change. Just as in the earlier phase, the therapist systematically responds to the family issues by directing the conversation toward building competencies that mitigate risk factors in ways that match the family. Now, with identifiable change targets in those more relational features of the family, and a more complete understanding of the way in which the identified problem functions in the family, the therapist initiates the behavior change phase. When the therapist redirects a conversation to specific changes in targeted risk behaviors, the family can draw on what they have accomplished already. The hope and involvement generated in the earlier phase provide the motivation, and the family-focused definition of the problem provides a rationale so that the behavior change interventions make sense to the family and are thus more likely to be carried out.

The FFT therapist is equally as active in behavior change as he or she was in the earlier engagement and motivation phase. However, the focus of the therapist's activities changes to accomplishing the goals of the behavior change phase. It bears repeating that to move ahead, the therapist must have made a clear relational assessment and evaluation of existing risk and protective factors. These assessments are the basis for an individual change plan that involves specifically identified targets and a relational strategy to accomplish them; both of these must match to the unique relational system of the family. The organizing theme established in the engagement and motivation phase serves as the rationale for the change plan (i.e., it should be logically related). The therapist needs to answer three critical questions:

- What are the most therapeutic behavior change targets? That is, which behavioral changes are mostly likely to reduce risk and build within-family protective factors?
- How can behavior change interventions be used in a way that matches the family?
- How can the therapist help the family do these new behaviors amid the powerful pull of the their relational patterns, history, and emotional intensity? In other words, how does the therapist position the targets of behavior change so that they make sense, given the way in which the presenting problem has been framed in the early engagement and motivation phase of therapy?

The intervention targets in this phase are of two types: reducing risk and/or increasing protective factors common in adolescents and families with behavior problems (e.g., communication, parenting, problem solving), and making changes in specific behaviors that are key points in the problem sequence. These skills are implemented not as checklists but instead as a set of competences that the therapist brings to bear on the unique relational organization of the family.

Behavior change can occur both in session and as homework activities that the therapist asks the family to do before the next session. In sessions, therapists might target communication. When the family begins to discuss events or issues, the therapist focuses the discussion on enhancing communication. The therapist may coach, direct, refocus, and practice these new skills during the session, recommending that the family continue to practice them outside the session. The therapist should be careful to ensure that the objectives of the homework are presented clearly and specifically to the family, and he or she must have high expectations that they are obtainable and can be successfully completed by the family.

Intervention Targets: Parenting Skills

Parenting is based on a set of specific behavioral skills—skills that serve as protective factors within the family. These skills complement the attributional changes made in the engagement and motivation phase by making behavioral changes to the common risk patterns of the family. The behavior change targets are based on the current scientific literature aimed at understanding the factors most predictive of risk and representative of families and adolescents with behavioral issues. That is, the goals of FFT behavior change are not unique—many types of treatment models share these goals. However, FFT takes a different approach to these skills. The skills are seen as outcomes of the discussions between parents and youth, achieved through the therapist's use of techniques that alter parenting behaviors, thus impacting the behavior of the adolescents, or change the structure of family systems as a means to help change the behaviors of an individual. Behavior change is a therapeutic activity that requires great creativity on the therapist's part—it involves taking very general principles and matching them to the particular family.

Parents perform their roles as the teachers, monitors, and managers of homes in ways that can serve as either risk or protective factors, either increasing or decreasing the potential for externalizing behavior disorders in their adolescent children. Improving parenting practices has long been a primary focus for family treatments. Developmental research also shows the importance of parenting style (supportive and challenging versus authoritarian) and linked it to outcomes such as school performance and social adjustment (Baumrind, 1967; Maccoby & Martin, 1983). Clear standards, consistent enforcement of rules, and monitoring of children's behavior have long been highly predictive of fewer emotional and behavioral problems in adolescents (Block, Block, & Keyes, 1988; Loeber & Stouthamer-Lober, 1986; Patterson, 1982). Parent education may be the most effective intervention for younger children, but there is far less evidence supporting the efficacy of parent-training programs with adolescents and juvenile offenders. Instead, parenting strategies, implemented within family relational sequences, appear to be the most promising method for treating the behavior problems of adolescent delinquents. It is clear that effective parenting of adolescents, particularly those with behavior problems, is a complex process requiring the parent and the adolescent to work together. Like other approaches to parenting, FFT focuses on the implementation of three essential areas:

- Clear expectations and rules
- Active monitoring and supervision
- Consistent enforcement of behavioral contingencies

Clear Expectations and Rules

The creation and maintenance of expectations and rules, and communication concerning them, may be among the most difficult tasks for parents and adolescents. Almost by definition, adolescents and parents come to rule making with different ideas about what should happen. The goal is to find agreed-upon and developmentally appropriate behavioral expectations that are clear and concrete, and communicate about them clearly and directly. This happens most successfully when the problem-solving and communication principles described below are used. After discussing the rules agreed to in session, the therapist may even want to write them down to avoid discrepant memories of what was said. *Contracting* involves having family members identify specific things they would like other family members to do in exchange for mutual adherence to agreed-upon rules, expectations, and tangible consequences. Contracting is particularly important to adolescents because of its mutuality; it binds the parents as well as the adolescent. It is also useful in FFT because contracting requires all participants in the system to get involved. Contracting should initially be conducted within an FFT session where the therapist can guide the process. Initial attempts should be as positive and successful as possible.

Active Monitoring and Supervision

Parental monitoring, broadly defined, is a skill that is relevant from infancy through adolescence, and perhaps even into young adulthood. Although the specific methods and foci of monitoring change at different developmental periods, the function of these activities is essentially the same: to facilitate parental awareness of the child's activities and to communicate to the child that the parent is aware of and concerned about the child's activities. As a prevention activity, monitoring means being involved in the teen's life. It includes being an interested, active listener. Just by listening to the adolescent's accounts of his or her day, the parent can show the adolescent that he or she genuinely cares about what happens to the teen. It may only take fifteen minutes a day of the parent's undivided attention. What classes does she like? How are things going with his friends? What problems is she having?

Supervision is similar to monitoring in that it requires being actively involved in knowing where the adolescent is, who his or her friends, are, and the degree to which the teen is fulfilling his or her required tasks.

Active monitoring and supervision often involve being able to answer four questions at all times: Who is the teen with? Where is he or she? What is he or she doing? When will he or she be home?

Consistent Enforcing of Behavioral Contingencies

Consistent enforcing of behavioral contingencies through the use of developmentally appropriate consequences is an important parenting tool. In fact, many parents come into therapy saying they want new ways to use consequences. Unfortunately, many times what they really want is a bigger hammer to force adolescents into compliance. Despite the attention that many models of therapy and many parents have paid to achieving parental control through consequences, with adolescents this is far more difficult than it may seem. Ultimately, most adolescents can't be controlled by their parents. If they choose, they have the capacity, despite any degree of negative consequences, to ignore the parents' rules or consequences. Thus, the use of consequences needs to be undertaken with care and based on alliance. In most cases, the way that the consequence is implemented is what makes it successful, rather than the exact nature of the consequence. Any consequence should be brief, done without anger, and linked to the behavior in question.

Intervention Targets: Improving Communication

Identifying and enhancing communication is a common activity in almost all therapeutic approaches. In the behavior change phase of FFT, the goal is to identify those aspects of existing communication patterns that can be altered and built upon to promote successful and effective communication patterns in families. It is important to note that in FFT, communication skills are rarely the primary behavior change target. The idea of "communication" is not specific and precise enough by itself to be a sufficient target to improve the relational functioning of adolescents and their parents, particularly with the adolescents that FFT is employed to help. Instead, communication skills are more a means to an end, rather than the end product. Parenting, problem solving, and conflict management all depend on and are enhanced by improved communication skills.

Effective communication is based on a number of core FFT principles (Alexander, Pugh, Parsons, & Sexton, 2000; Sexton & Alexander, 2004; Sexton, 2009) and involves a number of specific learned skills.

- *Source responsibility* is important to help foster individual ownership of requests and impact statements. Family members are encouraged to own and take responsibility for their words because keeping communication at a personal level helps reduce blame and defensive reactions. The family need not use the traditional "I" statements, although those might be a helpful way to express source responsibility. Instead, they need to find a way within their own interaction style to make it obvious that the communication, the request, the statement they are making is theirs, thus avoiding statements like "In this house . . . ," "Kids shouldn't . . . ," and "It would be nice if parents in this house were like Jack's parents."
- *Directness* is an important complement to source responsibility in that it specifies the intended recipient of the communication, thereby avoiding third-person comments, innuendo, and unhelpful generalizations. The goal is to reduce statements like "No one around here . . ." and "He never . . ."
- *Brevity* is important to give messages a chance to be understood and acted upon appropriately. Communications need to be short to avoid overloading the recipient with information and to make it easier to identify the key point of the

message. Brevity involves using as few words as possible to deliver the message specifically and effectively.

- *Concreteness and behavior specificity* are particularly important in negotiations among family members. The goal is to translate broad statements (e.g., "Do the right thing") into specific statements that can be understood, acted upon, and measured. Training in specificity often involves the therapist in helping family members translate their feelings and demands into specific requests that facilitate negotiation, contracting, and presenting alternatives.

- *Congruence* is important because it helps decrease resistance and eliminate confusion regarding the message. Because of the often high levels of emotion and the family's long history of struggles, simple communication often contains, or is perceived to contain, mixed verbal and nonverbal messages. The goal of coaching in congruence is to help decrease the discrepancy between messages, thereby reducing the likelihood of confusion, misunderstanding, or a seemingly inappropriate response to a request.

- *Active listening* is an important complement to all communication. Simply by actively listening to a statement or a request, the recipient demonstrates involvement and collaboration. Like impact statements, active listening must take a form that fits the family. Thus, it may not follow the prototypic "What I hear you saying is . . ." For example, active listening may be communicated without eye contact or restating, but simply with a grunt that acknowledges that the message has been received.

It is important to remember that traditional communication training and teaching, while compelling and familiar, are not the primary means of behavior change. Instead, principles of successful communication are used to make the core skills of developmentally appropriate parenting and problem solving more successful. This is because communication is core to every activity in the family, whether it be problem solving, negotiating, conflict management, or anything else.

Intervention Targets: Problem Solving

Problem solving is a central parenting skill. I discuss it here in a separate category because of the belief that, with troubled adolescents, problem solving must be a relationally oriented and mutual activity that is not just the parents' domain of responsibility. To be successful, problem solving between adolescents and their families must prevent problems and fix any problems that have occurred. Sometimes issues arise that require a more formal or defined procedure if they are to be resolved, but since problems and struggles are an everyday part of life for all families, developing an effective problem-solving strategy helps families engage these struggles in a way that maintains alliance while generating change. As noted, successful problem solving builds on the skills and strategies of positive communication. There are a variety of problem solving models available, but the system described below contains the critical elements of successful problem solving (Alexander et al., 2000; Sexton & Alexander, 2004). The steps include:

- *Identifying the problem.* The first step is to identify the specific problem to be solved by describing it in behaviorally specific and concrete ways. Point of view is a real issue here. Identifying a problem to be solved can be more difficult than it may seem because, as we have seen, each party is liable to see the other as the problem. For this reason, problem solving needs to be alliance-based ("We've got a problem") and approached collaboratively. Thus, the approach to identifying the problem must also be based on source responsibility, active listening, and the presentation of alternatives.
- *Identifying the outcome desired* is a critical step in getting everyone involved to work toward the same end. As with problem identification, identifying the desired outcome will require specificity. Outcomes must be determined through open discussion and the examination of alternatives.
- *Agreeing on what it takes to accomplish the goal* should clarify any subordinate goals (e.g., the steps involved in completing each individual's task). It may also include contracts that specify time frames and agreed-upon steps and outcomes.
- Before problem solving ends, it is useful to *brainstorm all of the obstacles* or ways that the plan might go wrong. When these issues are identified, the plan may need to be negotiated further. This precaution helps sensitize all involved to potential pitfalls, and it enhances successful completion of the process.
- *Reevaluation of outcomes* to see if goals have been met allows for accountability and helps problem solving be seen as a collaborative process that engages adolescent and parents in a process of constant improvement.

Problem solving (whether to prevent problems from developing or to solve ones that already exist) is successful when it takes place within a relational context of alliance and collaboration. It is an extremely effective strategy for altering risk behaviors when used as part of a comprehensive behavior change plan that matches to the family. Thus, problem solving is best initiated after communication training and within a session guided by the FFT therapist, to ensure that it is experienced as a useful alternative. Thereafter, the family may take the strategy and use it in programmed ways as homework.

Intervention Targets: Conflict Management

There are times when past history and rigid, entrenched, and problematic interaction patterns make it quite difficult to solve problems or negotiate to a successful resolution. Given the strong emotion that accompanies therapy, it is no surprise that some issues of long standing seem almost impossible to change by traditional means. Conflict management is a strategy to use in these situations. By managing conflicts to keep them from getting out of control, the family creates the emotional and psychological space to find new ways of working together that ultimately *will* overcome past hurt and struggle. Conflict management is not a strategy to "solve" the problem; instead, it contains the struggle so that it does not interfere with other behavior change activities.

In many cases, the best way to manage the types of conflict not open to negotiation and problem solving is to avoid the situations and triggers that start the automatic chain reaction of spiraling negativity. Whether this can be done often depends on the therapist having clearly identified the central problem pattern (see the section on relational function assessment, above). If the spiral is triggered anyway, the therapist or a family member may have to interrupt the pattern. This might take the form of the therapist ending a conversation between a parent and the adolescent and calling for a time-out when it gets to a certain level of negativity. It might involve a parent not asking about a "hot" topic, or an adolescent not bringing up old grievances and events that serve as triggers. The goal is to avoid the automatic verbal or physical triggers that cue up the pattern and start it running.

When conflict management is successful, it might happen that the family will eventually be able to use communication or problem-solving skills to identify a more long-term solution. Containing conflicts also prevents them from "infecting" other successes and objectives in behavior change. The steps described here have been previously described in various FFT publications (Alexander, Pugh, Parsons, & Sexton, 2000; Sexton & Alexander, 2004). Containing such a conflict requires the therapist to help both parties accomplish three things:

- *Remaining focused on the issues.* This helps reduce conflict by keeping it to a specific issue and not "the whole deal" or "everything that's happened." The goal for the therapist is to clarify the issue at hand and isolate it from other areas of the family's life.
- *Adopting a conciliatory mindset or a willingness to talk*, which communicates an emotional tone that contributes to a climate that promotes reduction of conflict.
- *Staying oriented to the present* keeps the focus on conflict reduction rather than on "rehearsing" and solving.

When one person feels the conflict and is unable to use other solutions (e.g., negotiation), it might help if the therapist (or parent, or even adolescent) talks the issue through by directing the person through the following questions. These are rhetorical questions—it is the asking, not any specific answer, that can help the person get unstuck and promote movement toward an issue-focused, present-oriented, and conciliatory climate.

Exactly what is the issue of concern to you?
Exactly what would satisfy you?
How important is that goal to you?
Have you tried to get what you want through problem solving?
How much conflict are you willing to risk to get what you want?

Intervention Strategy: Matching the Change Target to the Family

The behavioral skills described above are helpful in any relationship. They represent effective ways for adolescents and their parents to work together to meet and successfully overcome the problems they face, whether minor or major. In therapy, however, these skills have a different role. By the time a family gets to FFT, their problems have grown and become highly emotional, with meanings that go well beyond the scope of the skill itself. Thus, to use these skills therapeutically, it is essential to know how to help families successfully implement them.

Someone observing an FFT behavior change session would see some relatively simple skills in use. For example, the therapist would coach ("Why not try it this way when you talk with her?"), direct ("Wait, use the problem-solving steps"), and model when families bring the problematic events of the week or the day into the therapy room. What would not be visible, however, is the therapeutic "calculus" that goes into determining how to successfully implement a change in communication, parenting, or any other new behavioral skill. That calculus requires the therapist to match the specific change target to the family. As behavior change sessions unfold, the therapist may model new skills, ask the family to practice a new behavior or interaction pattern, or provide guidance in the successful accomplishment of these new behaviors. The ideas below can help therapists match the skills described above to the family.

In therapy with real families, it becomes clear that idealized prototypes of common relational skills do not correspond to how families really use the behavioral skills. Thus, the first step for the therapist is to get beyond his or her ideas about how communication or problem solving should look for a "healthy" family and focus instead on how that skill might look in this specific family. To illustrate these points, consider a common behavior change: communication change. Many therapists hold the belief that yelling and anger are disrespectful and inherently block honest, open, and "healthy" communication. Because of the belief that yelling is "bad," the therapist may target reduction of this behavior regardless of how the behavior may function in the family. As a result, families who have a style of loud and passionate arguments that do not interfere with their relational functioning are put in the same category as families in which yelling is coercive and blaming.

Making new behavioral skills "fit" the family relational system allows the therapist to take the path of least resistance and maximizes the likelihood that the family will be successful. There are three places where the therapist applies the specific skill to be implemented and, using coaching, teaching, and/or modeling, tries to help families adopt the skills as a new option in their core relational way of interacting. These include:

- *Matching to the problem sequence.* This requires that the therapist find the best place within the problem sequence to ask the family to try the new skill. This is an analytic task the therapist completes during treatment planning and carries out in the session. From the sequence the therapist can prioritize which behavior change target is most relevant and most obtainable, and at the same time can "make a difference that makes a difference" (Bateson, 1972).
- *Matching to the relational functions* of the parent and adolescents. This usually involves adjusting the intensity, frequency, and quantity of the skill application suggested to the family. For those relationship dyads where the common pattern is characterized by high contact between parent and adolescents, the therapist may describe the problem-solving activity as requiring frequent contact that includes expression of the core emotional meaning of the event to

each another. Those adolescents and parents who are considered more relationally independent might be told that problem-solving sessions should be
short, occur once a day, and be done with a focus on the content rather than the
emotional reactions surrounding it. For example, in one family the implementation of communication change might take the form of a close-up negotiation
of changes so everyone feels connected and part of a collaborative relationship.
In another family with a different relational profile, the same communication changes would look more disconnected and distanced, with information
exchanged via notes instead of conversation. Therefore, the goal of the behavioral intervention is to change not the relational functions of behaviors but,
instead, the manifestation of these outcomes.

- *Matching to the organizing theme* provides coherence and makes a link between
  the work of the earlier phase and behavior change. Conflict management may be
  described, for example, as an opportunity to honor and respect the importance
  of the issue for another family member, or as protecting the parent from pain.
  Reframing is the most likely method to link the work on the behavioral skill
  and the work done in the previous phase. For example, in one family, changes
  in family problem-solving style would be defined as "a way to work things out
  together," while in another family, it might be described as a "method for the
  parents to teach their children the lessons of being a young adult."

Reframing, Again and Again

While certainly central to engagement and motivation, reframing is also an important tool to help families use the new skill for behavior change. Reframing helps focus
the family's struggles and salient issues toward the goals of behavior change (e.g.,
competency development). Used in this phase, reframing follows the same steps as
described in Chapter 4 (see Figure 4.3) but may be done for a different purpose. What
is different is that in the behavior change phase, the therapist can build on the work of
engagement and motivation. New problems that arise can be reframed so as to focus
the discussion and reattribution on the organizing theme developed earlier, rather
than create a new theme; this helps solidify and build on the organizing theme. In
the behavior change phase, reframing can be used to focus on the need to change
a specific set of behaviors. Here the therapist can explicitly challenge the family to
use, for example, new communication skills, or negotiation, or conflict management.
Used in this way, reframing becomes a bridge into an action stage.

Case Example

Behavior change is most successful when it is specific and individually tailored
to the unique family. It was early in the first session that Simone's therapist
identified two potential behavior change targets. Over the course of the engage-
ment/motivation sessions, the therapist reframed these potential targets so that
they more clearly fit the sequence of the family. Fighting was very relevant;
preventing it was greatly desired, obtainable, and clearly connected to helping

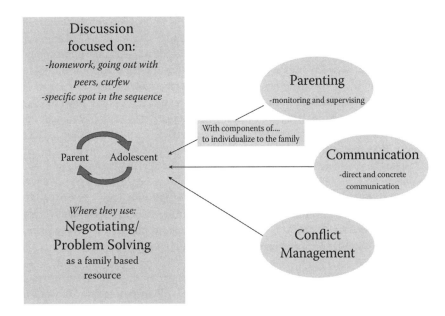

FIGURE 5.2 Targets of FFT behavior change.

Simone and Bernard. What was unique was the special way in which Bernard and Simone needed to implement problem solving. It needed to match the relational functions—this made it fit the outcomes of the sequence. It also needed to include some additional skill components, including communication and conflict management, to help it succeed, given the powerful relational sequence the family experienced. Figure 5.2 illustrates the specificity of behavior change targets in a clinical setting. For problem solving (fixing) and negotiating (preventing) to work, Bernard needed to make more direct and concrete requests, Simone needed to respond more actively, and both needed to employ conflict management skills.

Outcomes of the Behavior Change Phase

As they move through the engagement and motivation phase, families experience significant relief. The levels of negativity and blame surrounding the problems they face go down, a sense of working together increases, and the idea that "we are all in it together" begins to emerge as a family focus to the presenting problem. When successful, the behavior change phase of FFT brings an additional layer of change to the family. In this phase the family uses alliance and their family-focused problem definition to home in on some very specific behaviors; when successfully attempted, frequently practiced, and consistently implemented, these solve some of the immediate problems they experience and provide a protective buffer to the challenges in the future.

As a result of this phase of treatment, both parents and adolescents become more competent in specific skills that are empirically linked to helping adolescents with externalizing behavior disorders: parenting, the use of rewards and punishments, communication between adolescent and parent, and the negotiation of limits and rules. These new competencies help change the specific problem behavior for which the family was referred. But maybe even more importantly, this phase helps the family translate these seemingly simple skills into a mode of application that matches the way the family functions, how they think about themselves, and the less apparent but important relational functions.

Despite these sometimes dramatic changes to the family, they still have problems. The outcome of the behavior change phase, or any other phase of FFT, is not a total elimination of problems. Instead, what the family walks away with is the capability to solve many different problems now and in the future. FFT therapists don't attend to and target every risk behavior in each family. Instead, the goal is to successfully change a few central risk behaviors that can be built on and extended in the generalization phase.

For Simone and Bernard, the behavior change portion of FFT was surprisingly successful. They were able to maintain a more stable alliance-based way of working while trying various iterations of strategies to prevent and fix problems they encountered often. Both were able to stay focused on a single topic and use behaviorally specific language in working together to determine the specific problem, alternative solutions, barriers, and come up with an agreement. Over the course of four behavior change sessions, they applied variations of this new behavioral competency to various situations, including issues with her curfew (there were three instances where she overstayed curfew) and immediate arguments that happened at home. Each session began with a discussion about the situations that took place. Each time the therapist focused the discussion on trying problem solving or using negotiation. Over time, the arguments were reduced; Simone and Bernard found good solutions in most of their daily interactions. The biggest challenge for the therapist was to determine what was enough. Was success at a joint problem-solving skill within a more alliance-based and family-focused climate sufficient to stop Simone from fighting? Could the reduction of within-family risk and the promotion of within-family protective skills be enough to reduce the possibility of Simone having more behavioral difficulties in the future? The answer is actually in the last phase of FFT—the generalization phase.

Challenges of the Behavior Change Phase

Like the engagement and motivation phase, the behavior change phase of FFT has its challenges for the therapist. In fact, the biggest obstacle to successfully implementing this phase is its familiarity. The specific skills that FFT therapists help the family incorporate into their way of working are common to many therapeutic models. Skills such as these are often part of graduate training programs in social work, counseling, family therapy, and psychology. This means that the therapist comes to the phase with a number of preexisting ideas about how these skills typically look when successfully used, and with tried-and-true ways of helping people adopt them. These preexisting ideas pose a significant challenge to the relational and family-focused way that FFT approaches the same skills.

Successful FFT therapists implement behavior change phase in accordance with the core principles described in the first section of the book. Each skill is a relational one that fits within a larger and more complex relational pattern. To change these seemingly discrete skills, they must be considered as single behaviors within a relational context. Change requires the therapist to abandon the curriculum and instead focus on matching to the family. To do this, the therapist must check his or her values, beliefs, and cherished methods of implementing skills at the door, so to speak.

Conclusions and Reflections on the Middle Phase

The field has a rich tradition of parent training, parent education, and parenting strategies for working with adolescents and their families. There is good reason for this emphasis. The vast majority of the research literature has identified parental monitoring and supervision, family communication and bonding, and the ability to effectively solve problems as essential elements in families who can overcome the burdens of the behavior problems experienced by their adolescents. In fact, these skills seem to act as protective buffers, helping empower the family to be able to handle future problems. FFT brings a relational and family-focused approach to these tasks. For FFT therapists, how the changes happen is critical to whether or not the family can incorporate these skills over the long term. However, as the adolescent follows the very natural developmental trajectory toward independence and competence, the parents' ability to control their child's behavior quickly diminishes.

FFT is successful because it offers an idiographic, family-focused plan for how to change the essential behavioral skills necessary to help adolescents. FFT sees behavior change not as a technical activity but as a powerful relational and therapeutic process in which the therapist pursues the development and establishment of new protective behaviors within the core relational pattern of the family. Fixing problems is a secondary concern during this process, but in fact it will occur naturally if behavioral competencies are developed. FFT therapists pursue behavior change by following principles rather than relying on tools or pat interventions." While more technical than the engagement and motivation phase, the behavior change phase of FFT requires the same level of creativity and personal involvement by the therapist, making it a relational process between therapist and family. During this phase behavior change interventions are integrated into the change process, building on the important work in the engagement and motivation phase and laying a foundation for successful generalization and family empowerment in the final FFT phase.

The behavior change phase of FFT is also unique in that it is not limited to a discrete and finite set of skills. Instead, the targets are empirically validated skills from the emerging literature on adolescents. As such, this phase is inherently evidence-based. It is also an open system. As new risk and protective factors are identified, they too should be included in FFT's set of behavior change goals. What is most important is that the way in which changes are made must be uniquely crafted to fit the relational functioning of the individual family in treatment.

The next phase of FFT is one that takes us yet again in a different direction that is critical to long-term family change. Now that the family has reduced the within-family risk factors and built a set of new skills that helps solve problems in a way that fits them, they are ready to become self-sufficient and independent. If their therapist continues to respond to the problems the family brings to the discussion by helping them come up with solutions, the family can become dependent on the therapist. The family can easily fall into a "revolving door" mindset of turning to the therapist each time there is a problem. But acquiring self-reliance and empowerment is not only a natural process—it requires a systematic effort with specific goals and skills that the therapist can use to help families both generalize the changes they have made so far, maintain those changes over time, and support changes by incorporating family, community, and potentially other professional help.

6

Supporting, Generalizing, and Maintaining Family Change

Youth and families who struggle with the types of behavior problems described in Chapter 1 tend to be involved in the juvenile justice, mental health, or child welfare systems. Each system provides different kinds of support, treatment, and help, each having the common goal to provide enough help in a way that meets the unique and special needs of the family so that they get along better, are more self-sufficient, and leave the system of care. This means that to succeed, service providers need to help families change and at the same time empower them to function independently so they don't need to access the system again.

This type of empowerment is a noble therapeutic goal. However, the mechanisms that help families develop the ability to initiate and persist in translating changes made in therapy into their daily life are surprisingly complex. Every family therapist has had cases where, despite significant within-family change, at the very next instance the adolescent and family seem unable to use what they learned and how they changed in therapy to combat the challenge. We have all had cases where the family, faced with a new problem, repeats the same pattern and struggle. Other families fail to recognize the common elements that link problems in school with problems with peers and problems with prosocial involvement, when that recognition would allow the family to act in effective ways. Sometimes this happens because families in treatment got enough immediate relief that therapy ended, yet they were not counseled about how to handle future problems. For other families going through difficult situations, change somehow became linked to the person or place helping them, to the extent that they turn to the helper each time there is a problem; they are unaccustomed to dealing with problems on their own. In each of these situations, the same piece is missing—helping the family to generalize, maintain, and support the success made in treatment to future, potentially problematic situations.

In the absence of attention to the multisystemic context of the family, therapy does not provide a foundation for their interacting with and using external systems to help support and maintain change.

Yet there is a paradox that faces therapists in the final stages of helping families. Families do make significant changes as a result of the reattribution, reduction of negativity, and rallying around one another that occur in the early phases of FFT. Families can add important and specific behavioral skills, particularly when those are matched to how the family works and not applied in a cookie-cutter manner. At the same time, newly "graduated" families are at risk, and it is highly likely that they will struggle to maintain the change and use it in increasingly diverse life situations. Early family therapy models held out the belief that small changes in the family would naturally ripple out to impact other areas of life. Yet other approaches argue that it is the family's responsibility to take what fits them and apply it to their life in their own way when ready.

Over the years, FFT has evolved into a model that systematically addresses generalization, support, and helping maintain changes over time as issues integral to the change process itself. Parsons initially proposed the idea of the "family case manager" as a template for the generalization phase. The idea was that the therapist adopts the role of a case manager and helps link the family with community services. We quickly found that while helpful, this perspective was not enough to prevent relapse and build long-term empowerment. What did work was to focus on within-family factors that contribute to the reduction of relapse and the long-term maintenance of family changes. These components were added to the descriptions of this phase in more recent publications (Alexander, Pugh, Parsons, & Sexton, 2000; Alexander & Sexton, 2002b, Sexton & Alexander, 2002; Sexton & Alexander, 2005). What emerged is a comprehensive, family-based approach to helping families feel empowered to successfully navigate their unique social context.

The generalization phase is founded on the observation that families take two steps when making changes that last. In the first step, the families change the relational interactions and adopt alliance-based skills in their daily interactions. The second step is to bring this same attitude and skill set to other naturally occurring issues that confront the family. In this step, the successful family becomes consistent over time and learns to handle the emotional discouragement of relapses. The generalization phase is built on the principle that small changes can have a multisystemic effect when accompanied by systematic attention to generalizing, maintaining, and supporting the family's changes. These changes often don't happen naturally. Thus, specific strategies for generalizing new skills, maintaining change, and supporting those changes with the aid of informal and formal community support systems help create the necessary system change for long-term success.

This finding is consistent with the multisystemic core principles presented in Chapters 1 and 2 that suggest that if family changes are to be maintained over time, they need to be embedded in the natural systems outside and surrounding the family. In addition, Henggeler, Melton, Brondino, Scherer, and Hanley (1997) suggest the importance of creating and maintaining successful interpersonal ties and links to community resources to help support changes within the family. The generalization phase is intended to avoid the familiar phenomenon of the "revolving door syndrome," in which each time a family receives services they learn to depend on that organization or person as a "needed resource." When caught in the revolving door syndrome, the family is inadvertently robbed of the opportunities to learn to access appropriate support systems. They don't build new skills or adapt those gained in earlier phases of therapy, and they feel little sense of efficacy or confidence in their ability to manage problems independently. FFT aims to help families learn to rely on their indigenous environment of community, extended family, and friends as a source of natural, reliable, and effective support, giving them the resources necessary to be self-sufficient in managing the normal challenges of family life.

This chapter describes the therapeutic process that expands the family's use of skills gained in the behavior change phase and maintain the family focus of the engagement/motivation phase by helping them act on their environment in increasingly functional ways. In this phase the focus of therapy moves from inside the family to the interface between the family and those systems that surround it. It requires a shift in direction for the therapist in regard to clinical assessment and intervention: now the therapist responds to events in the family in ways that help them become ultimately self-sufficient and empowered in their interaction with the surrounding context. The therapist shifts his or her attention away from helping the family solve immediate problems to a discussion about the role of peer, school, and extended family and community interactions as they relate to the family's ability to continue reducing the likelihood of future problems. The therapeutic goal is to help families generalize from the few problems and solutions discussed in the therapy session to the many similar ones that will apply to the daily life of the client for quite some time. These changes can be supported by identifying needed resources to build more prosocial links to peer, school, or community systems and developing effective ways to access those supports. When problems come up during this phase, the therapist uses the problem as an opportunity to help the clients build a sense of being efficacious managers of their future.

Final Phase of FFT: Generalize, Maintain, and Support Family Change

The major question facing the FFT therapist in the final phase of the model is how to help the family take the small and specific new skills that were learned in response to a specific problem and apply them more consistently, steadily, and with the expectation of success. In the generalization phase, the therapist aims to address three primary goals:

- *Generalize* the changes made in the behavior change phase to other areas of the family relational system
- *Maintain* these changes through focused and specific relapse prevention strategies

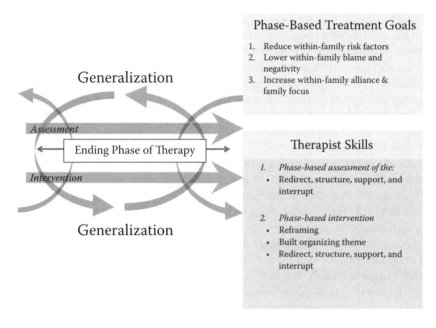

FIGURE 6.1   Phase goals and therapist skills in generalization.

- *Support and extend* the changes made by the family by incorporating relevant community and family resources into treatment

Case Example

David lives with his mother, Alice, his grandmother, Francine, and his younger sister, Aliene. David is 15, Aliene is 9, Alice is divorced, and Francine raised five children as a single mom. David's family is African American and lives in a large metropolitan urban setting. They are poor; the family income level is below the poverty line. David was referred to therapy by his mother. He is not involved in the juvenile justice system but he did participate in various different therapeutic services. Alice brought her "David folders." These were the records from the four different counseling services David and his mother have attended in the last year. He has worked with psychiatrists and family therapists. He had a mentor for more than two months, but they have not continued because of a "lack of interest" on David's part.

Twelve sessions of engagement/motivation and behavior change helped David and his family make a number of small yet significant changes. They had initially begun by blaming: "David just needs to be a man . . . he doesn't even want a relationship with me" (Alice); "You just have to cut loose when it isn't going to work out, just cut out . . . let him go . . . he doesn't like you anyway" (Francine); and "Why don't you all put me away? . . . Have you ever met some-body that doesn't even like their mom? . . . I am a little crazy" (David). Over the course of the sessions the negative emotional intensity has been replaced with more frequent, realistic acceptance that each of them is part of the problem and each needs to contribute to the solution. In the behavior change phase the therapist helped David and Alice implement more effective parenting strategies (monitoring and supervision) by helping improve their communication and conflict management skills. Francine remained skeptical, saying, "Whatever, as long as you help these two—that is all that is important. I already raised some—this is not mine to do."

The major question for David, Alice, and Francine is what it will take to help them build on the successful changes made thus far and translate those changes to future situations and their normal routines. For the therapist the question is what it will take to embed the therapeutic changes in the core functioning of the family so that it helps maintain and stabilize change. To achieve these goals David and his family need specific additional help from FFT to build on what happened in the earlier sessions. They need to learn to:

- *Keep it up.* David and his family face many more struggles. There will be a tendency for them to fall back on old ways of handling problems. What they need is to find a way to continue the changes they made in therapy despite new problems, the return of old issues, or other risk factors that may get in the way. For this family, this is most likely to occur if they know where to apply skills, what to bring to discussions (family focus and alliance-based perspective), and how to continue with the organizing theme built in the engagement/motivation and behavior change phases.
- *Handle more and different problems.* From the family's perspective, new problems have the tendency to look different. There's no real way to have a specific new approach for all of them; in fact, the more skills the family needs to employ, the lower the chances of success. So instead of getting endless new lists of skills, David and his family need to expand their existing skills to new problems in a way that seems manageable. They will be most successful if they can apply the small steps of behavior change to an increasingly wider range of issues in daily life.
- *Be consistent.* It isn't realistic to expect the family to be able to make a total change. There will be times and situations where despite their best efforts, things will be a struggle. They will be most successful in overcoming these situations if the family focus and behavioral skills are attempted and maintained, even if they are not totally successful. This helps them overcome the natural discouragement of the ups and downs of change. One of the most difficult parts for Alice is the competing "pulls" she feels from work, David, her mother, and her daughter. If she remained consistent instead of giving up when she was tired, it would actually be easier.
- *Adapt and adjust when things come up.* It is not uncommon to see the specific change strategies used in FFT evolve as the family uses them. Families tend to come up with unique family-based, alliance-based

solutions that include social skills that fit into the protective factors category. David and his family will be most successful if they are able to adapt both the cognitive changes and the behaviors that they acquired to the new situations they face.

- *Address other, bigger issues.* There are a number of risk factors that still face David and his family despite their success in the first two phases of FFT. The impact of negative peers and problems in school performance loom particularly large in David's life. These represent two major areas of interaction between the family and the world that can pose a challenge for the family in knowing how, when, and where to interact with the system in order to maintain the good within-family changes. How could David's family and the changes in the within-family relationship provide support and a source of alternatives for David in his peer group? The necessary parenting, monitoring, and supervision tasks that were addressed in connection with homework, school behavior, and the role of peer groups are also applicable in other future situations. The family has the greatest chance of success if this issue is addressed proactively.

- *Be realistic.* It's important for David that the family hold the belief that positive change is possible and that they do have the ability to succeed. The belief needs to be realistic, not one that sets them up for failure by being too positive. If the belief includes knowing that problems will come up in the future, that it won't be fun, but that with effort there is an alternative, then holding it creates the motivation to initiate new behaviors and put effort into persisting at them.

Integrating Assessment and Intervention in the Generalization Phase

In the generalization phase, the FFT therapist's task is to use clinical assessment and intervention to help the family develop consistency, independence, and the ability to take on a range of problems, accessing relevant community and family resources when needed. There is a pragmatic and functional reason for this shift in focus. Problems are a normal and expected part of life for any family, and the ultimate goal of FFT is to empower both individuals and the family to approach the inevitable difficulties in ways that minimize the risk of continued and future problematic behavior. Clinically, it is important to systematically prepare families to generalize the strategies they have developed and used inside the family to the natural ups and downs of change over time, and prepare them to handle potential lapses. In addition, future relapses are reduced if families develop and maintain both informal and formal support systems so that the changes they make can be sustained over time. Using social supports indigenous to the family lets them create a type of personal "continuum of care" that helps them withstand the natural challenges of the future.

On the surface, the generalization phase looks like the previous two phases of FFT. Families experience struggles and bring those problems into the therapy discussion, where the therapist redirects their efforts. In fact, for the therapist there is a complex decision-making process going on behind the scenes: Has the family assimilated the behavior change goals of the last phase into their relational patterns? Are they all ready to move on? What is the point of entry? What is the best way to redirect them from problem solving with the therapist to relying on their own newly acquired competencies? How to keep them motivated and engaged? How to set their expectations for the future? In addition, the therapist introduces the necessary informal and formal community resources and support to the family. The generalization phase has specific assessment and intervention techniques associated with it. Each is aimed at bringing therapy to a successful close by developing a motivation to continue with positive change, generalizing change, preventing relapse, using informal social networks, and identifying relevant formal support services.

What to Look For: Clinical Assessment

There are three domains of assessment in generalization: motivation to go on, within-family assessment, and an assessment of the systems that surround the family. The goal of clinical assessment in each area is to identify current risk factors, develop opportunities for support, and implement new competencies to interact with these systems.

Assessing Motivation

At first it may seem that developing motivation at the end of therapy is unnecessary. But taking the family's perspective makes it easy to see the importance. For them, things have improved: they experience less negativity and blame, more cooperation, and more skillful ways of dealing with each other and with the environment. As a result, families often consider themselves "done" with therapy. This is the same understandable mistake that leads people recovering from a bacterial infection to stop taking their antibiotics when they stop feeling sick but before the course of therapy is complete, thereby allowing the infection to come back stronger and more treatment-resistant than before. The therapist must take care to ensure that the family completes the course of FFT therapy to prevent relapses and the recurrence of problematic behaviors. Thus, developing and maintaining the motivation to continue with treatment is an important challenge for both the therapist and the family in this phase. Reframing is a valuable tool in this task. The organizing theme, developed in the early engagement and motivation sessions, once again helps mobilize the family. The therapist can use it to lay the groundwork for new ways of acting, by establishing that struggles are normal; what matters most is how the family handles them.

Assessing Family Relational Patterns

Assessment is geared to helping determine the ways in which the central relational patterns of the family may represent barriers to generalizing and maintaining change. Three particular elements are important here—the ability of the family to generalize the small changes of the behavior change phase to other situations, the manner in which the family handles the up-and-down pattern of change, and the future risk factors they may face and how to protect against them.

There are a number of risk factors specific to the generalization phase (see Table 1.1). Some are factors that have been present in the family since the beginning of treatment (e.g., ADHD or learning disorders, cognitive functioning, etc.). There are others that became apparent through the course of therapy or that have not yet been the primary target of therapy (e.g., association with delinquent peers, gang involvement, social rejection, and lack of involvement in conventional activities). These factors now become important because they are part of the way in which the family interacts with outside systems. Thus in clinical assessment, it is important to determine the degree to which these risk factors may play a significant role in pulling this family back to the ways of functioning they exhibited before therapy. Which of the risk factors are important, and how can the family use the skills formed during the behavior change phase to address these? It may be that a specific strategy is generated to address a risk factor. It may also be that a risk factor is targeted in relapse prevention or the other specific interventions of the phase. In each case, the risk factor is addressed in a way that puts the responsibility to initiate and maintain effort in this area with the family.

Assessing Relevant Outside Systems

The generalization phase is the time to think about how this unique family system interacts and works with the larger system of family, community organizations (e.g., schools), and community. FFT holds that symptomatic behaviors are linked to both within-family (relational patterns and functions) and outside-family (ecosystem) factors, both of which need significant attention. The goal is to determine which systems pose risks and which might serve to provide protective benefits of generalization and support. Long-term maintenance of specific behavioral changes depends on understanding which systems offer strengths to build upon and which might be barriers for maintaining change. It is important to understand the risk and protective factors in the school and peer group, larger community attitudes, values and beliefs about the youth, availability of prosocial community involvement, and extended family involvement.

This type of assessment requires the therapist to look to informal and formal support systems that are relevant to the family and available either routinely or in times of need. Frequently families either lack social support systems or have social supports that don't contribute helpfully to problem solving. The social isolation and turmoil that often accompany behavior problems are a significant risk factor for many other psychosocial problems (Henggeler et al., 1997; House, Landis, & Umberson, 1988), including domestic violence, child abuse and neglect, and mental health problems. Social isolation puts undue pressure on parent–adolescent relationships, so that meeting even the most normal challenge becomes a potential source of difficulty. Social isolation can limit the availability of informal and formal resources in times of need, and/or create a form of "learned helplessness" in the family, making them less able to access the resources that might help them.

At other times, the family's existing social support systems may withhold help or even act harmfully. For example, sometimes members of the extended family remain pessimistic and suspicious of the adolescent and put pressure on the parent to seek residential or out-of-family care. Other times, difficult interactions with spouses, friends, neighbors, therapists, or social service personnel create stress that can negatively impact parent–child interactions (Wahler & Hann, 1987). In yet other instances, friends of either the parents or the adolescent may provide access to the substances or activities (e.g., drugs or alcohol) that contribute to problem behaviors and family difficulties. Such risk factors represent undeniable challenges, but finding and successfully using the support systems that are available to help the family maintain change remains a critical goal in this phase.

The therapist should also look to ways in which neighbors might be a part of the problem and/or the solution—for example, by monitoring the adolescent when parents are working, or by engaging in antisocial activities. Another resource might be relationships that parents have in the workplace, which may be one of the parents' few opportunities for constructive peer interactions and sources of informational support in understanding the events in their family. Similarly, community caretakers and gatekeepers, typically encountered through local churches, neighborhood organizations, and local aid agencies, may support either the problem or the solution. Once the therapist understands the relevant community systems that may either support or become obstacles to maintaining change, they become targets for the therapist and family to build upon.

To connect the family with resources outside the therapy room, the therapist begins to use his or her assessment of the family's context to think about specific ways in which informal and formal social support systems can be made available to the family. Accessing formal social support usually happens through referrals to additional professional services. Whatever the type of support they offer, the goal is to help anchor the family to the larger community support system, thereby sustaining positive change over time and preventing relapse. It is important to consider three issues before connecting the family to a community resource:

- What type of support do they need (i.e., information, emotional support, or instrumental assistance)?
- What is the most appropriate and accessible place to receive such support on a timely basis?
- What type of support system is most likely to provide the needed help while at the same time matching the relational functions of the family?

Case Example

By the time the generalization phase arrived, the therapist had gathered a great deal of information about the areas necessary to be successful in the last phase of treatment. In planning for the generalization phase, the therapist pulled her thoughts together to try to answer questions that might help her focus the next session on the goals of generalization. Fortunately, there had been enough change to the family relational system that much of the negativity and blame were gone. Francine and David had come to a truce. Alice and David had found their way through the feelings of being lost and were now more engaged with each other in the daily activities that faced them. Alice grew increasingly able to see David as capable but struggling with his independence. Similarly, David knew his mom cared in her way. Both used better communication skills to sort through conflicts. Alice was more active in her monitoring and supervision of David, and he was responsive. Each time there was a problem, Francine told them to "get over it . . . just do what they told you to do when this happens."

For the generalization phase, these positive outcomes suggest an important intervention target: motivation to continue. In fact, the therapist did spend much time helping them stay involved enough to finish. Her biggest worry was that there was neither the cumulative self-efficacy to help them persist in their new efforts nor confidence about Francine's role and how she might help further support Alice in keeping the course. Finally, it was clear that Alice felt pulled between the demands of her family and the demands of her work, and she needed additional support to help with the burden of someone to watch over David.

What to Do: Intervening to Create Long-Term Empowerment

The therapist has to be guided by the goals of generalization and use the information gathered from clinical assessment to intervene in ways that ultimately help the family to increase their own efficacy in managing difficult situations. The overarching goal of therapy is to help the family become sufficiently self-reliant and competent to deal with the many challenges they will face in the future. The work of this phase can be difficult for two reasons. First, the therapist may find it hard to stay focused on the phase goals if the family continues to bring in new problems. In some cases, the therapist can be drawn back into problem-solving and behavior change activities. Second, the family's success to date may leave them feeling ready to end therapy, especially if they are no longer presenting specific issues or problems. Nonetheless, the therapist must motivate them to remain in therapy and prepare for the future. At times this can be difficult because from their perspective, things feel and are better between them and they don't see the relevance of further counseling. Remember, however, that a full course of FFT therapy involves remaining in treatment for a total of 8 sessions for minor clinical problems, or as many as 17–20 total sessions for families facing serious and pervasive problems. To motivate families to remain through this phase of treatment, the therapist relies on the organizing theme. It may be also helpful for the therapist to use his or her knowledge of the family to predict possible future events or contexts in which it will be difficult to maintain the changes.

There are seven major intervention strategies used by FFT therapists to accomplish the goals of the generalization phase:

- Create continuity and build on success
- Reframe to refocus
- Generalize therapy gains
- Prevent relapse
- Build family self-efficacy
- Connect to community
- Refer to other professional services when appropriate

Some of these strategies are familiar from other phases; the rest are unique to the generalization phase. Like behavior change, these "interventions" are really actions that can be taken by the therapist either in response to the family event or as a hypothetical situation initiated by the therapist.

Create Continuity and Build on Success

One of the advantages of FFT is that there is great attention given to the continuity between phases. The momentum of the first two phases is a useful engine to help drive the generalization phase. The cognitive and emotional changes of the first phase build expectation and motivation. The second phase adds relevant behavioral skills to the core patterns of the family; here families are motivated by the action. The generalization phase is most successful when linked to these changes to take advantage of the success and motivation that has been generated. The organizing theme can serve as the central thread in this phase as well. It can become the reason to keep working, suggest the places to apply those changes, and point the way toward accomplishing them. The organizing theme can help make the generalization goals relevant by linking them to the concrete struggles experienced by the family. Linking also occurs when the same behavioral competences developed in the behavior change phase are the targets of the generalization phase. For example, families who adopted problem-solving skills could use them to work with the school or child welfare office, to get help with rent or electricity, or to help gain access to needed resources that may help support the adolescent.

Reframe to Refocus

The negativity and blame of earlier sessions may also appear in sessions at the end of therapy. If negativity and blame arise or resurface with a new problem, the therapist must first acknowledge the struggle and pain, then reframe and reattribute the meaning of the event and redirect the discussion to focus on the challenge to the family of using some of their newly developed prosocial behavioral competencies in these new situations. It is important not to see reframing as a return to the engagement and motivation phase; the point is not to develop new themes but instead to reframe the meaning of current emotions and attributions and match to the organizing theme developed in the early stages of therapy. This allows the theme to become a new story that can continue to help the family in the future.

Generalizing Therapy Gains

Similarly, the family has to learn to experience any new problem as similar to ones they have already successfully overcome. To do so, they must be able to identify problems as they arise, then classify the new problems as similar to old ones they have successfully solved. The organizing theme is an important tool the family can use to classify problems in this way. When successful, the organizing theme becomes a new story or explanation of the family and its struggles; it motivates them to persist by casting the issue as solvable when approached in a family-focused, nonblaming way. Generalizing this insight leads the family to classify and identify the inevitable problems of life as solvable problems, now and in the future. The critical ability to identify and classify new problems in a helpful way doesn't develop on its own; it requires systematic work by the therapist. Figure 6.2 illustrates the generalization process.

Generalizing changes also can help extend the positive outcomes of therapy to the way family members interact with their social environment. The same prosocial behavioral skills that are necessary for good within-family functioning (e.g., communication, problem solving, etc.) and within-family change can have a positive impact on the way individuals connect with and interface with the "real world." Thus the therapist can help the family use the same communication and problem-solving skills needed for within-family interactions with the critical community institutions

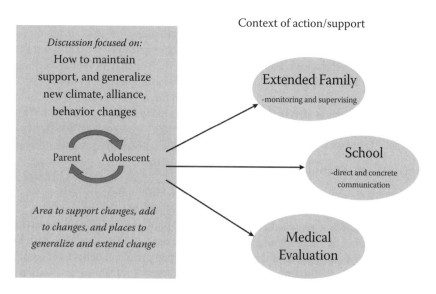

FIGURE 6.2 Targets of FFT generalization phase.

involved in their lives (school, the justice system, and the mental health system), thus further generalizing change.

David and Alice had most success at generalization when they were able to perceive new problems as similar to the ones the family members have already experienced and had success with. This perceptual ability was enhanced by using the organizing theme as a way to link categories of events into similar categories. It is aided when the family is able to face the new situation with the same family focus they used in the behavior change phase.

Preventing Relapse

Relapse prevention refers to a wide range of strategies designed to prevent relapse in the area of addictive behavior change. The concept has great utility for application as an intervention to help families (1) prevent the occurrence of initial lapses after embarking on a program of FFT change and (2) prevent any lapse from escalating into a total loss of their new direction and skills.

New challenging situations serve as stressors to the new relational pattern of the family. Marlatt and Gordon (1997) suggest that both intermediate elements of the relationship (high-risk situations, intractable problems with the youth, high expectations) and more indirect antecedents (relational events or historically and emotionally charged behaviors or words) can set off relational sequences that build negativity and cause the clients to lose the family focus. These elements are common to all relapse prevention programs, but programs can be further customized to meet the particular characteristics of a disorder. For example, prevention of depression or anxiety may focus on becoming aware of thoughts as passing mental events rather than facts about self or reality. Learning to identify bodily sensations that accompany maladaptive thoughts is also important for preventing depression and anxiety. Treatment of addictive disorders concentrates on reactions to social pressure, interpersonal conflicts, and negative emotional states as part of a relapse prevention plan.

Much of the early research in the field of substance abuse treatment focused on developing techniques for assisting individuals to stay drug-free or alcohol-free after successful detoxification. This work came from a simple observation: stopping and staying stopped are different processes. Empirical evidence supports the development of relapse prevention as a construct as well as a set of assistive strategies; it has been one of the most important advancements in the treatment of substance abuse disorders. The work of researchers, including Alan Marlatt, Kathleen Carroll, and others, helped move these techniques into the mainstream of substance abuse treatment.

The relapse process is familiar to anyone who has tried to change any type of behavior. It is particularly important in regard to therapy. During therapy clients build an increasing sense that they can have control over situations that were previously marked by distress, anger, negativity and blame. Each experience of success adds to the individual's and the family's perception of self-efficacy. This spiral continues upward until the client or the family experiences a high-risk situation that threatens their perceived control, decreases self-efficacy, and makes a relapse more likely. When a person copes effectively with the high-risk situation, the outcome is likely to be an increased sense of self-efficacy. The longer the new behavior lasts and the more experiences the family has of coping effectively with high-risk situations, the less likely the chance of relapse. However, failure to master a high-risk situation tends to decrease feelings of self-efficacy and create a sense of powerlessness. At this point, a relapse is likely. If a slip does occur, the person often suffers from a sense of cognitive dissonance that contributes to adopting a more individual and blaming attribution, thereby increasing the probability of a full-blown relapse.

Marlatt's original work involved asking relapsed individuals at follow-up to describe the situation that triggered their relapse. This research was the foundation for a major part of the relapse prevention model, key components of which are that the person should be able to foresee and identify high-risk situations, should have developed skills to deal with those situations, and should expect that using those skills will result in a positive outcome.

In FFT relapse prevention occurs when the therapist responds to the family's new challenges by reframing them as a normal part of the broader change process (e.g., "There will always be problems; it is how you respond to them that matters") and tries to build the family's confidence in their ability to manage new problems and "stick with the program" (not return to their previous, painful pattern of negative and blaming interactions). Successful relapse prevention requires that the therapist take the initiative and direct a discussion that helps to:

1. *Identify high-risk situations.* The discussion should include an analysis of the cues, initiating situations, family conflicts, and patterns of high-risk situations that may undermine the family's ability to continue with their established changes.

2. *Learn alternative ways to respond.* Once triggers have been identified, the susceptible person must find new ways of coping with those situations. The easiest coping mechanism for high-risk situations is to avoid them altogether. This may include avoiding certain people who have a negative influence or avoiding locations where the symptom is likely to occur. In some instances, avoidance is a good strategy, but the person needs additional strategies because avoidance is not always possible. These include identifying ways to cope with the negative emotions that arise around these situations, both for individual family members and the family as a whole; determining ways to deal with interpersonal conflict by applying conflict management principles; and discovering strategies to cope with social pressure that may involve both proximal and distant support systems.

3. *Reduce unnecessary stressors.* Besides preparing the family for high-risk situations, relapse prevention also focuses on general principles of mental health that, if followed, greatly reduce the likelihood of symptoms. These include factors such as balanced nutrition, regular exercise, sufficient sleep, health education, reciprocally caring relationships, productive and recreational interests, and spiritual development.

4. *Develop a support system.* Many research studies have demonstrated the importance of social support in maintaining a healthy lifestyle. Individuals who are socially isolated tend to display more symptoms of mental disorders. Conversely, individuals with mental disorders tend to have more difficultly initiating and maintaining relationships due to inappropriate social behavior. For such people, a support system may be nonexistent. Research suggests that support systems are most effective when they are naturally occurring—in other words, when a circle of family and friends who genuinely care about the individual is already in place. However, artificially created support systems are certainly better than none at all. For this reason, relapse prevention programs strive to involve family members and other significant people in the treatment program.

In order for coping with risk to successfully become part of a family's skill set, the family actually needs to relapse at some point, so that they learn how to apply the strategies to actual events and problems in their life. It is often useful to titrate down the "dosage" of sessions over time, typically by reducing their frequency. By increasing the length of times between sessions, it is more likely that the therapist will be involved with the family at critical points where relapse might occur and can help the family apply relapse prevention strategies.

It was Alice who struggled the most with relapses. It was difficult for her to bring forward her new way of thinking about David and apply it to situations as they came up in everyday life. If he had any trouble at school, she quickly wondered if he was "losing it." She learned that the highest-risk time for her was when David first let her know about a problem. She knew not to follow the initial fear she had, but instead to think of alternatives. She often went deep into worry and despair. Specific conversations in the conjoint sessions during the generalization phase helped her gain perspective. Each time a "David problem" ended up turning out okay, she was reminded of what she needed to do when afraid.

Building Family Self-Efficacy

One of the critical elements in continuing changes into other domains is the confidence and belief that it can be done. According to Bandura (1982), expectations of personal efficacy determine whether coping behavior will be initiated, what level of effort will be put into it, and how long the effort will be extended. The expectations that individual family members hold concerning their ability to act successfully in different ways (self-efficacy) have a direct impact on whether they will try something new and the degree to which they will persist at that effort. The FFT therapist can talk with the client about the importance of having options/alternatives and knowing what to expect; verbal persuasion is a powerful source of change. However, even more concrete and lasting changes come from those expectations built on actually trying something new and being successful (performance accomplishment). Persistence is most enhanced when the situation is challenging—somewhat difficult, threatening, or uncomfortable—but can be mastered, as a sense of efficacy develops further and defensiveness goes down. For the therapist, this means helping coach, teach, direct, and encourage the family to take new opportunities. Efficacy is also built from less direct and more vicarious experiences within the family session, or more symbolically through live modeling of successful experiences where their emotional arousal (from the personal nature of the discussion) can be guided by a reliable source of information.

David and his family fit what Bandura (1982) found in his early studies of self-confidence: They are more likely to generalize changes to other situations not only when they know what to do but also when they know how. There was no question that they knew what to do—each could recite the steps in their new communication pattern without fail. For this family the "how" came not from talking but from modeling and mastery. David, Alice, and Francine needed concrete, personal, and direct experience of a method to get through the difficult situations. Over time these experiences generated the mastery they needed to keep them going. For them, generalizing occurred when they knew where and when to act, knew what to do, and felt that they could be successful.

Connecting to Community

Most effective treatment models for adolescent behavior problems are multisystemic in nature (see Chapter 2). One element of this multisystemic network is the set of informal social networks to which the family belongs. High-quality social support from extended family, friends, coworkers, neighbors, and community organizations are strongly associated with favorable family functioning and the capacity to promote prosocial behavior (Harrison, Wilson, Pine, Chan, & Buriel, 1990; Reiss & Price, 1996; Vondra & Belsky, 1993; Weisz & Tomkins, 1996). Families with strong and available social support networks have access to more resources, and the availability of resources predicts differential responses to changing environmental conditions and traumatic events (Hobfoll, 1991).

The social support systems needed may range from formal (professional services such as mental health care or alcohol and drug treatment) to informal. The family's own social support network can range from those with fairly close ties (e.g., extended family, friends, neighbors, coworkers) to more distant formal relationships with community-based resources, either public (juvenile justice system, child and family services) or private (e.g., Big Brothers Big Sisters). Whether formal or informal, these sources provide one or more of the forms of support that Henggeler and colleagues have described as:

- Instrumental support (e.g., financial assistance, help with transportation, parenting assistance)
- Emotional support (empathy and caring)
- Informational support (e.g., help finding the best prices on food, need-based school assistance, places to get rent and utility assistance)

Clinical work suggests that informal social networks provide the most effective support for a number of reasons. As part of the family's existing social context, informal networks are more familiar to the family and have the potential to overcome barriers to help. Informal supports are more likely than formal supports to meet the family's immediate needs. For example, the family's most pressing need might be for $25 to buy gas to get the children to school and the parents to work. The money might be more readily available from a family friend than from an agency operating under city or state funding, with no flexibility to spend money outside its charter of narrowly defined needs. Informal supports are more likely to provide resources that are timely and easy to access. At one o'clock in the morning, a single mother struggling with her adolescent is more likely to obtain emotional support from her sister, friend, or neighbor than from a mental health worker. Most importantly, informal supports are more likely to continue after treatment ends than are formal supports. Informal supports rarely run out of federal, state, or local funding just when a family needs to buy gas or pay the rent.

Once established, social relationships are maintained by a relational mutuality and reciprocity, or the offering of tangible and emotional resources that is predicated on the expectation of receiving something in return (Uehara, 1990). These findings suggest that to maintain social supports for the long term, families who receive support must give something in return. This is not to suggest that informal support operates simply as a barter or payment system; rather, it works when there is a sense of alliance among people or an informal way of working together that is mutually beneficial rather than individual and one-sided.

To connect the family with help, the therapist must take on some of the tasks of a family case manager. The family therapist best fits this job because he or she understands the relational system of the family and can match it to available resources. In transitioning from the behavior change to the generalization phase, the therapist acts in this role more and more often, thinking and learning about the possible range of services outside of therapy that may augment what has been learned by the family. It is critical not to "pile on" all available services but to thoughtfully and systematically select the services and activities that both fit the family and provide opportunities for continuing and supporting what has already gone on in FFT. FFT helps families develop partnerships with potential resources such as local law enforcement, community organizations and activities, parks and recreation services, area churches and youth groups, area schools, mental health services, boys' and girls' club directors, YMCA/YWCA or other youth recreational program coordinators, and educational/vocational service providers.

Referral to Other Professional Services

There is no question that some families or family members may need professional services in addition to the informal social and community support services available in the family's social environment. Many types of professional referrals might be helpful in supporting the changes families have made in FFT. Maybe it is individual therapy for a depressed father, a parenting group for both parents, or an anger management support group for the adolescent that will add just that ounce of additional support needed to solidify change. It might also be psychiatric care for a medication review for attention deficit disorder (ADD) or a referral to a learning specialist for help in building reading skills. Regardless of the type of professional service, the manner and timing of this service relative to the family treatment is most important. Making referrals as a way to provide for the needs of a family is not new. In fact, many systems now employ wrap-around services where the available community resources are fitted to the family upon their entry into the treatment system.

Experience suggests that referrals are most helpful when used systematically as part of a broad treatment plan. For example, I find that sequential rather than simultaneous treatment interventions are more beneficial to the family. What this means is that the family derives more help from experiencing one treatment modality at a time. This reduces the chances of receiving inadvertent mixed messages from multiple treatments with different goals and intentions. Consider a case where the family is in family treatment and one parent is receiving individual counseling. The family therapist may advocate for a shared problem definition, emphasizing everyone's responsibility. The individual therapist, whose client is the parent, is likely to support the individual needs of the parent. Thus, the individual perspective may inadvertently work against the family therapy, and vice versa, compromising both interventions.

After a course of FFT therapy, the family therapist probably knows the family better than any other formal service provider accessible to and involved with the family. The therapist has a different view of the individual problems of family members that helps determine if individual symptoms were mitigated by changes in the family or if additional services could help. The family therapist can specifically match the style and functional (relational) needs of the family to a specific professional. That is why I think that making relevant referrals for families should be the domain of the family therapist and should come at the end of a course of FFT treatment.

Case Example

It was near the end of the generalization phase of treatment that the FFT therapist was able to clearly identify the two remaining issues she thought critical to address if David's family was to be able to maintain the changes over time. Alice worked until 8 o'clock each evening. While the family was able to successfully reduce within-family negativity and improve the clarity of their communication, the time between 4 o'clock (when David came home) and 8 (when Alice came home) turned out to be important. This was the time when most of the home struggles began. By the time Alice came in tired and hungry, she was confronted with the emotional and practical problems of a fight between David and his grandmother or sister. David needed a sort of buffer that would help him keep out of situations that would go badly.

The therapist knew that a local youth center was within easy walking distance from the family home and that it was open until 10 p.m. But she also knew that suggesting that David utilize this center would be a difficult discussion. For Alice the center was to be feared because it might "expose David to the bad kids." The family was very proud, which often made it hard to ask for help and use community resources. She also knew that all of them, particularly David, were easily frustrated and often didn't do well with filling out applications. The therapist called on some of the communication skills the family had developed in the behavior change phase to help prepare the family to enroll David in the after-school program. In the third week, they were successful in gaining access to the youth center program, a community resource that could help support the within-family changes.

The second related, critical issue was Alice's depression. In early sessions, the therapist had clearly recognized that Alice was experiencing symptoms that met the diagnostic criteria for depression. Because she was already perceived as a major problem in the family and because her symptoms did not greatly alter how she functioned, the therapist, in consultation with her FFT supervisor, decided to revisit the issue of depression later. It is not unusual for symptoms that fit mental health criteria such as depression to be connected to the relational problems in the family and to diminish in proportion with the family conflict. In addition, if the therapist had decided to make depression a major issue early in the therapy, it would have been difficult to create a family-focused problem definition that did not exclusively target Alice's deficits, thereby reducing the sense of shared responsibility among other family members. During the generalization phase, it was clear that Alice's depressive symptoms had persisted. In session the therapist used reframing to suggest that she seek professional consultation for depression. That took the form of saying, "Getting help for your feelings of sadness and loss is a way that you can support yourself and the rest of the family in maintaining the important changes you have made for the long run." Getting outside help was framed as a contribution she could make to the work that all of them had done, rather than as the "cause" of the family problems. By waiting to make the referral, the FFT therapist was also able to link Alice with a therapist who would match well with her quiet, somewhat vulnerable presentation.

Outcomes of the Generalization Phase

The ultimate goal of the generalization phase is for families to develop the skills and abilities they need to successfully confront and master the problems they will inevitably encounter in the future. The strategies of this phase are designed to stabilize the emotional and cognitive shifts made by the family during the engagement and motivation phase and the specific behavior changes made during the second phase to alter risk and enhance protective factors. This is done by helping the family develop a sense of mastery around their ability to address future situations. In addition, the goal is to maintain the changes through the roller coaster of life events, using relapse prevention techniques. Finally, the hope is that the family will be able to act in self-reliant ways by identifying and using relevant community resources. When successful, the family:

- Attributes the change to their effort
- Is realistic about future struggles
- Has a plan for how to continue to apply what they have learned to new situations
- Continues to maintain a within-family alliance and a view of the family based on the organizing theme developed early in therapy

Evidence of successful generalization work would be a family who faces struggles but is able to solve them—the family knows that problems will occur in the future and wishes that were not so, but they know what situations pose the highest risk and what course such situations might take. They know which skills to use and how to manage the social and interpersonal conflicts that may accompany such situations. In a successful family, the members think about themselves and other family members in the nonblaming terms of the organizing theme.

Evidence of success of the generalization phase can also be seen in the family's perspective on the future. A realistic and family-focused perceptive is one that acknowledges that there will be problems and that change, while not comfortable, is possible if all the family members work together. The way to think about these problems is as a family challenge, with everyone's efforts rooted in goodwill and noble intention.

The outcomes of FFT therapy are enhanced when the family has developed needed support networks and possesses the skill and confidence to use them when needed. Support from friends and extended family is the most powerful of these networks. Community-based services in the local community are also potentially powerful. The goal is to help the family use the behavior change skills they have learned as a way of accessing help and becoming successful consumers, able to identify and effectively access the services they need.

For David, Alice, and Francine, therapy ended having made many important changes. They felt better, they were more confident, and the dread they formerly felt had lifted. In their own ways, all of them demonstrated that they had gained much of what the final phase has to offer. Each was able to weather the natural ups and downs of change. Alice knew where and how to turn for help. Her mother was her first resource, but Alice knew that when she requested help from her mother, her requests needed to be focused and clear. Alice and David both knew the first step was always between them—they had to find different ways to talk and feel the other's real intent. When they worked together, it was difficult, but they always made at least some progress toward getting to the bottom of things. Both knew what was their individual part of a problem, what was their shared part, and what was the part that wouldn't change and just needed to be worked around. And the therapist recognized feelings she had had before at the end of successful therapy, suggesting that it was time to move on.

Challenges of the Generalization Phase

Like each of the other phases, the final work of FFT also poses challenges to therapists and to families. One clear challenge to successful generalization is the motivation to take further action. From the perspective of the family, they have made changes and things are better. For them, that is success. Quite understandably, the immediate experience is not one that naturally points them to more work. As we've seen, this phenomenon is analogous to taking antibiotics for an infection. The first few days of taking the medication can result in a dramatic improvement. However, unless the medication is continued, the sickness will return with an acquired resistance to the last antibiotic, making the infection more difficult to eliminate. In family therapy that starts well, there is a similar process. Clients feel success and are naturally drawn back to daily life, while the therapist can be lulled into being happy with the success already seen. Either reaction results in relapses that are even more difficult to overcome.

The ending of therapy also confronts the therapist with the challenge of becoming less important to the family and to the change process. Over the previous two phases the therapist was centrally involved in therapy. With successful engagement and motivation, the therapist experienced a very personal journey with the family through the emotional turmoil surrounding their daily functioning. The therapist was there as they become more alliance-based in dealing with their challenges. The therapist introduced new behavioral competencies to the family and coached them in using those techniques, helping the family members find a way to integrate these skills into their common patterns of interacting. Both phases involved close and central involvement. Now the therapist needs to, in essence, become less important. Rather than being in the middle, the therapist directs the process back to the family ("Good point. And what will you do as a family about this?") and sits back, intervening only to help them stay on track. It isn't always easy for a therapist to step back in this way. This step is a bit like undoing the close relational ties, exiting the family system, and becoming a consultant from the outside. An observer watching a FFT session in this phase might see the therapist much less involved in terms of frequency, intensity, and quantity of discussion, instead making more process comments that refer to future challenges, direct the family to outside systems, and make suggestions about overcoming obstacles.

There is also the challenge of what to do if the family comes back. Sometimes the family or referral agent makes a request for additional services or seeks out the therapist in future times of struggle. In FFT these requests are viewed as opportunities for additional generalization sessions. The therapist would of course engage, motivate, and reduce any negativity and blame that are apparent; however, rather than starting anew, the FFT therapist would move quickly to reestablish the original organizing theme, include new elements, and focus on generalizing behavior change accomplishments to the newly presented issues. It is rare that an FFT therapist would "repeat" therapy or go back to behavior change. Instead, he or she would use what had previously been done (e.g., organizing themes and previously established competencies) to push the family to generalize their skills and use available community resources. It is also possible that in some families "booster sessions" might be used to anticipate problems that are likely to occur. Booster sessions are purposeful contacts with the family and have been found to be increasingly helpful in maintaining and supporting therapeutic change. In many settings FFT therapists systematically conduct booster sessions as extensions of the generalization phase.

The therapist also needs to know when the change is big enough—when families consistently use in daily life the features that they gained in therapy. As in each of the other two phases, there needs to be, as suggested by Bateson (1972), a "change that matters." This refers not to the quantity of changes but to the changes that have the most impact, are the most meaningful, and are the most relevant to the family. In the generalization phase the goal of FFT is helping the family know where to use different cognitive and behavioral competencies, know how best to implement them, and develop experience adapting them over time. The family does not need to "fix" their every problem; instead, they need to have a way of changing that has a high probability of success. The goal is not to change the family from "dysfunctional" to "healthy" but instead to make specific cognitive, emotional, and behavioral changes that, added together, increase the likelihood that the family can successfully solve more and more of the challenges they face.

Conclusions: Reflections on Ending Therapy

Stopping and staying stopped are not always the same process. Even with significant success in adopting new cognitive and behavioral competencies, the families will still face difficulties in the future. The final challenge of therapy involves maintaining the direction and process of change, using those changes in ever-increasing and diverse situations. Success is doing so with consistency over time, using relevant community resources to help support specific and more general changes. Thus, the generalization phase is more than icing on the cake of a successful change process. It moves the efficacy and locus of control from the therapist to the family, integrating the changes made within the family and the changes in dealing with the surrounding context of the family. The goal of generalization is to help families to be better prepared to manage the future and its inevitable problems and challenges, capable of living productive lives in their own unique way.

In reality, using the generalization phase in a systematic way is difficult. It requires the simultaneous tasks of clinical assessment and systematic intervention on events that can help the family successfully move the changes of therapy into their world. I have worked with therapists in many different types of treatment settings and have found that a systematic approach to treatment requires planning to go along with the thinking and doing. Planning can also help promote positive outcomes when it is done in a way that matches to the model and translates to the specific family, their way of working, and the context in which they live.

In the next chapter the tasks of thinking, doing, and planning will come together. The focus is on applying FFT in realistic clinical settings. These are settings that require a significant amount of case planning to provide the structural support for the individual activities of any single session. The chapter introduces some tools of systematic treatment planning through two cases of FFT, each of which will be described through each phase. Each family presents unique challenges and the goal is to illustrate the ways in which the therapist needs to adapt FFT to fit what is happening in the therapy room at any given time. Following whole cases is intended to give a sense of the dynamic and evolving clinical process that revolves around core principles and specific change phase goals and directions.

7

Therapist as Translator: Implementing FFT in the Therapy Room

One of the appeals of FFT is its inherent logic and simple representation of therapeutic change as existing within three phases, each with clear goals and identifiable therapist skills. The elements of the FFT theoretical and clinical model that make up each phase are described in the earlier chapters of this book. The clinical model that serves as the therapist's map to guide diverse families to lasting change is built on theoretically sound, scientific knowledge. In each phase of the model, families change outlooks and behaviors and pass important milestones, each time adding another unique piece to the family's ability to handle outside systems and new problems; this process reduces the potential of future behavior problems in the adolescent. Yet when presented in discrete phases, the model can appear static rather than as the continuous, evolving, dynamic, and personal process that unfolds in the room with clients. It is in the room that FFT goes from a series of discrete phases to an emerging and evolving relational process between the therapist and the family, and this is where the therapist plays an important role as translator.

Remarkably, little attention has been given to studying what is necessary to make therapy models come alive in the room. Traditionally, psychotherapy models are tested with clinical trials to prove effectiveness—but these are unrealistic conditions. Between 1998 and 2008, the FFT Dissemination Project, under the direction of Jim Alexander and Tom Sexton, trained more than 5,000 therapists in upward of 250 organizations in more than 20 states and five different countries (the United States, Sweden, the Netherlands, Ireland, and the United Kingdom) to do FFT. We created a standard dissemination process that involved teaching, working with local organizations to adjust service delivery systems, helping therapists to integrate FFT into their daily work, gathering quality improvement data, and working in close clinical supervision with therapists in all stages of learning FFT. A central part of FFT training was devoted to an externship program in which therapists from around the country came to a university-based clinic to work with actual families over time. (See the discussion of the Family Project in Chapter 8.) Sessions were conducted with live supervision. With each case we had the luxury of planning the sessions, watching each session to see how the plan materialized, and working out ways around barriers in each of the phases. We gathered information on how FFT was practiced, therapists' decision-making processes, and the outcomes on diverse families.

What stood out most during those experiences was that the job of translating FFT into clinical practice belongs to the therapist. Through thinking (clinical assessment), planning (session and treatment plans), and intervening (systematic clinical intervention), the therapist moves FFT from the first to the final phases of treatment. Over the course of working with families, observing the struggles of hundreds of therapist trainees learning the model, and sharing experiences with numerous others with expertise in Functional Family Therapy, we have developed a number of guidelines to help the therapist translate the FFT model into the clinical realities of working with families. While they remain principles to test in science, they have relevance in clinical practice and are founded in the core principles (defined in Chapters 2 and 3). These clinical guidelines address the real struggles of making FFT work. They formed the foundation of the FFT Training Program for the decade of FFT's primary community-based development (Sexton & Alexander, 2004, 2005).

This chapter turns its attention away from the academically oriented theoretical and clinical principles to the therapist and the clinical translation process that must occur if FFT is to be effective. There are three main foci for the chapter:

- To consider the role of the therapist in FFT as the "translator"
- To show the dynamic nature of the treatment mode as it emerges over time in a case study
- To identify lessons for translating FFT to the real world

The chapter pulls together the phases of the model and brings them to life through real clinical practice.

The Role of the Therapist

It is increasingly clear that the therapist plays an important role in all types of therapy. For example, Blatt, Sanislow, Zuroff, and Pilkonis (1996) found significant differences in therapeutic efficacy among therapists, even among the experienced and well-trained therapists they studied. In addition, they indicated that these differences were independent of the treatment model, the setting, and even the experience level of the clinician. Wampold (2001) estimated that therapists contribute at least 6–9% of the outcome variance in psychotherapy, a considerable amount accounting for some 30% of the outcome in therapy. According to Sprenkle and Blow, the therapist's ability to identify and maximize these change opportunities largely determines the therapist's—and hence the therapy's—effectiveness. Even a recent task force established by the APA acknowledged the critical role of the therapist:

> The individual therapist has a substantial impact on outcomes, both in clinical trials and in practice settings. . . . The fact that treatment outcomes are systematically related to the provider of the treatment (above and beyond the type of treatment) provides strong evidence for the importance of understanding expertise in clinical practice as a way of enhancing patient outcomes. (APA Task Force, 2006)

Yet the field knows little about the variables and characteristics that exemplify a skilled and effective therapist. We know even less about how these therapist variables interact with varying therapy approaches, clients, or presenting problems. We know surprisingly little about the role of therapy, or how the therapy interacts with therapeutic practices.

Because of its dual focus on process and outcome, FFT has always attended to the role of the therapist. This is one of its strengths. Over time it has become clear that it is in the complex relational process between the client and the therapist that the power of a model is transmitted to clients in need; this is where the therapeutic efficacy of the FFT model is achieved. It is the therapist that brings and creates the necessary connections for the model to be translated to the client (Sexton, 2009). The success or failure of the FFT therapeutic process rarely lies in the model or in the clients; rather, most often it depends on the way the therapist translates theory into practice. The relational way in which the goals and mechanisms of the FFT phases are put into action in the room will ultimately determine the success of the therapy.

We know there are a number of variables that affect the relationship between treatment and outcome. *Moderators* influence the impact of the intervention to promote good outcomes; *mediators* create conditions that enable the therapy process to work. Moderator variables might include the therapist's knowledge level, adherence to the FFT model, ability to demonstrate basic good-practice skills, clinical expertise, a broad and specific knowledge base, and knowledge of and sensitivity to the client's unique cultural worlds. The ability of the therapist to understand and share the goals of the model (phases, goals, techniques) is also a moderator. In each case, moderators are necessary yet not sufficient conditions for change.

In their relationship with clients, therapists create mediators that are cognitive (a common direction), emotional (the personal nature of the conversation), and behavioral (the changes). These mediators create the connection between therapy goals, moderators that the therapist brings, and the family. The nature of the therapeutic relationship, the direct and proneness of the therapy session, and the cocreation of the organizing theme all serve as features of FFT that cannot be brought to the therapy but must be created in the therapy.

Through mediating and moderating influences, the FFT therapist acts as a "translator" of the clinical model into the world of the family. Consider the role of a translator. The linguistic translator bridges the gap between two speakers of different languages, carrying over not just the literal, dictionary meanings but a true sense of what the words mean in the speakers' different cultures. In bridging the gap between the FFT theoretical model and the clients' world, the therapist needs to understand the ideas, beliefs, and relational goals of each family member that constitute the meaning of their experience. At the same time as the therapist both brings and creates critical parts of the change process, she must also feel the ups and downs of the family's experience—she must be moved by the emotions in the room and must show a genuine and personal understanding of what it is like for the family. At the same time, the therapist needs to be focused and purposeful. Through his or her choices, decisions, and methods, the therapist is the vehicle for translating the theoretical principles and clinical directives into the treatment room.

Case Example: *Nigel*

Case examples are a useful way to illustrate how the therapist works, contingently responding to the client while following the model and making many kinds of necessary clinical decisions. The case is intended to illustrate how the therapist responds both to the goals of the particular phase and to the family at the same time, showing how clinical assessment and intervention intertwine. Finally, the case is designed to show how cases unfold over time, giving a taste of the dynamic nature of FFT.

The case of Nigel and his family represents the dynamic unfolding of FFT in an actual clinical setting with an adolescent experiencing multiple problems. This case has been discussed in other settings in different forms (Sexton, 2009). Here the explanation of the case is expanded to include a detailed, clinically based discussion of how FFT may assist the therapist in helping a difficult youth and family at great risk. The case also illustrates how adherence to the core principles of FFT can bridge the gap between cultures and ethnic differences between therapists and families, and the degree to which the FFT therapist matched interventions to these demands. Nigel was a 17-year-old male client referred to a forensic psychiatric treatment group in a major European city. I worked with Nigel in 11 family sessions over a 6-month period.

Nigel was born in Colombia and adopted by Dutch parents when he was 6 months old. At the time of the referral and first FFT session, the process of removing Nigel from his home and placing him in residential care had already begun. Nigel had been expelled from school 3 years before. Since then he had become a chronic runaway and a frequent offender, in constant contact with the police for theft, fighting, and habitual drug use. Both Nigel and his parents referred to him as a "street kid." FFT was considered the final option before residential placement. During the initial assessment period at the forensic psychiatric center, Nigel had been diagnosed with conduct disorder and depression, and the psychiatric staff was considering a diagnosis of bipolar disorder. Nigel had been unresponsive to any of the treatment options presented.

Nigel lived with his two adoptive parents. His mother, a homemaker, also worked part-time in a bookstore; his father was a salesman who was often away from home. The day before the first session, Nigel and his parents got into a major argument—Nigel got angry, a screaming match with his parents began, and he declared that he would not attend the family session, saying that he did not want to talk with an American that he didn't know, so just "take me to prison." His parents became equally discouraged and wanted to give up. Both parents had for some time believed that they had done all they could do and Nigel needed residential care. Thus, this case began with many initial challenges, which is not unusual for the cases typically seen in an FFT practice. In fact, it is not uncommon for FFT to be given to a youth and family as a last resort. In that case, the anger between family members, the anger directed against the system, and the hopelessness that accompanies the interpersonal struggle are all significant barriers to motivation and hope. In this case neither Nigel nor his parents have a therapeutic motivation—a belief that things can get better, a sense of working together to accomplish that goal, the idea that they know where to go and what to do.

Engagement and Motivation Phase

The first two sessions of FFT were conducted in the first week of this treatment. For me, early sessions are guided by the phase goals of FFT, and so initially I had one primary aim—to engage the family in treatment and build motivation to change. To accomplish this task, the FFT model identifies four early-session process goals that by now are familiar to the reader: identify and reduce the within-family negativity and blame, create a family focus for the presenting problem, build therapist-to-family alliance, and build family-to-family alliance, all through the use of reframing. In addition, I intended to make a systematic assessment of the ways in which the presenting symptoms were represented in core family relational patterns that were held together by the relational functions (relational outcomes) for each family member.

Because FFT is also about applying these common goals to an individual family with a unique background, culture, family process, and individual and family skills and abilities, I had to take care to adjust both the style and manner of intervention to match to the family in a culturally sensitive and competent manner. Pathways to the model-prescribed goals of engagement, motivation, a family focus, and so on are never apparent; they emerge within the room as the therapist begins to understand the family and its unique organization, values, and beliefs and at the same time looks for opportunities to reduce negativity and blame, build within-family alliance, and generate motivation.

After a brief introduction, the first session quickly moved toward the phase goals. Nigel came to the session wearing a traditional Colombian coat. I took this opportunity to engage Nigel in a brief exchange about his coat, which turned out to be one of his prized possessions; according to Nigel, it made him distinctive among other street kids. (The Netherlands has a significant Turkish, Moroccan, and Sudanese population.) This exchange was a brief but purposeful attempt to engage Nigel on his own terms. In a similar manner, I asked both parents about their English-language ability and the difficulties inherent in the challenge of talking about their family in a second language, and I talked about my own struggle to learn Dutch. Again, these interactions were a brief (one to two minutes) but purposeful engagement strategy, intended to identify potential cultural and cognitive barriers and put them on the table. I deliberately spoke to each individual family member to begin to create a family context.

In this case I moved quickly from these brief engagement discussions to a focus on the family and the presenting problems by saying, "I have been told that all of you were very reluctant to come today, and that you are considering having Nigel live somewhere else. Can you help me understand what goes on between the three of you that ends up in this level of discouragement?" The initial question, while subtle, represented an important core principle of FFT: presenting problems are relational, not individual. The question directly identified what I knew about the issues in non-blaming ways, while giving them a family focus.

As is common in an FFT session, the parents responded with their perception of the presenting clinical issue. The father said that Nigel didn't follow the "rules" and was "rude and disrespectful." For the mother, the issue was the violent fights that occurred between her and Nigel that started "because he explodes" whenever she asked him to do anything. Listening to these descriptions, Nigel said nothing. From an FFT perspective, these statements represent the problem definitions of the parents. I listened for the attribution element (who is blamed) and the corresponding emotional and behavioral outcomes (what they feel and do about this attribution). In this case, both parents attributed the problems to Nigel (blaming) but in ways that initially did not include high levels of negativity (emotional or behavioral).

The early focus in this phase is on changing the external attributions from laying all the blame on the adolescent to trying to find a part of the problem that belongs to the parents. Thus, the response to such opening blaming statements is to talk to the speaker about his or her part in the problem, building a more complex family-focused definition. Using reframing, I first acknowledged the father's attention to detail and the fact that, despite the discouragement he clearly expressed, he had not given up. I went on to acknowledge the father's struggle to understand why a smart, resourceful young man like his son was unable to follow simple rules and suggested that, as a father, his apparent anger also contained a component of hurt. Through a series of interchanges I tried to introduce the theme of hurt behind the anger into the conversation. Similarly, I talked with the mother about the hurt behind her anger, a hurt that comes from a mother who has invested much in her child and is devastated at being unable to reach him. When his mother talked of exploding, Nigel laughed. His view was that his mother yelled and that when people yelled at him he became "crazy." Reframing again, I began with an acknowledgment of his assertiveness, a style necessary on the street, where he was the "man" among his peers. The reframing was focused on his difficulty hearing his mother as a parent instead of as a peer who was challenging him; that is, hearing her anger as pain and frustration at not knowing how to reach him except by yelling. For him the struggle seemed to be making the transition between his street side and his home side. Nigel began to cry as he said that he had lost one mother (his biological mother) and he was not going to lose another, and that his parents saw him as a "bad guy" but inside he was a boy with a heart.

Developing Organizing Themes

Organizing themes, an outcome of early sessions, emerge in the conversation between therapist and family through therapist reframing. In any therapy session, there are many different themes that may fit. In this case what emerged from the conversation was that this family, despite their attempts to stay together, had lost something: their core desire not to give up and not to let go, in spite of all the work that each individual had done to overcome the challenges they faced (adoption, delinquency, etc.). Their desire had gotten lost in the problematic events and angry explosions.

The intent of these early reframing interventions is not to take away the responsibility for bad behavior from either the adolescent or any other family member, but to expand the problem to include everyone, thereby building alliance. This required being sensitive to and understanding of the parents while attributing their behavior and emotions to a cause (the theme of loss, bafflement, and hurt) that motivated reactions that were not always helpful but were understandable and guided by good intentions. This nonblaming and supportive way of discussing their part in the problem helped build alliance and created a purposeful yet safe environment in which to discuss important issues directly. In addition, if family members view the therapist as taking a family focus rather than letting the problem be defined as only one person's fault, it has a positive effect on their engagement and motivation. Nobody wants to be a scapegoat.

Reframing is not an interpretation or positive spin that the therapist "gives" to the family. Instead, reframing is a relational process in which the therapist offers a theme hint, the family responds with their interpretation, and the therapist uses the response to change and expand the theme until a new family-focused problem definition emerges. Because the therapist's hypotheses must be shaped and focused throughout the conversation with the family, the result is that things are said more than once. The process must, however, be focused and evolving, not just repetitive. Each response by the family requires the therapist to determine how his or her response to this statement can promote the process goals of the phase.

One of the outcomes of reframing is the creation of an organizing theme. An organizing theme (described in Chapter 4) is a family-focused explanation of the family and its current struggles that explains the motivations and behaviors of family members by way of their noble intentions while still acknowledging specific behaviors, events, and reactions. When family-focused, nonblaming, and linking family members together, organizing themes do just as their label implies—they organize the family's understanding of the problem and useful and reasonable goals for the future in a way that creates greater opportunity for success.

Organizing themes are not found or given as directives but instead are emerging beliefs. Simple ideas or reframings of individual events grow until they become stories that acknowledge family members' noble intentions. In Nigel's case, the theme grew from a simple notion that the family had lost something and feared losing each other to a more complex description of the intentions, challenges, and struggles of each family member and the whole. In this case, the common themes of loss and protection linked Nigel and his parents together in the problem and in the solution. As an early theme hint, the broad frames of protection and fear were used as kernels of more complex stories that explained their behavior and the challenges they face. For example, Nigel's struggle was in his parents seeing him as someone who had learned lessons, did love his parents, and yet had a life. He struggled with making the switch from his "tough guy" persona on the street to being a son of a mother and father at home. His intense anger reflected a fear that he would lose his parents. For his father, the organizing theme focused more on him being caught in the middle—supporting his wife and trying to help his son, all from a great distance. What looks to others like inconsistency is his constant moving back and forth between supporting each.

The growth of a theme from fear and loss to something more specific, engaging, and family-focused is best illustrated in this case by a set of interactions in the therapy room between me and Nigel's mother. Early in the first session I had reframed the mother's anger as hurt and fear that her son, in whom she had invested so much, was struggling. In the second session, the discussion of an argument between Nigel and his mother that week helped add to the theme. Nigel and his mother got caught in the core sequence that characterized their escalating cycles of anger and blame. I responded to the mother with a reframing for both her and Nigel:

I can see that this discussion, this struggle between you often happens, and now I have a much better idea of how it works. In a funny way, both of you are saying the same thing and struggling with the same issue—because [turning to the mother] when I hear you get angry, what I hear is a mother who is scared for her son, who can't seem to find a way to express that fear, who comes to anger very quickly. It is as if the fear is no longer there—just the anger. That is what I think gets lost between you two.

There was a long pause, and both Nigel and his mother looked at me. Nigel's mother said:

That is right. . . . I have invested a great deal in him, and when I see him not changing I get scared. I just don't know how to handle it.

After a moment Nigel said:

I don't know. . . . I just don't like people yelling at me. It makes me want to explode. I know she is saying it with love—she is just not acting that way.

In the reframing process, themes are mutually developed and become the way the family understands themselves and the framework for how the therapist understands them.

Cultural Differences

It is difficult for a brief narrative to express the significant challenges involved in overcoming cultural barriers. In Dutch culture, public expression of pain and struggle is not common; typical prototypes of parenting are different (the Dutch ideal is tolerant yet firm), and the early independence of youth is common. It was challenging for me to try to understand the family from the inside out rather than impose American expectations and values on the behavior of Nigel and his parents. To overcome these barriers, I purposely adopted a questioning style, trying to learn and understand the cultural differences, making them the life experts. In addition, I openly discussed the differences and my lack of knowledge, but retained the role of directing the conversation as the change expert. This stance created a collaborative atmosphere in the room.

Relational Patterns

While focusing the conversation on the relational process via reframing, I also gathered information about the common relational patterns between Nigel and his parents—the sequences in which the delinquent behavior was embedded. It is important to remember that problem sequences don't need to be determined in significant detail or through detective work within sessions. As noted in earlier chapters, understanding the relational pattern or problem sequence happens over multiple points of observation, taking on increasing detail over engagement and motivation sessions. During each session the family expanded on details or presented additional situations that helped further illustrate the core relational pattern, and so by the end of the first session I understood portions of the sequence. After the second session, I was able to piece together additional pieces of the sequence, and by the end of the engagement and motivation phase I had an even more complete understanding. Details of the problem sequence are most helpful in the behavior change phase.

Relational Functions

In addition, I began to hypothesize about the relational functions or outcomes of these patterns for each individual. The problem sequence is a useful window into the relational functions that provide consistency to the relational pattern. Looking at the sequences, the therapist can wonder what the youth and parents might experience as best characterizing their relationship with other family members. I was able to hypothesize relational functions for Nigel (relative to his father and mother), the mother (relative to the father and son), and for the father (relative to the mother and son). Relational assessment allows for the therapist to understand the core outcome of the relationship. It is this core that must be matched in any behavior change or engagement/motivation activity.

Clearly the central pattern concerned the escalation of anger between Nigel and his mother. Occasionally the father would step in to support either the mother ("Nigel has to follow the simple rules") or Nigel ("We need to be patient and understand him"). This pattern was central to their interaction, regardless of what content (e.g., staying out too late) came up for discussion. What emerged was an assessment of relational functions that hypothesized that the pattern between Nigel and his mother was midpointing from Nigel's side (both in terms of need for contact and psychological distance) and more psychological distance (or independence) from his mother's perspective. The father was psychologically distant (independent) from both his wife and his son. (See Figure 2.4 and the discussion of relational functions in Chapter 2.)

It is important to reiterate that these are hypothesized relational assessments; they are not definitive diagnostic categorizations. Relational functions are not the targets of change in FFT, but instead serve as descriptors and as early indications of potential ways of making behavior changes that match to the family. Reviewing my clinical observations, I decided that the goals of the engagement and motivation phase had been accomplished: Nigel and his parents had lower levels of blaming and negativity, they had formed an alliance among themselves and with me, and we had crafted a family-focused problem definition. I had identified specific behavior change targets and made a relational assessment. It was time to move on.

Behavior Change Phase

The targets of behavior change are specific behavioral competencies that would serve a protective function for the family. In the case of adolescents with externalizing behavior disorders, these tend to be related to the broad areas of communication, problem solving and negotiation, conflict management, and parenting. The most difficult aspect of behavior change phase is finding relevant targets. Relevant behavior change targets are those behaviors and events that feel to the family as if they are important and central to their struggle. It is through these targets that the therapist helps the family develop the behavioral competencies that will serve as within-family protective factors in solving current and future problematic situations. To be relevant, behavior change targets need to be directly linked to the problem sequence, be important to the family, and be obtainable.

With Nigel and his family, the initial focus of behavior change was on interrupting the escalating interaction that occurs when Nigel comes home. I noted initially that two specific competencies might be helpful: negotiating the limits of Nigel's being out on the streets, and conflict management when he came home late. These targets were acceptable to the family because they were logical given the organizing theme of grief and fear of loss that had developed in the engagement and motivation phase. Each target represented a different potential place for behavior change to occur and a specific behavioral competency to be added to the core relational pattern. With the first target, the focus would be on preventing problems by having Nigel and his parents work out plans before he goes out. A different target would intervene when Nigel comes home late and there is an explosion of anger between him and his mother; that target would focus on solving the problem that had developed. Finally, it might be that a reduction of the escalation of conflict would be a possibility for a third target. With three choices, the therapist must prioritize the opportunities by determining which will be most relevant to the family, obtainable, and able to develop a long-term protective behavioral skill.

In the fourth session, the family came in upset about a recent incident in which Nigel had been late and not let his parents know; when he came home, the typical "volcanic explosion" occurred between the mother and son. The father stepped in to lecture Nigel about rules and to counsel the mom to become more patient. From my perspective, this sequence of events represented a common relational pattern in this family. Now, instead of reframing, I focused the conversation on teaching a skill and helping the family enhance their ability to solve this situation. I said, "I think this is a common struggle among the three of you. I want to ask you to try something different in your discussion of this event. First, it seems that this is an opportunity for you, Nigel, and your parents to negotiate a time to come home so that they are not worried and scared. In addition, negotiation might help all of you to find a way to identify a common set of rules that might serve as a basis of what you can expect to occur. So here are the steps in negotiating . . ." What followed was a teaching-focused discussion of negotiation: Make concrete and specific requests, present a set of alternatives, discuss one alternative in depth, and make a contract indicating what the agreed-upon choice was.

It is important to note that what agreement is negotiated is much less important than helping the family to follow a negotiating process that helps develop a competency. Thus, it is not uncommon for the therapist to serve as a teacher, coach, and director of relational processes rather than a mediator and problem solver for the family in this phase. In this respect, the therapist's goal is not to help "find the middle" or come up with an agreement acceptable to both sides in that session. Instead, the desired outcome is to have the family know how to negotiate for themselves in the future. This requires in-session practice, where the family struggles with the content they brought into session; working on their specific issues develops the needed skills. Meanwhile, the therapist's challenge is to focus on the specific phase goals of competency building in ways that match the relational functions of the family.

In the three behavior change sessions with this family, I used their most salient presenting issue (escalation of anger around Nigel's return home) to focus and structure a conversation during which they practiced and refined the negotiation and conflict management strategies that I had introduced. In the end, it took all of us working together to tailor these competencies to the family in such a way that they could successfully replicate the new skill in multiple situations. The remaining two sessions of behavior change focused on applying negotiation and conflict management skills to numerous problem situations the family raised. In each case, my goal was to help develop a within-family process change, not to produce specific outcomes. The events the family brought into therapy provided a chance to experience a change rather than just talk about how it might be done. Once the family had experienced multiple successes in using the skills of negotiation and conflict management and had demonstrated the ability to handle situations that previously would have ended in explosions and threats of Nigel's removal, I decided to move to the final phase.

Generalization Phase

It should be apparent from the discussion above that three behavior change sessions did not resolve all of the specific struggles in Nigel's family. In addition, he had school and learning problems associated with his attention problems, which had not yet been systematically addressed. However, the family was feeling better and had actually canceled a session because they were busy. I was faced with a set of challenges common in FFT: generalizing the behavior changes to other areas, building motivation to complete the last phase, preparing them for future problems and relapses, and identifying other services or resources that might be needed.

I opened session six by saying, "The good news is that you are feeling better. The bad news is that there is yet another problem you as a family have yet to face." Puzzled, the family asked what I meant. I said, "While you have had great success, there will be additional problems you will face." Nigel was quick to say, "I have really learned that the way we had been working together will not work, so I know I won't do what I did before." Similarly, the father suggested that he was now convinced that Nigel had learned and that they were now able to work things out. The subsequent discussion focused on the many ways in which the strong emotion generated by their volcanic reactions is likely to pull them back into old patterns. In the two following sessions, the family did in fact experience additional struggles, to which I responded by reframing their discouragement as normal and challenging them to use their newly discovered skills again. Additional areas of concern arose, particularly around Nigel's drug use. Rather than initiate a new behavior change strategy, I helped the family generalize the same negotiation skill to this different area of concern. My primary concern was helping the family generalize existing skills and systematically learn and practice relapse prevention. Accomplishing this would empower the family to solve current and future problems themselves.

It was also important to help the family support the changes they had made by calling upon outside resources. I began a conversation about Nigel's school and learning difficulties. Because of the between-family alliance they had developed, the family took this as a common and joint problem. The parents quickly moved to use the resources of the mental health center to access a psychiatric consultation; it resulted in medication for what was now diagnosed as Nigel's attention deficit problems. The psychiatric consultation reversed the earlier concerns about bipolar disorder and found that no further treatment was required. In addition, the family identified a contained classroom (operated by the mental health center) and Nigel enrolled. Accessing these resources on their own marked an important success for the family. The goals of the generalization phase had been accomplished.

Outcome of Nigel's Case

During a follow-up appointment 6 months later, I discovered that Nigel had been arrested once for a minor curfew violation. While discouraging, this represented a small problem, given Nigel's history. In addition, the mother and Nigel had experienced a few explosions; after extensive fighting among themselves in session, the family was able to reapply the skills they learned in FFT to overcome these problems. More importantly, the family had successfully managed their discouragement about any setbacks by using the conflict management skills they had learned during the behavior change phase of treatment. Nigel was successfully meeting the requirements of the special school program, coming home close to the expected time, and taking his medication as prescribed. He used illicit drugs much less frequently. Most impressive to me was the fact that despite the challenges, his parents had not threatened or asked to have Nigel removed from the home, which represented a major positive change for the family.

FFT with Nigel and his family resulted in significant, lasting, and obtainable changes in the family. Their initial blaming and negativity turned to within-family alliance, which enabled them to work together using both enhanced and newly developed behavioral skills or competencies. They were able to stick with therapy even after they felt better and generalized their skills to other areas. They gained the confidence to keep at it when additional problems arose, and identified and used available and relevant community resources to support what they had done. From an FFT perspective, lasting family relational changes are the most enduring and empowering changes that therapy can make.

Lessons Learned

What were the conditions that made the case above successful? Certainly following the phase goals of the model helped provide direction. The principles also gave guidance in how to accomplish those goals. There are some practical hints that also help stay focused on FFT amidst the very real struggles within the immediate interactions in therapy.

See Through the FFT Lens

Consider how looking through the FFT lens helps in translating the model. During the engagement and motivation phase, while a family member talks about problem situations and why he or she believes the family is in therapy, the therapist knows to listen to the content of the problem and translate it into the goals of the phase. For example, the therapist might ask him- or herself:

- "What does this tell me about what is important to this person?" The answer to this question helps the therapist know what to acknowledge in reframing.
- "What does this tell me about their relational patterns and how they link the family members together?" This assessment helps the therapist develop a family-focused way of understanding how the presenting problem functions.
- "What does this tell me about the biological, historical, and relational things that family members bring to any interaction that will help me understand why they are reacting this way?" This assessment helps the therapist determine

where the energy and emotion might come from and also helps identify what to acknowledge in the reframing process.

- "To what cause are they attributing the problem? What is the problem definition?" This assessment helps the therapist identify the target for blame and form a target for reframing.

In the behavior change phase, the therapist would translate the same or newly occurring content into different questions:

- "What is the specific behavior change target that might interrupt the problem sequences between family members?" This assessment helps the therapist focus on a specific behavioral protective factor that might be increased.
- "Where in the problem sequence is it most relevant to intervene? What is most likely to obtain a positive change?" This assessment helps the therapist know where to build in new skills and competencies.
- "What relational functions (i.e., outcomes of the family patterns) are represented? How can I match a specific behavior change to those functions?" This helps the therapist know how to make an intervention match the family in terms of frequency, intensity, and quantity.

In the generalization phase, the therapist translates the problem description and its discussion by the family member by asking:

- "What is the barrier here to using the new behaviors developed in the behavior change phase for this new problem?" This assessment helps the therapist know how to generalize the new family competencies into new situations and contexts.
- "How is this issue like other problems the family has faced?" This question helps the therapist know how to use reframing to link what seems to be a new problem to ones already described in the organizing theme.
- "What outside support could help the family maintain the gains they made in this situation?" This question helps the therapist identify community resources and informal supports that might be relevant to link to the family.
- "What barriers are there that might keep the family from using community resources?" This assessment helps the therapist know what new skills to help the family develop and use in order to overcome barriers to accessing other community-based services.

Plan Treatment Systematically

Treatment planning is the way to bring the content and the process of therapy together. There are two types of treatment planning: thinking about the last session and planning for the next. Session planning requires assessing the goals of the previous session and the change in progress toward those goals, and coming up with new ideas about ways to accomplish those goals in the next session. Session planning is based on two elements: matching to the model (for goals) and matching to the client (for how to implement those goals). The plan takes short-term process goals from the model, and then the therapist specifies how those look and can be accomplished with this unique family, and gathers more information about the family and how they work. FFT therapists are constantly thinking (about how they work, how problems function, core patterns, relational behavior change targets, obtainable outcomes). As a result of session planning, the therapist asks him- or herself questions to bring to each session, such as: "What does alliance look like with this family? How can I be credible with this family? What is the father's problem definition? What is important to the person identified as the cause, so I can include it in the acknowledgment part of reframing? What competencies will help in monitoring and supervising the adolescent? What school resources are available for the adolescent's reading difficulty?" These and similar questions help fill in the ongoing assessment of the family, individual, and context.

Long-term planning involves creating what Bruce Parsons labeled as an "outcome sample" (Alexander & Parsons, 1982). Outcome sample is a qualitative picture of how the family might look or act if, for example, they reduced the blame and negativity between them, had family-based alliance, or reduced hostility. As therapy moves along, the outcome sample might include a picture of how the family might operate differently if they used negotiation as a parenting technique to help them better monitor their adolescent. Near the end of the therapy, the outcome sample might include how the family and the school might work together and what it would take from both the parents and school to start and maintain that outcome. This isn't an objective assessment of the client. Instead, it is a clinically based representation of how the family would work, look, and act after having implemented certain changes. The qualitative picture that emerges is a guide for therapists as they try to move the family toward different patterns. In addition, the picture grows in detail and clarity with each encounter.

Neither treatment or session planning is done in the room while interacting with the family. It is a process that takes place in the treatment planning time allocated to or by the therapist to prepare for the next session. However, while FFT therapists do approach sessions with a specific plan, they also stay open to new opportunities that arise in the session to work toward the goals in a slightly different way than initially planned.

Responding Contingently

In the room, the therapist responds to events in ways that accomplish particular therapeutic goals. Events are occasions when members of the family bring up something regarding a problem or issue to be solved, or an interaction occurs within the discussion which provides an opportunity to intervene, or an event is reported (e.g., a positive drug screen or a school problem). Events can be therapist-generated ("I remember when you told me about the problems in school") or family-generated ("We had the worst week—we fought all week"). Events may occur as spontaneous interactional sequences that provide an opportunity to achieve phase goals by making the discussion personal and relevant to the clients. To FFT therapists, events are a rich source of information about how the family works, the nature of the current problem, and ways to work with the family.

The most powerful events are those than can engage and motivate the clients enough to be the engine that drives therapy. The FFT model can help direct the strong emotions and personal experiences of the family toward different process goals. The therapist's responses within these interactions are what make the conversation at the same time strength-based and alliance-focused. An observer watching a good FFT session could see the session as a series of events and actually map the events and the therapist's responses. The observer would see continuity among the responses: Each time the family brings something up, the therapist responds personally and directly but with a common theme. In other words, in an FFT session the therapist focuses on responding consistently and idiographically to the events that emerge from the discussion. Powerful events provide a pathway to achieving the goals of the phase in which the event occurs.

Because it is a phase model, FFT might look like a linear process applied in rote ways regardless of the family, but that is a misleading perception, as the previous case examples have demonstrated. FFT is both systematic in its approach and contingently directed and dynamic in its application. For example, sometimes FFT is an eight-session model of home-based therapy. Sometimes the total therapy consists of twelve sessions, four in each phase, delivered in a community-based setting. Other times FFT is sixteen sessions, half of which focus on engagement and motivation, while four sessions are devoted to each remaining phase. The decision about the best way of delivering FFT depends on the nature of the family and the circumstances of the case.

The idea of contingent responding applies to all interactions between the therapist and the family. For example, we think the first phase of FFT actually begins well before the first session with a family. The initial phone call to a family is a therapeutic opportunity to make contact, engage, motivate, begin reframing and directing the conversation, and building an alliance with the family by demonstrating responsiveness and understanding. In a recent study (Sexton, Ostrom, Bonomo, & Alexander, 2000), we tracked the number of phone calls prior to a first session. In a large multiethnic, urban, clinic-based setting, the average number of phone contacts made before a first session was eight. This effort demonstrated the principle that the therapist (not the family) should work hard to overcome all barriers to initial contact. The outcome of this effort was an exceptionally low dropout and nonengagement rate for the project (22% and 11% respectively).

The contingent nature of FFT is also illustrated in the transition between phases. Decisions about when to move on are made contingent on in-the-room markers; the length of each phase is goal-driven rather than time-driven. Transitions occur when the goals of the phase have been accomplished. For example, one family's negativity and blaming may be so intense that the therapist spends significant time (3 to 5 sessions out of 12) on the first phase, realizing that without the necessary level of motivation on the family's part, moving into behavior change would likely result in noncompliance, not change. In another family, it may not take long to address the initial motivation level, family focus on the problem, and negativity. In this case, the therapist may move quickly to the behavior change phase, where developing specific competencies and the building skills perhaps takes significant time (4 or 5 sessions). In yet another family, both early phases may be accomplished fairly quickly; it will take the most time and energy to maintain change in the family's difficult peer and community environment. In each example, the model has retained its direction and the goals of each phase were accomplished; however, the distribution of effort was contingent on the needs of the family.

Act Purposefully

The process focus of FFT allows the therapist to take part in a genuine, personal conversation with the family and at the same time attend to a different internal dialogue: "What phase am I in? What do I need to assess/understand? What response can I give in this moment that will move the client toward the goals of the phase? How do I match what I need to do to the unique clients sitting in front of me?" The internal process-focused dialogue is phase-specific. For example, in engagement and motivation, the internal dialogue of the successful therapist is filled with assessment questions regarding the levels of negativity and blame, the degree of family focus, the level of alliance between family and therapist, and the level of alliance between family member and family member. The therapist's mind is also filled with such details as attention to reframing, the family's response to a reattribution, deciding on what might be added to the acknowledgment portion, and how to change the meaning of a behavior, emotion, or intention.

Move Quickly

For FFT to be effective, it has to begin immediately. There is no time for long diagnostic and psychosocial assessments. There is no time to do what some of the traditional family therapies suggest and "let the family show who they are" or "let the family tell their story so they can be heard." We work with very difficult adolescents and need to seize the opportunity and emotional power of the moment if there is to be forward movement. For us, the issue is not whether the family story is important; it is. It is not as if families can't tell their stories; they should. In fact, for us, within the words of this story lie the values, experiences, hopes, and frustrations of each member. These features are critical for reframing and creating alliance-based motivation. However, we think it is critical to move quickly because the core patterns to change are those on display in the immediate moment. If the therapist misses the first opportunity, the very patterns that need to be changed occur again, and they set off the very same emotional processes that they do at home. Thus, in FFT the therapist must listen and understand, but he or she must also use the data quickly to facilitate change. Otherwise, the family's experience in therapy is no different than at home, and they have no reason to muster up the courage to really take part in the conversation or to come back to the therapist for help. It is through simultaneous assessment and intervention that the therapist creates space for the family to tell their stories.

Act on the Best Guess

In FFT therapists often must act, sometimes with little information, responding to the actions of a family member in ways that have a high probability of accomplishing the phase goals of that session. Doing so is part of trusting the model, following the phase goals even before the therapist knows everything about the family. To act without jumping to conclusions, however, the therapist must adopt the approach of making and testing a hypothesis. For a researcher, hypotheses are essentially educated guesses that are then tested by collecting and comparing data about the outcome to the guess. If events and data support the guess, the researcher elaborates on the hypothesis and looks again. What is critical in testing a hypothesis is that the researcher is not only open to data that will contradict his or her educated guess but is in fact looking for it. Furthermore, the researcher constantly reformulates the hypothesis to fit what he or she finds.

Therapy follows much the same process. Therapists listen to clients and make educated guesses about what they hear. For example, during the initial phase, the therapist might have a guess about why something is important to the father. When acknowledging the father's struggle as a parent, the therapist bases the first reframing of the father's behavior on this guess in a way that acknowledges that the behavior may be problematic but also suggests a more strength-based motivation than is apparent on the surface.

In a behavior change session, the therapist may initially focus on the target of improving the quality of family communication. The therapist begins working on changing the within-family communication patterns following the principles discussed in Chapter 5 by having the family adopt a more positive tone with each other as they discuss the problem at hand. However, over time the therapist might find that the original hypothesis about the relational functions between father and children appear to be incorrect. In the therapist's original assessment, a pattern of intense verbal anger was intended to create distance between them. Actually, it functions as the only means—albeit a painful one—that they have to pull each other in. As a result of testing this hypothesis, the therapist adjusts the communication target to make it fit the revised assessment of the family's relational functions. In both cases, the therapist has to intervene before he or she knows all of the relevant information. By generating and testing hypotheses, the therapist is able to begin the change process and yet remain open to the revisions that are naturally to be expected as he or she learns more about the family.

Challenges of Implementing FFT in the Room

The chapters in this book lay out the principles, describe models, and identify goals and interventions; along the way, these assertions are backed with observations drawn from clinical experience and research. This information aims to help clinicians to anchor themselves in a perspective when they work with families. Regardless of the clarity of the explanation and the comprehensiveness of the informational support, such explanations fall short when therapists enter a session. This is not because the FFT model is unclear or inaccurate. It is because what happens in the room is the relational interchange, and reality is bigger than any theory.

Among the significant challenges to implanting FFT is that the conversation is fast-paced, the emotions are powerful, and it is difficult to predict exactly how the interactions between family members and therapist will go. In the middle of this whirlwind of activity, it can feel as if the therapist is losing his or her way, as if there is nothing to hold on to, and as if there's no way to know what will happen. Because I have been doing FFT long enough, my experience as I sit in the room is more like being in the eye of the storm, a calm place from which I can be both present and planful. I have come to this ability by way of clinical experience. But my feeling of calm comes from trust as well. I trust that the mechanisms and goals of the particular phase of FFT will give me correct directions and that if I stick to the associated therapist skill, the process in the room will come to a positive resolution. I have come to trust the model and believe in it, knowing that if I focus on what is needed in the moment, the session and the therapy are highly likely to reach a successful outcome.

It is a challenge for the therapist to trust a model as a guide when he or she is in the room with real people experiencing strong emotions. A lack of trust in FFT creates the most difficulty at the times when the relational interchanges in the room are most powerful. It is in these difficult moments, when the therapist needs the model most, that he or she is most likely to throw it overboard and fall back to a more natural, instinctual, but often less effective response. This is to be expected; if any of us were drowning, we would probably cling to the nearest object for support, regardless of its ability to keep us afloat. Changing the nautical metaphor, learning to trust the model is like having an anchor in a stormy sea. An anchor holds the ship steady and allows it to hold its ground, regardless of the size of the waves and the strength of the wind. When therapists trust the FFT model, it anchors them to the very change process that will provide the most help in the most difficult of times.

A therapist has to be brave to do FFT. Bravery consists of being willing to move toward the painful experiences discussed, feel their impact, and change the pattern that leads to their occurrence. The notion of moving toward the pain is somewhat counterintuitive; in painful situations, the most natural thing to do is to move away in order to protect either oneself or another. It is no different in therapy; as change agents, therapists often "move away" by halting, ignoring, or dismissing the difficult things that occur or by prematurely suggesting behavioral solutions.

While conceptually easy to grasp, having courage enough to move toward anger, pain, and negativity is much harder than it seems. Real courage at such times means that the therapist must put him- or herself in the client's place and feel the pain and the anger, so that when the therapist acknowledges that struggle, he or she does so in a way that really makes a difference but does not blame someone else. Trying to understand clients and their pain is not unique to FFT. Most therapists are taught to be empathetic. However, FFT clinical experience suggests empathy is not enough; it requires courage to experience, discuss, and acknowledge the family's difficult experiences, even if they may not be willing to do so themselves.

Bravery also requires the therapist to let the pain, anger, and hurt in the room exist. Therapists must be accepting of these strong emotions, both personally and professionally. Personally, the therapist must be willing to bear the discomfort of experiencing emotions, behaviors, and actions that might be personally offensive or alien to his or her own experience. Professionally, the therapist must respect the family enough to let these events occur, knowing that this is part of what the family is going through. While this advice seems like common sense, it is one of the most difficult tasks for the therapist. Many therapists feel the need to "protect" one or more family members, either by moving beyond the pain or anger being expressed or by using their position to rule out expressions of these emotions. While well intended, this protection is often more for the therapist's sake than for the client's. These feelings and behaviors are not new to the family; in fact, they are how the family is used to working. From an FFT perspective, change happens when the therapist embraces these difficult scenarios and turns them (in the judo metaphor presented earlier), rather than pushing them away. In the end, the therapist must believe that the therapeutic (healing) intervention is turning the expression of the family's very real emotions in a new direction rather than preventing it.

Developing credibility through bravery means that the therapist must also be very direct. Being direct means being willing and able to talk in a straightforward way about the specific events that have occurred in the family. In contrast, not being direct comes across as "talking around" the issue or reluctance to deal with difficult issues. In FFT, our "not if . . . but how" approach suggests that the test of the therapeutic value of a discussion of problematic behavior is what happens by the end of the discussion. If an adolescent has hit a parent, if someone's behavior harms another person, or if someone in the family has engaged in other bad behaviors, the therapist must be willing to bring up such incidents, talk about them, and talk about what they mean to each member of the family. Then, depending on the phase goals, the therapist works to change the impact of that event. In an engagement and motivation phase session, for example, the therapist discusses the violence directly and then reframes it, not to remove individual responsibility but to reduce blame. In a behavior change session, the therapist may directly discuss the adolescent's drug use and take it as an opportunity to practice negotiation and communication skills. In a generalization session, after discussing a father's angry outburst in depth, the therapist might refocus the discussion on the conflict management skills developed in the behavior change phase. Regardless of phase, when the therapist is direct, the family experiences his or her willingness to discuss the salient issues in their life and finds that therapy offers them a helpful place with a credible and capable helper.

Finally, it is not always easy to embrace the circular nature of the FFT conversations. This process of moving two steps forward and one back actually distinguishes good FFT therapy from less helpful therapy. This natural back-and-forth process suggests another nautical metaphor. Because the sailboat gets its power from the wind and the direction of the wind can't be changed, to get anywhere, the sailor must harness the power of the wind and work with it, rather than wait until the wind changes to a more favorable direction. To accomplish this, sailors use a technique called tacking. Tacking involves changing directions relative to the wind, moving one way and then the other across it to gain power from the wind in its current direction. However, following the wind alone is not enough. To be successful in going to a specific location, the sailor has to keep an eye on the target and anticipate the trajectory. Thus, sailors often pick out a marker on the distant shoreline; as they move back and forth across the wind, they use the marker as their ultimate target.

A similar tacking process happens in FFT. The direction of the emotion in the room does not always lead to the goal of the FFT phase. Consequently, therapists often mistakenly react to the crisis in the room by changing their goal. For example, anger is not an unusual emotion between parents and adolescents when behavior problems are an issue. In FFT a therapist might reframe a father's anger toward his son as the father's powerful and understandable feelings of loss of control, noting that it scares the father to feel this way. It is more common than not that the father, in the midst of anger, will not immediately agree with the therapist. As he struggles to overcome his anger, the father is likely to disagree with the therapist's initial reframing attempt. It is easy for the therapist to feel as if the reframing was not the "right" one and then try an entirely new one. The competent FFT therapist is able to contingently respond to the father's disagreement by acknowledging his disagreement (acknowledgment is the first step in reframing) and adding to the reframing rather than changing it. Competent therapists never take their eyes off the goal of the current phase; however, they do move back and forth—tacking into the wind, so to speak—constantly changing the pathway they are following to get to that goal.

Conclusions and Reflections

Good FFT requires good therapists. FFT is only effective when the therapist translates it to the client effectively. Thus, FFT therapists carry much responsibility. They must possess an understanding of a model, its principles, and its practices, and they must have a personal presence in the room. The therapist's presence gives the therapeutic process that often difficult-to-capture value that makes the model come alive. That is because therapy is a dynamic, interactive, emotionally powerful, and immediate experience between a professional who is the change expert and a suffering family seeking help to change their life together. The therapist comes into the interaction prepared with the knowledge, principles, and clinical intervention procedures of his or her operative change model. The family comes with their past experience, their emotions, their desires, and hopes. Good therapy comes from the relational interactions between these two very different perspectives.

To do FFT successfully, a therapist has to go beyond the simple descriptions of the phases and the academic knowledge of the multisystemic perspective on externalizing behavior problems and *really* be in the room. This requires courage, planfulness, patience, relentlessness, careful listening, and contingent responding. It requires leading families through each phase of the model. Success in the room is like all other aspects of FFT—it requires being both model-focused and client-focused in a relational, personal and highly emotional way. The FFT therapist uses specific clinical skills and interventions to accomplish model-specific goals and objectives. The FFT manual he follows, and subsequent training activities he undergoes, integrates theory, research, and years of clinical experience with diverse populations. Together the training and experience provide specific direction to the processes that go on between the therapist and the client/family. However, FFT is not a series or compilation of intervention techniques, even though as a "manualized model" the training and application of FFT may seem internally contradictory. In particular, the FFT clinical model is best captured by seemingly contradictory descriptors such as:

- Simple yet complex
- Systematic and formalized yet flexible and individualized
- Grounded in theory yet pragmatic in application
- Requires high adherence yet depends upon individual creativity and clinical wisdom
- Comprehensive and orderly, yet much more than a paint-by-numbers approach or curriculum-based intervention model

Success in the room is like all other aspects of FFT—it requires being both model-focused and client-focused in a relational, personal, and highly emotional way.

As a family therapist I have always been most interested in the principles that work "in the room." The guidelines presented in this chapter come from experiences implementing FFT in community-based settings, as noted above. However, in the course of those implementation experiences we learned some additional lessons regarding FFT that are not essentially about the family or the therapist, but instead about the powerful impact of the context in which FFT is implemented. We learned that there are particular features of the organization in which the therapist works, the "tools" available through those organizations to help anchor the therapist in the model, and the nature of the clinical supervision that have a major impact on the therapist's ability to do FFT well. These lessons, along with three implementation cases studies, form the topics of the final section of the book.

III

Translating FFT Into Community Settings

EMERGING EVIDENCE SUGGESTS THAT EVEN though evidence-based family treatments may be effective in research trials, they don't always translate well to programs in community settings under less controlled conditions (Hoagwood et al., 1995; Rowe & Liddle, 2003; Sexton & Alexander, 2002b; Henggeler, 2007; found that effects are consistently lower for EBTs implemented in real-life clinical settings compared to laboratory settings and that those reductions were on the order of 50% lower. Similarly, Weisz, Jenson-Doss, & Hawley, 2006). Despite thousands of studies on the dissemination of innovations in health and mental health services, there is virtually no definitive guidance for the implementation of specific evidence-based practices (Goldman et al., 2001).

These findings are equally true for FFT. Despite FFT's long history and great promise as a treatment model, there are significant challenges in demonstrating that the same successful outcomes found in research on FFT can be achieved with the model in community practice. Two issues seem to emerge as most salient: the role of the therapist and the specific mechanisms of training, quality improvement, and data monitoring required to fit FFT into the various treatment systems in which it operates.

In the last decade my colleague Jim Alexander and I developed a systematic, process-based model of dissemination as well as a model-specific clinical supervision approach (Sexton & Alexander, 2004, 2005). This opportunity came at the invitation of the Center for the Study and Prevention of Violence, which played a leading role in moving EBT to community settings. The chapters in the final section of the book address what we learned about the issue of translating FFT to community settings in such a way that its potential is realized. Chapter 8 examines clinical supervision and its role in creating, maintaining, and advancing FFT model fidelity in the diverse clinical settings in which it occurs. Chapter 9 addresses the multisystemic and relational process necessary for helping organizations in community settings adopt and effectively use FFT and discusses the "tools" of dissemination and the elements of a continuous quality improvement system. Each of these chapters also provides examples, in the form of case studies, of the myriad of settings in which FFT has been adopted. The goal is to provide the reader with examples of how FFT was adapted to unique organizational settings, service delivery systems, and community needs.

8

Translating FFT
Into Community
Settings

Despite their potential, clinical models are really only as good as their delivery to communities, families, and individuals in need. If a treatment model such as FFT is ever going to reach the adolescents and families it is intended to help, it must be translated from theory to practice (the subject of the last chapter) and from an academic to a community setting, from training and learning into clinical implementation (the subjects of this chapter). Translating the model involves a continuous, systematic process of ongoing learning, monitoring, and helping both the therapist and the organization integrate FFT into the heart of the organization's culture and treatment delivery system. Successful translating requires supportive organizational systems.

Only in the last 10 of its 35 years has FFT begun to be practiced in a systematic way in community settings. As the designer and director of the FFT dissemination projects, I led the effort to help FFT "go to scale" and find the best ways to train, work with organizations, and help therapists find a way to help adolescents and their families. In doing so, it has become clear that the manner in which FFT or any other evidence-based practice is implemented in the community may have just as much impact on those families and adolescents as the treatment itself. Transporting FFT into the community is a multisystemic, relational, and data-based process that requires a set of guiding principles and specific protocols, just like the clinical model itself. We quickly learned that moving FFT into community settings was as complex as doing the treatment itself. In fact, without systematic attention to this process, the people who most need FFT never receive the service and never have the potential to benefit from the changes in their lives that it can facilitate. We learned that some of our earlier ideas (e.g., don't have a session without the whole family, strength-based is enough) were rather simplistic and were not applicable or realistic in real community clinical settings. We also discovered that a practitioner could not learn enough just by attending a workshop and that merely wanting to do FFT, wanting to help youth, and being a family advocate were important but not nearly sufficient success factors.

Along the way we developed a series of training, supervision, implementation, and quality improvement protocols linking the science, clinical practice, and the needs of families and communities that struggle with complex and difficult situations. These protocols now guide the process of moving FFT from theory to practice. The challenge of this real-world translation confirmed to us what the U.S. Surgeon General (2001) has said, "Program effectiveness depends as much on the quality of implementation as on the type of intervention. Many programs are ineffective not because their strategy is misguided, but because the quality of implementation is poor."

As dissemination experience grew around the country, many of the model developers (from FFT, Multisystemic Therapy, and other evidence-based programs) discovered a number of challenges. For example, it was clear that the traditional means of teaching therapy (classes in graduate school, reading books, and attending workshops) are not enough to move models of treatment into practice. There are two reasons for this. First, we are all aware of how things go after classes and workshops. On Friday we go to a great workshop. During the workshop the video examples by a master clinician are engaging and impressive. On Monday we try a few things, but as the demands of clients and their crises multiply, most of us go back to what we know. By Wednesday we usually remember again that it would be nice to try the new things we learned, but the next Friday comes and little of the new approach has been tried or integrated. This is what families experience too—both with the therapist and in their own attempts to integrate the new insight. Implementing FFT and other evidence-based models brings the therapist face-to-face with the challenge that 25 years of health services research has largely failed to explain the critical moderators and mechanisms for a successful dissemination of efficacious and effective clinical models to complex real-world environments. Using an FFT lens, the therapist won't be surprised that we suggest that implementation is a relational process involving complex dynamics between the program implementers, the culture of the organization adopting the model, the background and training of the clinicians, and the characteristics of the clients.

Second, the great diversity of real-world settings and participants impedes simple knowledge transfer. The organizations, therapists, and clients at replication sites represent a very diverse cultural, community, and ethnic range. To date FFT has been used in agencies whose primary clients are Chinese Americans, African Americans, White, and Vietnamese, among others. In fact, on any given day FFT is delivered in one of eight different languages (Vietnamese, Chinese, Dutch, Swedish, Spanish, English, Arabic, Haitian Creole). The agencies in which FFT has been replicated range from community nonprofit youth development agencies to drug and alcohol groups to traditional mental health centers. The last three years have seen an increasing emphasis on statewide implementation of FFT in various treatment systems. For example, FFT has worked within the juvenile justice system in Washington State for over eight years. We had projects to train adolescent and family therapists in the New York mental health system, in the juvenile justice systems in Pennsylvania and New Mexico, and in the national forensic psychiatric treatment organizations across the Netherlands. The therapists at these sites are as diverse as the clients in regard to gender, age, and ethnic origin. At these sites the FFT program is delivered both as an in-home service and as a traditional outpatient program. Increasingly, it is being implemented in school-based settings (Mease & Sexton, 2005). Incorporating the diversity of client, context, and therapist into a systematic treatment model and transporting it to so many different organizations is, to say the least, complex. A successful outcome requires much more than just workshops, manuals, and individual learning. It requires practice sessions, feedback on how the therapists are doing and how they might improve, and ongoing training and supervision.

This chapter presents the lessons and best practices of a decade of community-based transportation of FFT. These lessons come from our clinical experience, transportation efforts, and knowledge of the interpersonal process necessary to build engagement, maintain effort, and change practice to the degree that it achieves the goal of helping youth. However, in this chapter the focus shifts from clients to communities, and to ways that models can live and grow within them, yet be followed with fidelity in a community-specific way. Why are such lessons important to a practitioner who may want to learn FFT? Because certain supports need to be in place if the therapist is to have a good chance of successfully using FFT and replicating the impressive outcomes demonstrated in the research studies—for which he or she may be held responsible.

The goal of this chapter is to illustrate what is needed, at the community and system level, to make FFT work effectively. It begins with a discussion of the process-based model of dissemination developed to guide our efforts, followed by a set of lessons learned and four case studies that show how FFT can be widely adopted at the level of a university-community partnership, in an individual clinic, and across a wide system of care. The diversity of examples illustrates the breadth of application of the FFT model.

Continuous Quality Improvement: Maintaining Model Fidelity While Meeting Family Needs

Successful community transportation requires aligning the multiple domains of the treatment system—therapist, agency, and service delivery system—to deliver the model with adherence (high fidelity to the model). Our definition of fidelity is similar to that of other researchers: It is the degree to which a given therapy is implemented in accordance with essential theoretical and procedural aspects of the model (Hogue, Liddle, Rowe, Turner, Dakof, & LaPann, 1998; Waltz, Addis, Koerner, & Jacobson, 1993). We became interested in the issue when it became clear that treatment fidelity is a critical factor in the delivery of effective programs (Henggeler, Melton, Brondino, Scherer, & Hanley, 1997; Hogue, Liddle, & Rowe, 1998; Koerner & Jacobson, 1994; Sexton & Alexander, 2002). Adherence has also been linked to treatment outcomes in family-based therapies (Henggeler & Schoenwald, 1999; Huey, Henggeler, Brondino, & Pickrel, 2000; Schoenwald, Henggeler, Brondino, & Rowland, 2000). Barnoski (2002), Sexton et al. (2002), and Sexton & Turner (in press) found therapist adherence to be the primary mediating factor in the successful delivery of Functional Family Therapy. Those therapists who delivered the model with high rates of adherence had significantly better outcomes than those who did not. Without therapist model adherence FFT did not produce results any better than treatment-as-usual conditions. Studies of model adherence in family therapy models for adolescent drug abuse and delinquency (Barnoski, 2002; Henggeler et al., 1997; Hogue et al., 1998; Huey et al., 2000; Nitza & Sexton, 2001; Sexton & Alexander, 2002a), demonstrate that complex, manualized treatments need to be implemented with a high degree of fidelity to ensure positive outcomes.

In community settings, developing and maintaining treatment adherence is difficult. Community projects don't have all of the controls and conditions that are in use in clinical research trials. It is up to the community organization to find practical methods to make sure FFT is delivered as it was intended. Consider all of the variables that may have an impact. The organization needs to have a service delivery system that matches the characteristics of FFT; for example, there needs to be a short time between the clients' referral to the agency and the beginning of therapy. For some service delivery systems, the traditional multiple-session intake and assessment systems come into contradiction with FFT. For example, many service delivery systems utilize a "wraparound" model where families and youths are given a number of services simultaneously. As noted below, FFT may work best in organizations that take a sequential approach to services delivery—for example, placing FFT as the first service, followed, if necessary, with additional services determined by the FFT therapist in the generalization phase. Finally, there is the issue of treatment planning and caseloads. The reality of working in community mental health and other types of psychological services is that therapists need to act a bit like lawyers, billing a significant number of hours of revenue-generating services each week. In FFT, the need for systematic treatment planning can sometimes exist in contradiction to the push for each hour of the therapist time to be billed.

So how can FFT be implemented in diverse community service delivery systems, unique and varied organizational settings, with therapists who vary in training, experience, and background, and still be successful? Successful implementation is much like good family therapy—FFT is implemented with high adherence while at the same time matching to the characteristics of the organization, the therapist, and the client. The treatment model retains its integrity and the organization retains its individuality.

Translating the FFT model with model-specific adherence is a relational process that involves therapists, supervisors, and organizations. In the dissemination project, we discovered that we were working toward developing organizational structures to help maintain the learning and treatment quality that came from training and supervision. It became clear that rather than monitoring, we were engaging in a more process-focused approach and continuous quality improvement where the experiences of each session and each case were gathered and used to further improve the work at the site.

Our approach is one based on the principles of continuous quality improvement (CQI). CQI is not new or exclusive to FFT. This philosophy gained wide acceptance in the health care sector during the 1990s (Deming, 1986; Ju-ran, 1964; Crosby, 1979). CQI is an approach to quality assurance that was originally proposed by Shewhart in *Economic Control of Quality of Manufactured Products,* first published in 1931. It has been defined as "a linear incremental improvement within an existing process" (p. 1) and focuses on doing the right things the right way the first time. CQI places responsibility for quality on personnel at all levels, not solely management, and it emphasizes process, not environment. Building on these ideas, the Institute of Medicine (2001) defined quality in medical services as the degree to which services and treatment increase the likelihood of desired outcomes and are consistent with current professional knowledge. In a CQI process, treatment quality is not just the responsibility of the therapist; successful CQI is an ongoing, organization-wide framework with a number of essential elements, described below.

- *CQI is organization-wide.* CQI can only be successful if the organization seeks quality in all that it does. It takes a total commitment to quality from the governing body and senior management, involves all employees including clinical staff (Berwick, 1994), and is rooted in a cultural setting that supports quality initiatives, teamwork, adaptability, and flexibility (Boerstler et al., 1996, p. 143). Management must commit resources and create an atmosphere conducive to continuous improvement in which quality is integral to the work of all employees and clinical staff. Employees and staff must commit to continuously improve their work results and the way they achieve results.
- *CQI is process focused.* CQI seeks to understand processes, identify process characteristics that should be measured, and monitor processes as changes are made to determine the effect of the changes. This results in more efficient and effective processes that improve productivity through better use of resources, generating higher-quality work products and service.
- *CQI empowers employees.* Process understanding and improvement requires a team-based approach in which employees are involved and empowered to effect change.
- *CQI must be ongoing.* The aim is to prevent poor quality before it happens and to seek opportunities to improve processes in an organized fashion.
- *CQI requires management to meet its leadership responsibility* to train employees, encourage innovation, worker participation and empowerment, and team building so that employees can contribute to process improvement problem solving, and to facilitate organizational change that leads to improvement.

In FFT our approach to CQI is based on three assumptions:

- Model fidelity must be measured from different perspectives (therapist, client, and outside consultant).
- Fidelity and adherence information should be readily available to therapists, supervisors, and program administers for daily use.
- Attention to fidelity and adherence should be a central part of clinical practice and supervision.

To implement this approach in community settings, we use four methods to monitor and track model fidelity: therapist progress notes, client report of experiences (CPQ), supervisor adherence ratings, and measures of short-term and long-term change. These instruments provide information from multiple perspectives (clients, therapists, and supervisors) about different activities (therapist intentions, family behaviors, and service delivery decisions and profiles) in order to develop a comprehensive view of model fidelity. These measures are also part of the clinical supervision model that is integral to CQI because of its primary focus on data-based interventions to promote model adherence and build competency. The CQI processes make up an FFT service delivery system (Chapter 9) built on a computer-based CQI system (FFT-Q System) These tools are the topic of the next chapter.

Principles of Effective Community Implementation

What does it take to translate FFT from ideas to everyday clinical practice? What does it take to implement FFT within an organization in ways that have the greatest potential to help youth and families? What follows are principles that now guide community-based training, quality assurance, and clinical supervision in FFT.

Systematic, Ongoing Training

As described throughout the book, FFT is much more than a set of tools to be learned and then applied at the will of the therapist. Instead, FFT is a systematic approach with a set of core conceptual and theoretical principles and a set of specific therapeutic procedures. These come to the therapist by way of systematic training and supervision. The real clinical application of FFT can't be learned from a book or from an introductory workshop; becoming competent and developing adherence to the model are outcomes of a systematic training program.

The goals of the clinical training program are adherence and competence by both therapists and site supervisors such that FFT becomes a lasting and self-sufficient intervention program within the agency. FFT training is conducted in three sequential phases, during which we:

- Focus on the therapists who will be implementing FFT. The primary goals are model adherence, accountability and competence.
- Focus on a site supervisor who is a member of the agency and who will take on the responsibilities of managing the quality of FFT at the site (see Chapter 9).
- Provide continuing education training to the community site as a collaborative partner.

The overall goal is to enable the participants to master both the knowledge and performance components of the clinical and supervision models. In our projects we have come to rely on a multiphase process of training. Distributing the training over time and providing sequential practice and adequate time for learning the principles of the model enhance success. The sequence is planned to fit the therapist's developmental learning curve. It should be accompanied by continuous practice (based on adequate caseloads) to move the training from a conceptual to an experiential realm.

FFT training is currently offered through three organizations. The Functional Family Therapy Training Institute is part of the Center for Evidence-Based Practices at Indiana University (www.cafs.indiana.edu). The center provides ongoing research, evaluation, training, and quality improvement services to organizations implementing FFT. The center has branches in the Netherlands and Ireland, as well as across the United States. Two private organizations also offer certified FFT training: Functional Family Therapy Associates (www.functionalfamilytherapy.com) and FFTinc (www.fftinc.com).

Alliance-Based Implementation

The concept of alliance has been well established in the psychotherapy literature in general and in family-based models as a critical component of successful outcome (Alexander et al., 1995; Alexander & Barton, 1996). However, the construct is equally important in implementation, where there needs to be an alliance between trainers, therapists, organizations, and the community in which there is agreement on the implementation goals, the tasks necessary to accomplish those goals, and the establishment of an emotional bond. To create implementation alliance, organizations need to work to find a place in the service delivery system, embrace the family-based goals of FFT, and develop and adopt the CQI principles *before* training ever begins. We now do an organizational assessment and work with organizations to identify the challenges and barriers that might get in the way of FFT adoption at an early stage of implementation. Sexton and Alexander (2004) suggested that the ultimate success of any dissemination effort is due to the development of a relational context in which the implementer, the administration of the organization, and the therapists themselves work together to accomplish the goal of successful adoption of the model.

Sexton and Alexander (2003) identified several common features that are emerging in the successful transport of evidence-based practices, including the need for treatment fidelity through quality assurance and adherence monitoring, a focus on the structures of organizations in which the programs are implemented, and the need to establish community–implementer partnerships. These elements are also contained in the dissemination work conducted by the Center for the Study and Prevention of Violence (Elliott & Mihalic, 2004) and now guide FFT implementation at community sites. This approach incorporates the principles of CQI and the lesson we have learned over the last decade.

Long-Term Commitment

Sustainability is one of the most important aims of any transportation project that brings FFT to a community. Therefore the project has to overcome its start as the "newest thing on the block" and become a regular and normal way of doing the business of helping families. This takes time—usually a much longer time than therapists, agencies, and even funders are used to considering as the break-in period for a new practice. The traditional ways of training in discrete units or hiring staff trainers don't seem to meet the dual challenge of model fidelity and sustainability in a satisfactory manner.

In the field of medicine, we are not surprised that making a good physician requires, after undergraduate training, an additional three years of medical school and at least one additional year of residency training, all involving careful oversight and evaluation. Of course, FFT is designed to be implemented by a much wider range of professionals, but as noted above, it is far too complex and demanding an intervention to be picked up and internalized quickly. That is why the introduction of FFT into a community setting requires a long-term commitment from therapists, administrators, and funders in the interest of creating a sustainable program. Training needs to be ongoing and be conducted in partnership with model developers. There must be a commitment from therapists, administrators, and funders to engage in ongoing quality improvement through data analysis, monitoring therapist adherence, and summoning the courage to actively help those therapists who are not doing FFT well and reward those who are. The commitment is to model fidelity as a means of ensuring good care to clients. To engage in this type of quality improvement, all levels of the organization (therapists, administrators, and supervisors) must share accountability because it takes all of them to create a successful treatment intervention. Finally, everyone needs to keep an eye on the long term. Rarely do therapists or agencies internalize a commitment to FFT immediately. In fact, their process is just like that of a family seeking to change the behavior of an adolescent member. That is, engaging in training is just the first step toward success. That engagement must be followed by specific behavior changes and continuous attention to overcoming challenges. In the long run, an FFT transportation project is successful only to the extent that it is sustainable and becomes part of the fabric of the organization and the community.

Matching the Treatment Model With Agency and Service Delivery Characteristics

The importance of matching organizational and service delivery characteristics can't be overstated. In fact, research evidence suggests that the structure and climate of an organization have a direct impact on client outcomes. Our experience suggests the same. In addition, we have found a similar impact on the initial adoption and long-term sustainability of FFT. While these ideas may not come as a surprise, their importance becomes more apparent given the usual context for the adoption of a new practice like FFT. Most often FFT comes into organizations through a grant or another form of start-up funds. Traditional approaches to such projects have led organizations to focus on issues such as training rather than the context within which the practice must fit. In addition, innovations are often championed either by an agency or service delivery director or by a few therapists; those who are less passionate and involved may not get involved or may be left behind. The outcome is often a discrete project that is not integrated into the agency's long-term plans or services. The therapists who must learn to adopt the practice may end up feeling as though they are swimming upstream—both learning a new intervention program and resisting the inertial pull of the context.

Glisson and James (1992) established an empirical link between organizational characteristics (culture, climate, and structure) and the successful delivery of children's mental health services, suggesting that these variables are indeed important aspects of the dissemination process. Organizational climate is a function of the way individuals perceive their work environment; it is represented by a set of measurable properties of the work environment perceived directly or indirectly by the people who live and work in this environment, and it is assumed to influence their motivation and behavior. Organizational cultures consist of the beliefs and expectations that prescribe how things are done in the organization, forming the basis for socializing new workers. The focus is on what the individual believes are the expectations and norms for the people in his or her work unit rather than on what the individual thinks is expected of him or her personally. Organizational structure describes the centralization of power and formation of roles in an organization. It includes participation in decision making, hierarchy of authority, the division of labor, and the procedural specifications that guide work-related interactions among the members of an organizational unit.

As noted above, one significant challenge in matching to organizations is integrating FFT with other services. When families are referred to FFT they are often simultaneously involved in other community services (e.g., for parenting, anger management, support, etc.) or professional services (individual therapy for parents and adolescents, group therapy, etc.). In fact, many traditional wraparound, court-mandated, and mental health systems purposely provide the family with a number of such resources. While helpful, these services require systematic coordination to avoid inadvertently sending mixed messages or countering each other.

This is particularly important with FFT. FFT is family focused, with its early therapeutic intervention oriented toward creating a family focus on the problem. Services with an individual focus generally place the locus of problem in the youth or parent, or they direct attention to something other than family relational systems. Such a focus will hinder the progress of FFT. As a result, we suggest that all other professional counseling services be terminated or placed on hold during FFT; if they are continued, the FFT therapist needs to link up with the service provider(s) to understand how the other service(s) might enhance or, more importantly, work counter to FFT. In addition, other educational services should be carefully evaluated to determine the possibility of delaying their start until after FFT. During the generalization phase of FFT, additional services can be matched to the family in a way that increases the impact of therapy, which leads to a more efficient use of community services. Delaying services in this manner often requires the FFT team to educate the community services providers by organizing a coordinated system of care.

Examples of Moving FFT Into Community Settings

The section below describes four examples of FFT implementation projects in order to identify the broad systemic level of issues that need attention if FFT is to work as intended. Each example illustrates a unique set of challenges and provides a specific set of lessons. Together the examples also illustrate how far FFT has come from its beginnings in the small academic training center at the University of Utah, where graduate students worked with mostly white youth from the Salt Lake City juvenile court, to its present standing as a model used in diverse and complex community-based organizations that represent the diversity of real-world practices. These examples also illustrate the process-based implementation model, to which they owe their success.

The first example is unique in that it was the first FFT project ever conducted, and it continues to be the largest. In a university-community partnership, I and my clinical team created the Las Vegas Family Project, a training, service, and research center implementing FFT to thousands of adolescents. The project combined quality FFT services to a local community with data-based monitoring and supervision, generating effectiveness-based research that has helped to test FFT and verify its model-specific change mechanisms.

The second example illustrates the nearly decade-long implementation of FFT across an entire state system of juvenile justice. The state of Washington was one of the first to embrace evidence-based practices. This project illustrates how FFT served to change the culture of an entire system and how a systematic evaluation of those efforts helped identify a critical element of community implementation—treatment fidelity. The last two examples illustrate how FFT can be used with culturally diverse groups of clients. One setting is a community mental health system that works with Hispanic, South American, African American, and Haitian youth in a large U.S. city. The other is an international project to implement FFT in a psychiatrically dominated mental health center in Amsterdam, the Netherlands.

Though they differ in many ways, each example illustrates the same need for a systematic approach to the transportation process and the need to think about the multiple systems that might impact the long-term sustainability of a treatment program. Following the examples are a set of lessons learned that are intended to serve as guiding principles for implementing FFT in community settings.

Family Project: Integrating Research, Training, and Community-Based Practice

The Family Project was created as a means to bring service delivery, training, and research together. It began as a partnership between the Las Vegas juvenile court and the University of Nevada, through my professional role there. It now operates out of Indiana University, providing the same link between research, training, and clinical practice. Beginning in 1998, therapists working in the Family Project have provided FFT to over 4,000 adolescents and their families. In addition, the project has provided real community-based training experiences to over 500 FFT therapists from organizations around the world. The project also helped solve some significant problems for the juvenile court. At the time the Family Project began, the Las Vegas Juvenile Court was doing initial intake assessments of more than 1,200 youths each month. The county detention facility was overcrowded, and the community service providers were unable even to keep up with the caseload, much less provide effective evidence-based treatment.

The services provided by the Family Project were unique. Its clients were referred as a result of direct court orders from the judge, as a result of initial screenings from the juvenile court intake process, from individual family-based referrals, and from residential treatment facilities in the area that needed community-based treatment settings for youths returning to their community. Clients ranged in age from 10 to 18, of whom more than 20% were Hispanic and 20% African American, with a range of referring problems from early at-risk behaviors (curfew violations and family conflict) to serious felony crimes (armed robbery, assault, and major drug crimes). Services were provided in an office setting by a group of experienced and licensed family therapists whom I had trained in FFT.

The service delivery system was unique in that we had only a short intake interview for the purposes of signing informed consent documents, followed immediately by the first FFT session. Therapists carried a caseload that gave them flexibility in scheduling, meaning that they could, if clinically needed, schedule families quickly and rearrange scheduled visits based on the needs of the family. The staffing and supervision process developed from our experiences supervising and planning for these cases contained the seeds of the FFT Clinical Supervision Model (Sexton, Alexander, & Gilman, 2004), described in Chapter 9. Delivering FFT through the Family Project taught us a number of things that became core elements in the current dissemination model:

- FFT was most effective when it was delivered immediately following the referral. In the Family Project, we evolved into a model where each family was contacted within 24 hours and had their first session within 48 hours following the referral. This model resulted in a cumulative dropout rate of less than 15%, far below the reported rates for other models and traditional services (Kazdin, 2007).
- To be successful, clinical supervision needs to be model-focused. Supervision for each case was based on developing model adherence while at the same time matching to the client and addressing the unique in-the-room challenges, and it was systematic. The result was an FFT supervision manual that detailed the relational process, different phases, and methods that ensure adequate model implementation.
- FFT could be used with diverse youth, with diverse problems, and diverse family structures. The Family Project took all adolescents who were referred. We worked with the part of the family system that we could get into treatment. Thus, we did not refuse treatment for a family that came without, say,

a stepfather or a sibling. Our notions of "conjoint" became more realistic, less rigid, and more engaging.

- Flexibility in service delivery was important. We discovered that the once-a-week session model so common in traditional services was not necessarily useful in FFT. Therapists in the Family Project were able to schedule more than one session in a week, could reschedule a cancellation or no-show for the next day, and were able to titrate out the generalization sessions to enhance the ability to do relapse prevention. This flexibility matched to the family needs and fit the principles of contingent decision making.

The Family Project also provided a unique opportunity for training. Through cooperative agreements at both universities and community organizations, therapists from around the world were able to join the treatment team and provide FFT, under supervision, to the families in the project. The training mission of the Family Project was modeled after the family institute model developed by the founders of Family Therapy. Much like the Philadelphia Child Guidance Clinic in the 1970s, the "externship," as it came to be called, was an intensive training experience where therapists came to the Family Project site for three to four days a month over the course of three to five months. Each case was conducted in front of a one-way mirror, observed by therapists in training, and videotaped for later review and analysis by the therapist. Each case and each session in the training process were planned in great detail, and each session was observed. Supervision of the cases was done live. We intervened in sessions as they were going on to redirect and refocus the discussion. This allowed us to have an immediate impact on the family and provide real-time feedback and learning to the therapist.

These training projects meant that we could, for the first time, watch the progression of FFT treatment in the planning stages, in individual sessions, and in the series of sessions over time (Alexander, Bonomo, Ostrom, & Sexton). It gave us what Hoffman (1981) describes as the view from behind the one-way mirror, where attention could be given to even the smallest detail in how something was said and how an intervention was implemented. For therapists in training, the externship opportunity was among the most valuable of all the FFT training procedures because it was real and applicable; it allowed them and us to find their strengths and challenges within the real work. It meant that supervision was no longer based on just the clinician's report but included actual observation.

We learned a number of lessons regarding training. For example, we found that therapists' descriptions of what they did in session did not always match what they actually did. This encouraged us to develop the clinically based adherence measures described in the next chapter. We found that therapists learned better from real clinical examples once they had the conceptual and academic knowledge gained from more traditional training. While it seems simple, we were quickly confronted with the fact that knowing and doing were very different. This encouraged us to expand our idea about what it takes to be a successful therapist. The next chapter discusses the outcome of this in our adherence and competence model of clinical supervision. In addition, many of the clinical guidelines for translating FFT from its conceptual model into real action, described in Chapter 7, emerged from this experience. We discovered that families like the help and involvement of a team. Almost every therapist in the training program began with a worry that the role of the supervision team, the ongoing supervision interruptions, and videotaping would reduce the family's spontaneity, make it difficult to engage in the process, and change the progress of therapy. This was not the case. In fact, families uniformly liked each of these features of the treatment they received. This experience encouraged us to promote the use of a similar type of open, live, collaborative supervision at the replication sites.

We learned a number of things about FFT. The Family Project created the largest set of FFT clinical data in existence, with a library of thousands of videotapes of FFT sessions showing, for the first time, the progression of the clinical model from the first to the last session. An impressive number of research-based findings emerged from this data library that have in some cases validated the FFT clinical model and in other cases helped us to further develop it. For example:

- Sexton and colleagues (Sexton, Ostrom, & Bonomo, 2000) found that youths in a community-based study who received FFT had between 25% and 40% lower levels of recidivism 1 year later than those in both alternative treatment groups. FFT was equally effective for a variety of presenting problems including drug offenses, violence, and property crimes. Now at Indiana University, the Family Project this study along with its recent follow-up (Sexton & Turner, in press) demonstrated that FFT remains an effective model even in a diverse community practice site.
- Sexton & Mease (2002) replicated earlier FFT results and found clinically significant changes in not just the broad outcomes like recidivism, but on parent and youth family functioning.
- Nitza (2002) and Nitza and Sexton (2002) were able to investigate the role of family negativity and its impact on dropout (see Chapter 4). Two critical practice implications emerged from this work. First, in-the-room negativity is important; FFT needs to have real events between family members. Second, it is important to reduce that negativity before the session ends.
- Sydnor (2007) and Gilman (2008) investigated the impact of critical components of FFT supervision. In studies of actual supervision sessions, these studies were able to identify the critical relationships between adherence and competence, and the impact of model fidelity. Both studies demonstrated the need for an active, systematic, and model-focused supervision process.
- Erickson (2008) found FFT to be effective with juvenile sex offenders. We found that FFT, delivered once a week over the course of 3 months, could produce results equal to those of a specialized sex offender treatment program requiring individual, family, and group therapy lasting 2 years. The potential cost-saving implications of this study are significant.

The work of the Family Project is ongoing. At the Center for Adolescent and Family Studies at Indiana University, we are now conducting major studies on the role of early alliance and dropout, on the changes in family blame and their impact on outcome, and on the necessary components of the behavior change and generalization stages of FFT. We are also expanding our FFT work to focus on young adults with families as they come out of the justice system. More importantly, the work of the Family Project illustrates the necessity of the ongoing study of the service delivery mechanisms, training principles, and research studies that are necessary if a clinical model such as FFT is to remain viable as a treatment model in community settings. It also illustrates the value of university–community partnerships in both delivering and improving treatment models such as FFT.

The Washington State Story: System-Wide Implementation of FFT

In 1997 the Washington state legislature took a bold step into the era of evidence-based practices. Fourteen juvenile courts across the state selected and began implementing FFT as part of an effort to make EBPs such as FFT the only services delivered for youth in the juvenile justice system. The demographically diverse sites were located in cities (Seattle, Everett, and Tacoma), medium-sized communities (Spokane and the Tri-Cities), and remote rural areas (the San Juan Islands). To build local sustainability, the 30 new FFT therapists were organized into six working groups, ensuring that no therapist would work in isolation and that all members of the units would attend training, case consultation, and follow-up training as a cohort. In the ensuing 10 years, this initial project has evolved into a comprehensive statewide system of FFT delivery and quality assurance. FFT is now institutionalized within the juvenile justice system and available to all youths who come into contact with the court. Its daily operations are coordinated by a statewide FFT quality assurance director (QAD) and conducted in partnership with the FFT model developers. The QAD monitors FFT services throughout the state using the FFT quality assurance database (see Chapter 9). A statewide quality assurance plan (Community Juvenile Accountability Act) was developed to guide the QAD's activities, providing steps for identifying and improving the performance of therapists who do not adhere to the FFT model. These steps include both informal and formal improvement plans that are oriented toward supporting and enhancing the work of community therapists rather than evaluating and punishing. The plan operates on the principle that therapists should receive specific, timely, and concrete information regarding their performance; be informed early when problems arise; and be helped to develop specific, individualized plans for improvement.

This project taught us a number of lessons that have been incorporated into the FFT training, supervision, and clinical models. It also generated a number of research findings that both supported and helped focus these efforts.

- The project was the first test of the FFT training model (Alexander et al., 2000; Sexton & Alexander, 2004). It demonstrated that the model of training, externship, supervision, and ongoing quality assurance was effective in producing positive client outcomes.
- FFT was effective with diverse youth with serious clinical problems (Sexton & Turner, in press). A review of this project is in the research section of Chapter

3. FFT had a 31% reduction (13.2% vs. 19.2%) that was a statistically significant [b = -.51, p < .033] reduction in being involved in the criminal justice system in the future. In addition, those in FFT experienced a 43% reduction in violent recidivism (2.5% vs. 4.4%).

- The role of the therapist was critical. The positive outcomes were only evident for those therapists who delivered FFT as it was designed. This suggests that quality assurance and implementation plans are critical to successful community implementation (see Chapter 9).
- Finally, these outcomes also translate into important cost savings, another way of measuring treatment effectiveness in a community setting. The total cost of FFT per family was $2,500, a remarkably low figure (costs in other areas would vary due to local conditions). Using the algorithm developed by Aos and Barnoski (1998), FFT saved the Washington State system $16,250 per youth in averted court costs and crime victim costs, not to mention the incalculable emotional pain suffered by family members. In the first year alone, this project presented $1,121,250 in cost savings. This same algorithm suggests that every $1 invested in delivering FFT returns more than $14.67 in savings.

The Miami FFT Project

As FFT model developers and therapists, we have become increasingly interested in the role of client race, culture, and ethnicity in the process and outcomes of FFT. The early outcome data suggested that FFT was equally successfully regardless of gender or race. Data from the Washington State FFT Project described above (Barnoski, 2004) showed no difference in outcome based on race or ethnicity. However, despite these preliminary findings, we believe more systematic study is necessary. Over the last 6 years, a highly successful FFT project has been developed at the Children's Psychiatric Center (CPC) in Miami, Florida. CPC works closely with the Dade County juvenile justice and child welfare systems in providing family-based therapy (FFT) to adolescents in need across metropolitan Miami and its surrounding areas. CPC is known for serving a diversity of Hispanic, Cuban, African American, South American, and Haitian families. Over the last 5 years, the CPC FFT project has served youth and families of whom 68% were Hispanic, 27% were African American, and 5% were Haitian American, with therapists who are equally diverse. As a result, this project is an important place to start examining the role of FFT with culturally diverse clients by looking at the rate of engagement and program completion of clients and the within-family changes resulting from FFT.

The project is unique in that it demonstrates how FFT can be implemented in a very diverse community. It also provided some initial experience in training culturally diverse therapists. At CPC, FFT was delivered in Spanish, English, and Haitian Creole. Because it implemented the identical training and clinical model used in the other community replication sites, the results of the CPC project provide some initial evidence on the cultural competence of the FFT model.

- Of the adolescents who entered the CPC program during the 5-year project, almost 80% completed FFT. There was no significant difference in completion rates for African American, Hispanic, or Haitian families in Miami compared to the same rates in other parts of the country—Las Vegas, for example.
- Families that completed the FFT program in Miami made significant changes in within-family functioning and individual symptom levels of family members. On a standard measure of within-family/individual functioning (Youth Outcome Questionnaire; Lambert & Burlingame, 2002), mothers and fathers of the FFT participants reported a clinically reliable change in their adolescent's behavior in a wide range of areas including intrapersonal distress, interpersonal relations, somatic and mental health problems, social problems, and behavioral dysfunction.
- In terms of reducing recidivism rates, FFT was equally effective with youth in each of the cultural groups represented in the project (Dunman, 2009). Thus, there is preliminary data to suggest that because of its family focus and individualized approach, FFT does cross cultural and racial lines.
- We found that racial or ethnic matching of the therapist and the family had no effect on the outcome. In other words, clients were assigned to the therapist with open spots; most often therapists and families were of different cultural and ethnic backgrounds (Dunman, 2009). While we don't know for sure, it is likely that this made no difference because matching to the family is a central part of the theory and practice of FFT.

Amsterdam Project: FFT in a Forensic Psychiatric Treatment Setting

Serious adolescent behavior problems have become an international concern, to which many countries have responded by implementing evidence-based treatment programs. In the Netherlands, juvenile crime is emerging as a social crisis. Over the last 20 years, both self-report measures and official police records indicate that approximately 37% of juveniles in the Netherlands admitted to having committed a criminal act in the previous year. In addition, the number of violent criminal acts among this age group has tripled over the last 20 years (Boendermaker & Van Yperen, 2003). In response to the growing trend of violent crime among adolescents and the accompanying societal attention to adolescent problem behavior, identifying successful treatment methods for juvenile delinquency has become a high priority in the Netherlands. The ministries of justice and health, in addition to the National Institute of Health Sciences and mental health service providers in the Netherlands, have searched for well-established, effective clinical intervention models. They turned to American models of clinical intervention because they come with a long history of systematic outcome research. As a result, the Ministry of Justice recently adopted Functional Family Therapy as one of the primary treatments of choice. The ministries have supported the training and implementation of FFT to diverse community providers. Local community providers found that FFT fits into a mental health institute because of its therapeutic focus, as opposed to the more common case management approach that other models employ. Functional Family Therapy is much more like traditional family therapy, which appealed to the professional staff.

Nonetheless, it was a challenge just to introduce a family model into this mental health culture. Medical approaches are based on diagnosing individual risk factors in adolescents (mental health problems, peer influences, etc.) and parents (relational conflicts, parental psychiatric disorders, family history, education levels). As noted, FFT takes a relational rather than individual focus, and it privileges ongoing assessment over diagnosis. Overcoming the culture clash required the development of trust between the FFT family therapy consultant (myself), local family therapists, and the psychiatric directors of the treatment facilities. We built a strong relational alliance by means of careful, patient development of a joint vision of the project, carried forth with a purposeful focus on creating a solid partnership during the implementation of FFT.

One goal of this project was to identify the cultural adjustments needed to transport a U.S. family therapy model to the Dutch system. Although the United States and the Netherlands differ in size, they share some of the same European cultural legacy: the value of the individual, the standard nuclear family (father, mother, and two children), and Christianity. Like the United States, the Netherlands is a multicultural society in which the church now plays a diminished role, and many single parents or postdivorce combined families live side by side with the standard family. There is an increasing multiethnic profile in the Netherlands; large Moroccan, Surinamese, and Turkish groups have immigrated and become Dutch citizens. Thus, cultural sensitivity was a critical variable in the successful transportation of FFT. After the first year of training, the treatment staff and I found, to the surprise of all, that FFT could be delivered in this international and culturally diverse setting with no changes to the clinical model. It is important to note that matching to the diverse families was a critical issue that required great clinical skill, however.

Over the last 6 years the Dutch FFT project has successfully trained over 100 therapists in more than 14 different treatment organizations. A Dutch "knowledge center" was established in which Dutch supervisors monitor treatment integrity, provide ongoing quality assurance and supervision, and help organizations fit FFT into their service delivery systems. During the course of the project, approximately 5,000 families with adolescents received FFT. The training and supervision are now done by Dutch organizations and "owned" by the treatment organization where services reside. This process illustrates how, with systematic planning, FFT can be integrated into a different treatment delivery setting and ultimately be self-sustaining. The Amsterdam project illustrated that the FFT treatment model can indeed span some cultural boundaries.

Conclusions

In a way, implementing FFT in community settings is just like doing FFT with families. It requires engagement and motivation, behavior change, and ultimately generalization as a process that brings the best of the treatment model and, through an alliance-based approach, integrates it into the treatment delivery system of an organization. At the center of the process are FFT and its theoretical and clinical model. Even we model developers have been surprised at the way in which FFT, when implemented well, can move so easily into vastly different community settings. In retrospect, this is likely due to the unwavering commitment we have made to treatment fidelity. In each project, doing FFT as it was designed was the major goal. Treatment delivery systems, therapist roles, and the workings of the organization all were aligned to promote the implementation of FFT in each of its core principles, its clinical model, and in the clinical guidelines that help therapists translate it to clients.

The main lesson we have learned is that models such as FFT need to take a comprehensive approach if adopters are ever to replicate the outcomes of developmental clinical trials in real community settings. As such, the traditional methods of training, supervision, and accountability no longer apply. Instead, successful clinical treatments now rely upon continuous quality improvement based on developmentally targeted training. Given complex cases involving adolescent externalizing behavior disorders, transporting the treatment model is a complex and long-term commitment.

In the real world, FFT is not delivered in sterile settings but instead in complex, diverse settings. Projects such as the ones described in this chapter illustrate the diversity of client, setting, and system in which FFT can work. FFT can be a perfect way to overcome the ongoing research-practice gap in the psychological sciences because it offers a clear and systematic model that can be used to provide services, training, and research in settings in which each of these domains is intertwined and interrelated. The outcome is better research with more clinical utility, relevant clinical training, and a view from behind the one-way mirror so that we can continually learn about what works. FFT applies to ethnically diverse clients both within and outside the United States. In fact, the FFT projects are among the first to demonstrate that an American treatment model can be successfully transported to other cultures and other countries.

Implementing and translating FFT to community settings is not easy. FFT is more than just a clinical model. It is a service delivery system that includes training, treatment, supervision, and implementation protocols. All of these elements are connected by the principles of continuous quality improvement; at all levels of an organization, the primary focus is on quality delivery of FFT, ongoing process and outcome data gathering, and learning how to improve practice therapists. This means that therapists need to be their own evaluator, not just for the work with their current client but with their entire caseload. It requires organizations to monitor and make constant adjustments to the ways they support therapists, the various treatment delivery systems, and the climate and culture that characterize the organization. It means that clinical supervisors perform an even larger role—both monitoring quality and using that data to systematically improve outcomes. The FFT service delivery system is the topic of the next chapter.

9

FFT as a Service Delivery System

In real practice, clinical models such as FFT are delivered within larger service delivery systems (SDS). A service delivery system represents the overall way in which an organization implements clinical interventions. Typically it includes how clients are assessed, how they are treated, the use of clinical supervision, and the monitoring of clinical process and outcomes. The organization's SDS covers the various elements of good treatment (assessment, intervention, clinical supervision) and is based on principles of quality assurance, as noted in Chapter 8. However, it is not uncommon to find that such systems are "disconnected" from and unrelated to the treatment approaches delivered within them.

We discovered that when implementing FFT with clinical fidelity and using the principles of continuous quality improvement, we were in fact promoting a service delivery system each time we transported FFT to a new organization. Over time we found that for FFT to be effective we needed to develop and implement a comprehensive system of assessment, treatment planning, clinical intervention, quality improvement, and clinical supervision. When most successful, FFT functioned to pull together the disparate parts of service delivery within an organization offering treatment services to adolescents and their families. In fact, whether in small or large organizations, we found that the ultimate success of FFT is in part determined by the degree to which the various elements of the SDS are linked together and the degree to which they are consistent with the principles of FFT. The system of care that surrounded FFT could help promote model-specific adherence and therapist competence specifically and efficiently.

Three areas are particularly important in a service delivery system organized for continuous quality improvement—clinical supervision, ongoing data monitoring and feedback, and matching to the context. During our very first experiences transporting FFT to communities, we quickly discovered that clinical supervision was more than just a tool to solve crises or discrete clinical problems (as it is usually used); rather, it was an essential element in the overall effort to maintaining the integrity and ultimately the outcomes of FFT. Supervision is one of the major ways that fidelity is managed in clinical trial studies, and it is a common procedure in most practice settings. In community settings, the tools and process of clinical supervision are often case focused and not specifically linked to the adherence and competence in delivering a specific model of treatment. This finding led us to develop a specific supervision model that focuses on the development of adherence and competence in FFT (Sexton, Alexander, & Gilman, 2004). This model of supervision has been a central feature in the dissemination efforts of FFT over the last decade. To be a true quality improvement activity, clinical supervision needs to have unique principles and practices that are, as suggested by Liddle (1986), isomorphic to the clinical model itself. When considered in this way, clinical supervision is a central part of the foundation of a "treatment model and functions as a central piece in a service delivery system that is able to maintain itself over time."

We also became aware of the need for methods to measure critical elements of the FFT model in order to inform a continuous quality improvement approach. As noted in Chapter 8, CQI takes an organization-wide approach to enhancing positive outcomes in adolescents and families. We first thought of CQI methods as "tools." Now we realize that they are elements of the service delivery system itself. For example, in research trials, we used numerous methods to measure model fidelity. Most involved complex videotape rating and coding where an expert rates the work of the therapist in regard to the overall FFT model and the specific phase within which they are working. However, in community settings these methods are not realistic or cost effective. What was needed were realistic, clinically relevant measures of therapist work and reasonable methods for both collecting and feeding back information to therapists so that they can be aware of their progress and can use that information to improve practice. This led us to develop one of the earliest computer-based systems to monitor and improve practice (FFT Q-System, Sexton & Wilkenson, 1999).

Finally, we found that as FFT became established in the organizational SDS, it needed to fit into the work of other professionals. Much like the principle of clinically matching to the client, as a service, FFT needed to match to the work of case managers, probation officers, psychiatrists, and other treatment providers in order to enhance the outcomes of FFT and to provide a systematic, integrated collection of services to clients. This work resulted in two model extensions, one that moved FFT principles to probation officers (Functional Family Parole) and the integrated case management approach (a case study later in this chapter). Chapter 8 contained number features of organizations that make them more open to FFT.

Thus, this last chapter focuses on the ways in which the theoretical, clinical, and organizational features of FFT come together into a systematic service delivery system that can help bridge the gap between the academic and research world, where models such as FFT have been tested and found effective, to the real clinical world, where they must be integrated into a broad range of treatment services in community-based organizations. These elements often do require a major shift in the way that organizations work, that therapists function, the role that clinical supervisors play, and the methods used for data collection and management. Thus, the ideas in this chapter are aspirational in that they propose a model and set of principles that could work despite the many realities of insurance regulation, funding requirements, and the necessary elements of mental health regulations. They aspire to bring about the conditions within which FFT has its best opportunity to reach and help adolescents and families. However, these ideas are reality based as well; they are in practice at many sites that use FFT on a regular basis, and they now form part of the FFT dissemination and transportation system protocols. They reflect what it takes for any clinical model to translate theory into practice: a comprehensive system of theory, clinical practice, supervision, and continuous quality improvement.

The chapter focuses on three distinct elements. The first section addresses model adherence and therapist competence, the most important elements of model fidelity within a service delivery system. The second section addresses the means to achieve adherence and competence: clinical supervision, comprehensive data monitoring, and information feedback. The chapter ends with a case example illustrating how these elements go together in a community mental health center setting. The center uses FFT as its core intervention model and case managers as adjuncts to expand the reach of therapy.

FFT Within Service Delivery Systems

If you search the literature on service delivery systems, you will find very little that attends to the integration of the actual core services within an organization providing treatment services for adolescents and families. There is a considerable literature on what have been labeled "systems of care" (SOCs) (Stroul & Friedman, 1986). This approach brings various types of services such as mental health, substance abuse, vocational, health, and social services together around the needs of the child and family in large, macro-level systems. The systems of care philosophy is intended to bring together various treatment providers to help the consumers of their service receive the least restrictive, most appropriate services in a coordinated fashion. While the SOC principles are appealing and helpful, they don't provide the specificity needed to enable each treatment component to build on the others, thus creating a comprehensive, systemic service delivery system.

What is apparent in the available literature is that client-focused, coordinated care is an important goal in any service delivery system. Coordination is often considered to be the communication aspect of the SDS. Our experience suggests that services can really only be coordinated systematically when they have a conceptual and treatment-oriented lens through which they consider what, when, and how each element of the treatment process takes place. Systematic care occurs when the various elements of treatment (assessment, intervention, measurement of outcomes, clinical supervision, and monitoring and evaluation) all come together to provide treatment that has a common philosophy and approach, with similar principles, and methods of focusing on the youth and family. Systematic care would mean that the goals of assessment and treatment match, that the focus of clinical supervision is aligned with the specific type of treatment being delivered, and that evaluation is aimed at measuring outcomes that fit the goals of treatment. Our experience is that FFT is often adopted by organizations as a single discrete treatment element, not integrated into the assessment, supervision, and evaluation functions in a systematic way.

Most of us in the applied psychological fields have been trained in the medical approach to service delivery, which works in linear ways. When a client comes for help he or she first receives a comprehensive assessment that results in a diagnosis. The diagnosis directs treatment choices. Care is offered and when other features of the problem arise, additional discrete care units are applied. Since every diagnostic system currently in use is individually focused, so are the treatments. The result is that problems are usually focused on individuals, diagnoses are individual, and different treatments are directed at different parts of the family system. For example, a typical youth referred to FFT has what many clinicians may call "anger issues." Indeed, many adolescents are angry and quite openly and honestly express their passionate feelings. In this scenario, that adolescent is likely to receive a diagnosis that locates the anger in him or her, and thus results in treatments for anger management or impulse control. If that anger was directed at the parents and there was family conflict, it would not be surprising to find the family receiving treatment for family conflict. If there is peer involvement in the anger, the youth may also be referred to a group such as Aggression Replacement Therapy (ART). Along the way, if the youth also uses drugs and or alcohol, he or she would be referred to specialized addiction treatment. In most cases, these services would be conducted simultaneously based on the prevailing philosophy of wraparound services.

Most organizations that have successfully integrated FFT into their SDS in a systematic, coordinated way work differently. They coordinate care using a sequential model, as discussed in Chapters 3 and 8. These organizations found it most helpful to organize treatments in a family-first way where treatments are sequenced logically. (In fact, FFT argues for a family-focused, systematic, simultaneous-care model where conditions permit. The case example in this chapter illustrates one such care model.)

Figure 9.1 illustrates how FFT helps to coordinate services sequentially within organizations. Note that in this model, FFT is the first treatment that clients receive. Assessment is multisystemic and based on the principles outlined in Chapters 2 and 3. When FFT begins, other treatments take a step back. As the generalization phase begins, FFT therapists begin to think about community resources and other services that families might need to successfully maintain changes (see Chapter 6). Referral and coordination of care is a central feature of this phase. What is most important about this model from an organizational perspective is that the essential treatment components have a common thread that guides continuous quality improvement (CQI). Clinical supervision and ongoing monitoring of clinical progress and model fidelity provide continuous, focused, and specific support for FFT, creating a feedback loop to help the therapist deliver the best treatment possible.

Most importantly from the client's perspective, it gives the family the feeling that they are at the center of treatment because each phase of the service delivery system focuses on the unique ways in which they function as a unit. Like SOC, this makes the family central to the treatment process, but in a way in which therapists

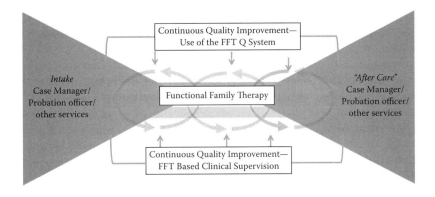

Primacy of Services as Youth and Family Progression through SDS over time

FIGURE 9.1   Integrated FFT service delivery system.

and organizations can still provide the most helpful and effective treatment. Unlike SOC, this approach means that families don't determine treatments but instead become the primary unit of analysis, with a voice in what is most relevant and central in their lives.

Central Elements of an Effective FFT Service Delivery System

Within the model described in Figure 9.1, there are three essential elements that promote continuous quality improvement and enhance the positive outcomes of FFT: the development of model adherence and therapist competence; ongoing monitoring and feedback on the progress of the process and outcomes of the clinical model; and model-focused, systematic clinical supervision.

Developing and Maintaining Model Adherence and Therapist Competence

FFT is most effective when it is delivered as it was designed (model-specific adherence), and it must be delivered well, with a high degree of skill (therapist competence). These are the specific targets of CQI because of their importance and direct link to client outcomes. *Adhere* is defined in the dictionary as "to be in accordance with," "to follow through or carry out a play without deviation," or "to cling, stick or hold together and resist separation." Each of these meanings fits. FFT therapists who demonstrate model-specific adherence make clinical decisions in accordance with the principles and conceptual foundations of FFT, conduct therapy in accordance with the clinical model, and work with clients guided by the goals of FFT. Similarly, adherent FFT therapists follow through without deviation, meaning that they stick to the goals and principles of the model when events, situations, and problems are presented to them. Finally, they cling to the model as the map for deciding what direction, goal, and outcome to pursue. Without the basic model elements, the work being done does not represent the intervention program as it was developed, and thus it cannot produce the potentially positive outcomes associated with the model. What is most important to remember is that model adherence is something between the therapist and the model, something that can be measured.

While clearly important, model-specific adherence is not enough. In any clinical situation there is more than just a therapist and a model—there is the family. Throughout the book, the primary principle in each example, each phase and each goal is that the interventions of the model and the therapist are only effective to the degree that they match to the client. This principle is what makes FFT effective in families from many ethnic, racial, religious, and cultural backgrounds, and it depends on therapist competence.

The dictionary defines *competence* as "the ability to apply knowledge, skills, or judgment in practice if called upon to do so." In FFT this means that the therapist is able to apply the clinical model, its core theoretical principles, and the specific clinical intervention skills in implementing FFT with a specific family. Therapist competence is, therefore, the ability of the therapist to match the model to the unique, complex, and multisystemic nature of the families they treat. It is important to note that our definition of competence does not mean the same thing as having competencies, that is, qualifications or abilities. In FFT competence is specifically the ability to apply FFT as a matching-to process.

While interrelated, adherence and competence are different. In fact, adherence is a prerequisite to the competent application of FFT, for reasons that are intuitively obvious: If you want to replicate the outcome, you have to replicate the model. As noted in Chapter 8, research coming out of the Washington State Project, during which 500 therapists were trained, found that those who delivered FFT with high adherence (as rated by their supervisor on a weekly basis) had significantly better outcomes (as measured by recidivism rates 1 year later) than a randomized control group. Those therapists with low adherence ratings had outcomes that were *worse* than traditional services, and of course, significantly worse than adherent FFT therapists, to the point that their clients might have been better off not receiving family therapy. It is important to note that the outcomes measured here were clinically significant ones, measures of arrest 18 months following FFT.

Knowledge and Performance

Adherence and competence are interdependent constructs, and they both are present when a therapist works successfully with a family and has good outcomes. Adherence and competence are anchored in and measured by the FFT clinical model. Each dimension has both knowledge and performance components. Figure 9.2 illustrates the relationship between model adherence, therapist competence, knowledge, and performance.

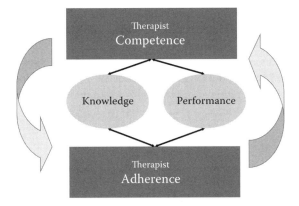

FIGURE 9.2 Case and session planning (therapist-level Q-system data). Adapted from Sexton, Alexander, and Gilman (2004).

Model Adherence

The *knowledge domain* of model adherence includes a basic working knowledge of the FFT core principles. They form the background of all the FFT therapist's clinical actions. The clinical supervisor listens for these principles in the therapist's discussion of cases; an accurate assessment of the therapist's mastery of them helps the supervisor systematically target his or her interventions.

The *performance domain* of model adherence requires the ability to put knowledge into action with a family. Basic performance includes the ability to execute the common elements of good counseling and family therapy. Adherent performance requires that the therapist be able to operationalize the core principles by approaching therapy in a way that is alliance-based, built on respect and understanding of the family's unique nature. Like the knowledge domain, the performance domain of model adherence is anchored in the FFT clinical model. The therapist needs to have the basic ability to engage and motivate the family, focus on specific, obtainable behavior change targets in ways that match families, and generalize changes.

Therapist Competence

The knowledge domain of therapist competence requires that the therapist have a complex understanding of two important aspects of FFT: client problems and the therapy process. Highly competent FFT therapists have the ability to understand the vast array of client problems and issues in very complex and idiographic ways. When highly competent, the therapist can place difficult presenting problems into complex relational patterns, sorting out the important details of relational functions. Having a complex understanding of clients and their problems allows the therapist the ability to respond in increasingly contingent ways that match clients. A complex, multidimensional understanding of client problems means the therapist is able to deal with a broader range of presenting concerns while remaining in the relational domain that is essential to the FFT model.

The performance domain is the principal domain in therapist competence. It is represented by the therapist's ability to respond in the room to families in ways that are highly attuned to the individual needs and presentations of the situation. The FFT therapist must demonstrate a complex ability to respond contingently while staying focused on the immediate and long-term goals of the model. An adequately complex performance domain is represented by a highly idiographic approach to accomplishing the goals of the FFT model.

Ongoing Monitoring and Feedback

The major goal of a CQI-based service delivery system is that clinicians are able to successfully learn, practice, and maintain the success of the clinical interventions in their organization. Sapyta, Riemer, and Bickman (2005) liken such a process to the learning of any other difficult task. Using archery as an example, they suggest that though some archers might be naturals, it takes practice, training, and information feedback to hone a skill. Systematic training, ongoing guidance, and comprehensive information feedback make the difference between trial-and-error learning and an efficient, effective pathway to skills development. In family therapy, the youth and families we work with need help and the consequences of ineffective help (e.g., violence, crime, school problems) are significant. These issues don't afford the family therapist the luxury of time to learn by self-guided experience and trial and error. This is an ethical as well as a practical issue.

The literature has numerous examples suggesting the need for systematic learning of clinical skills. For example, Grove, Zald, Lebow, Snits, and Nelson (2000) found that computers were more successful at certain diagnostic tasks than were experienced professionals. Despite the growing evidence suggesting that clinical decision making alone is relatively inaccurate, professionals continue confident in their abilities to make clinical decisions based on experience and judgment alone (Garb, 1989; Sapyta et al., 2005). The work of Bickman and colleagues (Sapyta et al., 2005) suggests that this is because clinical treatments are most often learned by experience instead of through the use of relevant, regular, and reliable feedback. Their work further suggests that feedback needs to be specific, process- and outcome-focused, and accompanied by help in using and integrating the feedback into specific clinical decisions and interventions.

Systematic monitoring is the flip side of systematic learning. Despite its importance, we actually know little about the methods for monitoring and using model-specific, clinical process, and client problem information in psychotherapy (Sapyta et al., 2005). Particularly promising are the efforts to use computer technology to monitor and provide feedback for both clinical process outcomes (Lambert, 2002; Bickman, 2009; Sapyta et al., 2005; Riemer et al., 2005) and model-specific adherence (Sexton & Alexander, 2004). These tools are useful in monitoring the ongoing relationship between client symptoms, model adherence, and other clinical processes (e.g., therapeutic alliance); increasing model adherence; and promoting the clinical adaptations necessary to increase model adherence and improve community-based outcomes. Thus, computer systems provide the technical foundation for finally moving continuous quality improvement into psychological service delivery systems.

The FFT Quality Improvement System (FFT Q-System) and the clinical supervision process work hand in hand to realize this potential. The FFT Q-System is an adherence and competence development tool intended to serve as a technical aid to building and maintaining the quality of FFT services. Recognizing that managing the multiple sources of information necessary to promote treatment fidelity is a daunting yet critical task, Sexton and colleagues (Sexton & Wilkenson, 1999; Sexton & Alexander, 2004) developed the FFT Q-System as an intuitive, user-friendly, but highly secure and HIPAA-compliant program used by community-based FFT therapists to record client information (e.g., contact information, demographic information, previous history), client contacts (visits, scheduled visits, phone contacts, etc.), assessment information (individual, family, and behavioral assessment), adherence measures, and outcomes measurements.

For the therapist, the Q-System is a treatment planning tool, used to record the events of each encounter with the family, make plans for the next session, and integrate each of the core elements of the clinical model into actual practice. It keeps therapists focused on the relevant goals, skills, and interventions for each phase of FFT. It integrates measures of specific model adherence, therapists' treatment planning, outcome measures, and risk and protective factors assessment with contact management tools. When used in practice, the Q-System tracks all clients, all sessions/contacts with clients, all client assessments, and all quality assurance information for each FFT case. Based on this data, the Q-System provides real-time feedback to therapists on their levels of model fidelity, ongoing indices of client outcomes, and service delivery profiles.

From the supervisory perspective, the Q-System addresses one of the most difficult tasks of any evidence-based treatment: ensuring that model fidelity is maintained each day with each case in each therapeutic encounter. It has the added benefit of providing the clinical supervisor with specific, focused, and session-by-session information that reflects how the therapist thinks, the decisions he or she makes, and the outcomes of his or her work. Access to this information helps focus and improve the effectiveness of the supervision process, further improving client outcomes (see the sections on clinical supervision, below).

The FFT Q-System is unique in that it is a *single* system that provides real-time information to therapists, supervisors, administrators, evaluators, and researchers regarding model fidelity, client outcomes, and service delivery profiles. As a result, the Q-System is both a monitoring and quality improvement feedback system providing all parties with a range of information that can be used to improve practice, determine supervision goals, and evaluate outcomes. The case study at the end of this chapter provides further information on how the Q-System is used and how it is integrated into the organization's SDS.

Data-Based Measures

As noted by Sapyta et al. (2005) and Rimer (2005), continuous quality improvement depends on more than just computer tools. Improvement in services comes when reliable, relevant, and easy-to-use information is provided as feedback to help redirect, support, or even correct clinical decisions before crises occur. We developed a series of such instruments that are the central data-based measures that make up the core of the Q-System. These instruments were developed by myself and are described in length in the Blueprints manual for FFT (Alexander, Pugh, Parsons, & Sexton, 2000) as well as in numerous other publications in the last decade (Sexton & Alexander, 2002b, 2004, 2007, 2009). These instruments are in use in over 300 community-based sites and are being used by thousands of FFT therapists every day. The following descriptions summarize those previous presentations.

Session Planning Tools

Session planning tools are an important part of adherent and effective FFT. Session planning is organized through a series of progress notes (PNs) that serve both as documentation for all FFT services and as a method to help therapists think about the session through the FFT lens. The progress notes prompt the therapist to consider the essential goals of the phase, the progress made toward accomplishing those goals, and future session plans—in effect, modeling how the therapist can/should think about the process aspect of the session. As such, it is a helpful guide for new therapists to begin to pull the process aspects of sessions into the foreground and let the content aspects drift into the background. (As with any tool, progress notes help to the extent that they are used.) They also provide immediate model-specific guidance on how to focus attention and direct their efforts in upcoming sessions. This technology allows the therapist to be focused on the clinical model well before feedback from the clinical supervisor, thus promoting his or her own self-sufficiency. Figure 9.3 illustrates the various tools available in the Q-System to help with session and treatment planning.

Model-Specific Adherence and Therapist Competency Measures

Given the specificity of the FFT clinical model, goal identification is an important measure of the degree to which the therapists pursue model-specific therapeutic goals and the degree to which these are accomplished. Adherence is measured from two different perspectives in order to capture a complete picture of the activities of the therapist behavior in regard to the treatment model (Sexton, Alexander, & Gilman, 2004).

- *Supervisor-rated therapist adherence.* The TAM (Therapist Adherence Measure) is a supervisor-rated measure of therapist adherence to the FFT clinical model. The TAM has two dimensions: a general supervisor adherence rating (TAM-G) and a phase-specific supervisor adherence rating (TAM-S). The supervisor rates both measures during the weekly clinical staffing using a 7-point Liker scale, indicating low, average, and high general model adherence.

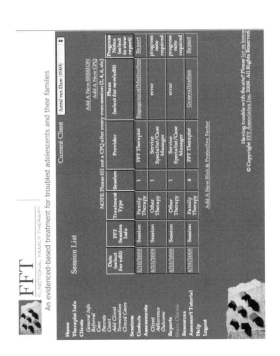

FIGURE 9.3 Therapist feedback reports.

In a study of FFT model adherence, Barnoski (2000) found the TAM to be significantly correlated with adolescent behavioral outcomes; high model adherence scores (as measured by the TAM-G) successfully predicted lower rates of criminal recidivism. The phase-specific therapist adherence measure (TAM-S) is a supervisor rating measure adapted from videotape adherence rating systems (Gilman, 2008). As a videotape rating method, the TAM-S has demonstrated high interrater reliability (.70–.85); the supervisor rating version of the TAM-S contains the same items and scale. Both general (TAM-G) and phase specific (TAM-S) supervisor ratings of therapist adherence are made during clinical staffing presentation of cases during weekly FFT clinical supervision. Supervisors trained in the TAM-G and TAM-S systems follow the FFT supervision manual (Sexton, Alexander, & Gilman, 2004), and rate the general therapist adherence for each case presentation and the specific elements of adherence for that phase.

• *Family/client-rated therapist adherence.* The Counseling Process Questionnaire (CPQ) is a family report of their experience in a particular treatment encounter with an FFT therapist. The CPQ (Sexton, Ostrom, Bonomo, & Alexander,

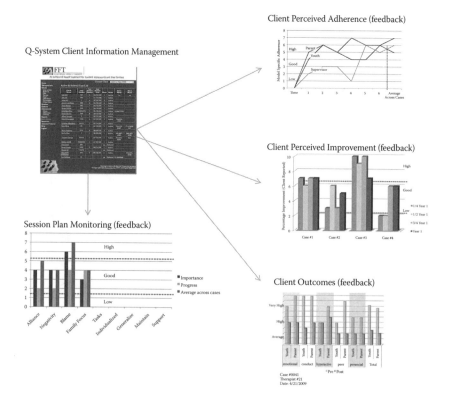

FIGURE 9.4   FFT clinical supervisor decision-making process.

2000) is an 18-item inventory completed by each family member. Six items per phase reflect the goals of each phase of FFT. In a preliminary study of CPQs from adolescents and parents (Datchi-Phillips, in process), the instrument has been found to successfully reflect families' expected experience in FFT (e.g., the mean scores are highest for the phase in which the CPQ was delivered) and to measure the extent to which the therapist implements interventions that activate FFT-phase-specific change mechanisms. In other words, the CPQ has been found to successfully evaluate the degree to which the therapist adheres to the model as it is described in the treatment manual. An initial factor analysis of data collected from 348 families after the first, second, or third therapy session yielded results in support of a three-factor structure of the CPQ.

Service Delivery Profiles

Because each FFT session and client contact is recorded in the Q-System, it is possible for FFT therapists to get the big-picture view of how services were delivered to individual families and across their caseload. Therapists can see the frequency of family sessions; what treatment phase families are in; when they cancel, reschedule, or don't show up; and who attended, among other features. These service delivery data points are fed back to the therapist in the form of a profile so that the therapist can better plan sessions. This allows both therapists and their clinical supervisors to pinpoint places in the model where the therapist has strengths (e.g., in early engagement) and/or places where improvements can be made (e.g., in promoting specific behavior changes).

Client Assessment and Outcomes Measures

As a comprehensive CQI tool, the Q-System displays the most current model-relevant client outcome measures in reports that summarize pre-, post-, and clinically relevant change levels. The measures provide the therapist with ongoing real-time feedback about initial areas of client need (initial assessment) and the outcomes of FFT therapy (final measures of change). With this information, the FFT therapist can plan better as well as obtain quality information critically important for further skill development. Outcome measures show pre- and post- change, clinically reliable change index scores, and changes in functional levels of the clients. The Q-System includes reliable, clinically useful instruments with low respondent burden and maximum clinical benefit. The measures of assessment and outcome include:

- Mental health measures (Strength and Difficulties Questionnaires, Parental Stress Index, Youth Symptom Behavior Inventory, and the Service Assessment for Children)
- General outcome measures (Strengths and Difficulties Questionnaire)
- Risk and protective factor measures (Washington State Risk and Protective Factors Instrument)
- Process variables critical to successful outcome (Peabody Alliance Scale, phase-based goals and improvement measures)

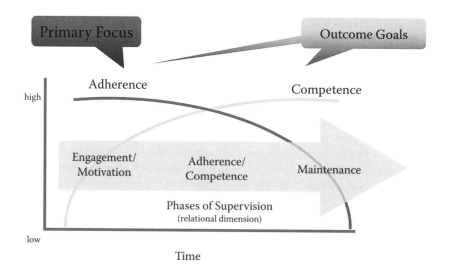

Primary Focus

Outcome Goals

Adherence

Competence

high

Engagement/
Motivation

Adherence/
Competence

Maintenance

Phases of Supervision
(relational dimension)

low

Time

FIGURE 9.5 Use of the Q-System in community-based service. Adapted from Sexton, Alexander, and Gilman (2004).

Feedback Reports

The Q-System was designed to provide immediate reports and summary tables of each of the elements described above to both the clinician and the supervisor. This means that therapists can turn to the Q-System to find out the current progress of the client (process measures), measures of client- and supervisor-based therapist model adherence, and the outcomes of treatments across one client, the therapist's entire case load, or across agency norms. The computer displays and summarizes session-level monitoring of service delivery. Figure 9.5 illustrates some of the feedback reports available in the Q-System. The use of these is illustrated in the case example below.

The FFT Clinical Supervision Model

Clinical supervision has always been an important part of clinical practice. In clinical training programs, clinical supervision serves as a bridge between the academic and the practice realms. In an agency setting, supervision often serves both administrative (e.g., focusing on the standards of practice set by the service delivery system) and clinical (e.g., helping clients) purposes. In the larger social context, clinical supervision is a central part of the licensing process and enables a therapist to practice independently. Thus, in a variety of ways, supervision is almost institutionalized within the profession. Clearly the type of clinical supervision a therapist receives can have an impact on his or her clinical decisions. Yet, despite its place in the field, the mechanisms and procedures of clinical supervision have always been a bit more elusive to define. In this new era of evidence-based and systematic clinical models, the role of supervision and its contribution to accountability hold great interest and importance.

Different types of supervision have different goals. Supervision aimed at developing the therapist often focuses on personal growth, professional development, and orientation to the profession. Administratively focused supervision is based on the criteria and standard practices of the agency or of licensing and billing requirements. Clinical supervision is often less specific in its foundation and in its goal. While oriented toward ensuring that the therapist provides the most appropriate and effective treatment, the basis of the questions and suggestions offered by the supervisor, and the process followed, seems to be less clear. Much like general therapeutic practice, the practice of clinical supervision has been based on a handful of broad conceptual approaches (see Bernard & Goodyear, 2004). What is missing in these approaches is a clear articulation of the specific clinical model upon which the supervisor is basing his or her suggestions and the goals to which the supervision is directing the therapist. Therefore, linking supervision goals, practices, and procedures with the clinical model is essential to improving practice.

The supervision and training of family therapy in particular has evolved over the last 30 years, through several eras with different emphases. It is now an area of clinical specialization, designated and certified by professional organizations, such as the development of the AAMFT standards for qualifying supervisors. Cleghorn and Levin (1973) outlined three family therapy skills essential to trainee development: (1) perceptual skills, which involve the ability to accurately describe the behavioral data of the therapy session; (2) conceptual skills, which involve the ability to take clinical observations and translate them into meaningful language; and (3) intervention skills that guide in-session therapist behaviors to modify family interactional patterns (Anderson, Rigazio-DiGilio, & Kunkler, 1995).

The FFT clinical supervision model builds on these earlier ideas. In FFT, clinical supervision is a key element in learning the model, maintaining good-quality practice, and extending the model to diverse clients and settings while maintaining model-specific adherence and therapist competence. Clinical supervision must be based on the same principles as FFT, must be aimed at the same goals as FFT, and must support the same relational clinical practices if it is to enhance the therapeutic work. The first formal articulation of the FFT supervision model was published by Haas, Alexander, & Mas (in Liddle, Breunlin, & Schwartz, 1988). As our experience with FFT in community settings increased, we found that more was needed—to be exact, a supervision model must address model-specific adherence and therapist competence (as defined above) in real clinical settings.

Sexton, Alexander, and Gilman (2004) were the first to describe a model-specific supervision model for FFT applicable to community practice. Because of the intense focus on these two elements of adherence and competence, it became clear that FFT supervision must encompass more than a focus on therapist development and the provision of a supportive environment. It must also include a teaching component and an emphasis on the interdependency between model adherence and developing competence at treating families, and it must embrace the multisystem context that includes the therapist, the treatment setting, the working group of the FFT team, and the supervisor.

Our approach has major implications for service delivery systems. An FFT clinical supervisor must first be a good FFT therapist, because good supervision is based on an expert understanding of what good practice requires. Thus, unlike what is customary in many organizations, FFT clinical supervisors are fully trained therapists with demonstrated ability to practice FFT at a high level. In addition, while acting as supervisors, they also continue to see clients and receive supervision for their own cases. The following descriptions of the role and process of FFT clinical supervision are based on previously published work by Sexton and Alexander in this area (Sexton, Alexander, & Gilman, 2004). This work is also built on the early work of Alexander in his University Training Clinic, from which he developed his descriptions of supervision (Alexander et al., 1988). In this work, three features of the supervision process become clear, distinguishing it from previous models: the role of the supervisor, the goals of supervision, and the relational process that is the "how" of successfully conducting clinical supervision.

Role of the FFT Site Supervisor

At a community-based FFT site, the clinical site supervisor is responsible for the quality of the FFT services delivered by the agency. The FFT clinical supervisor operates to promote three major goals across multiple operational domains, intervening where necessary to:

- *Monitor model fidelity and quality* of the service delivery in the clinical practice of FFT (i.e., provide quality assurance)
- *Promote adherence and competence* by guiding FFT therapists to consistently think through the FFT lens and to make clinical decision based on FFT principles (i.e., promote quality improvement)
- *Manage the service delivery context* so that it promotes the model and allows for delivery of FFT such that families receive the benefit of high-quality services

FFT clinical supervision accomplishes these goals through two basic activities. The first, *quality assurance*, is a monitoring process in which the supervisor's job is to constantly watch the adherence and competence of individual therapists in their working group. Supervisors do this formally through systematic rating mechanisms and informally through observation in case staffing. Their monitoring responsibility also extends to their agency and requires them to evaluate whether or not the organizational context (both administrative and structural) consistently supports the successful delivery of FFT.

The supervisor's second major responsibility is *quality improvement*. This is the primary objective of clinical supervision, improving the ability of both therapists and the site to deliver FFT as designed (model adherence) and in ways that successfully meet the needs of individual families (model competence). To improve quality, supervisors intervene with therapists, guided by the FFT supervision model and principles described below. The ultimate goal is high adherence to the model with high-quality service delivery. Quality improvement results from systematic supervision interventions taking place within a complex relational process between the supervisor, individual therapists, and the working group.

Core Supervision Principles

Like the FFT clinical model, the supervision model is based upon a set of core theoretical and philosophical principles that operate as the background for activities and the foundation of supervision interventions. In many ways, the principles are even more important than specific interventions because they set the parameters within which the supervisor works (Sexton et al., 2004). FFT clinical supervision is:

- *Model-focused.* The FFT clinical model (its central core principles and clinical protocol) is the primary basis for quality assurance and quality improvement; therefore it is the yardstick by which the therapist is assessed and the outcome goal to which the supervisor directs all interventions. Supervision is based on attention to model adherence (the prescribed goals and intervention strategies of the model) and competence in meeting these goals and using treatment strategies.
- *Relational.* The relational process between a supervisor, individual therapists, and a working group of therapists is reflected in the phasic nature of the supervision model. The relational process is founded on respect for the individual; it acknowledges the unique differences, strengths, and characteristics of each therapist. In addition, it is a relational process built on alliance in which the supervisor and therapist work together to the same end—successful implementation of the FFT model with families and youth.
- *Multisystemic.* Supervision requires attention and action in multiple domains: the therapists, the service delivery system, and the working group.
- *Phasic.* The supervision process unfolds over time, parallel to the treatment phases. Each phase has a set of goals, related change mechanisms, and supervisor interventions most likely to activate those change mechanisms.
- *Data-based or evidence-based.* Specific supervision interventions and goals are based on monitoring the therapist's service delivery patterns and consulting specific measures of therapist activities related to adherence and competence. Monitoring, goal setting, and ultimately intervention use data from multiple sources and perspectives. Throughout the phases of the supervision process, the supervisor constantly assesses adherence, competence, and the developmental status of the working group. Monitoring, decision making, and intervening are facilitated by evidence from multiple data sources including the therapist (self-report) and the quality improvement system (FFT Q-System).

These principles all cohere in the FFT supervision protocol.

Systematic Supervision Protocol

The role and principles of supervision form a protocol—a "map" or guide to help the FFT supervisor know where he or she is and where he or she is going in the process of supervision. The model helps set the agenda for an upcoming supervision encounter and identify specific goals for the encounter as well as supervisory behaviors/interventions mostly likely to promote the desired outcome. While the supervisor's primary responsibilities are quality assurance and quality improvement through the development of therapist adherence and competence, the supervisor must pursue these goals and tasks as a relational process rather than as scattered events. The process requires different roles for the supervisor and the therapist. Through performing their respective roles and working together, they help the families they serve to overcome their struggles.

As a process guide for the supervisor, the supervision model becomes the primary reality from which the supervisor understands what is occurring and provides a source of guidance. Consider what happens in a supervision encounter. FFT therapists, who work daily with very difficult families, bring in their struggles, emotions, or perceptions of the families with whom they are working. The supervisor focuses on the relational process of these content presentations and responds to the actions of the therapist (or group), guided by the session-specific, phase-based goals of the clinical model. This means that the supervisor must have a good understanding of the phases of the supervision model, responding one way in the early stages of supervision and a different way in later phases. Thus, the protocol operates as a map, helping the supervisor to focus on the most important immediate goals of the supervision encounter and stay on target.

The phases of FFT clinical supervision (as illustrated in Figure 9.5) are quite specific, direct, and prescriptive, and thus can look and feel like a curriculum. Do not confuse this with a paint-by-numbers approach, however. FFT supervision is based instead on the idea of pursuing specific goals in relationally responsive ways. Thus, FFT supervision, like FFT therapy, is both systematic and structured while being relational and responsive. Approached through this dialectic, the encounter never occurs the same way twice; the supervisor applies the phases and executes the accompanying strategies in ways that are unique to each working group and individual therapist.

Supervisor Interventions

Based on the profile of therapist adherence and competence gained from clinical supervision and tracked using the quality assurance tools described above, the clinical supervisor can attempt to improve a therapist's adherence and competence in a number of ways. The choice of interventions depends on:

- Whether the primary issue is one of adherence or competence
- Whether the domain is one of knowledge or performance
- The supervisor's relational understanding of the individual therapist

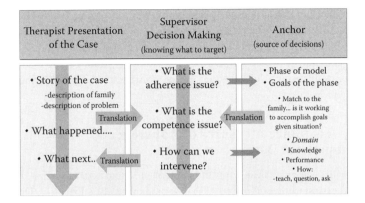

FIGURE 9.6 FFT clinical supervisor decision-making process.

In many ways supervision is an indirect process, and one that frequently differs from the earlier published supervision process and outcome research bases for the FFT designation as an evidence-based model. In some large community-based projects with widespread and geographically distant sites, the supervisor never sees what the therapist sees. Instead, the supervisor must make judgments based on what the therapist reports in supervision. While difficult, this can be done if the supervisor learns to hear the therapist's reports, decisions, and thinking in terms of model adherence and competence. Figure 9.6 illustrates how we have come to understand the translation process that the supervisor uses. Note from the figure that as the therapist tells the story of the case, he or she moves from the broad description of the family to the specific actions they took. This broad description provides an opportunity for the supervisor to listen for core principles, while the account of actions taken gives the supervisor the chance to determine if therapeutic interventions are faithful to the model.

To decide what to do, the supervisor must first look beyond the request that the therapist presents and determine whether model adherence or model competence is at issue. To make this judgment, the supervisor uses the clinical model as the yardstick, measuring what the therapist reports against what the model prescribes for this stage in therapy. Figure 9.3 illustrates this process.

There are two primary pathways of intervention to address these areas of quality improvement:

- *Teaching* is most appropriately addressed to issues that fall within the knowledge domain, such as a misunderstanding of core principles or the application of clinical procedures at either a basic level (adherence) or a complex level (competence). In both cases, it might be best for the clinical supervisor to focus on the conceptual principle behind an issue at the heart of the therapist's struggle. Teaching interventions are targeted primarily at improving the understanding of the therapist.
- *Case-specific suggestions* are a way to improve either adherence or competence, primarily in the performance domain. The clinical supervisor may suggest a

specific course of action or a particular way of reframing, add to the development of an organizing theme, or suggest an alternative relational assessment. When targeting competence, the goal is to help the therapist match to the client and apply the FFT model contingently. Suggestions can be made directly, imparted through role-playing and demonstration, or by describing necessary procedures.

Quality Assurance Measures of Adherence and Competence Data

Quality assurance data come from the content of case discussions that occur during formal case staffing and/or individual sessions with the supervisor. During case presentations, the supervisor listens for issues related to adherence or competence. In general, it is best to think about the level of adherence first, because adherence is a necessary but not sufficient condition of FFT. If and when adherence is evident, the supervisor considers issues of competence.

Supervision Planning and Staffing

FFT supervision staffings are more effective when the supervisor plans for each meeting. The supervisor starts by identifying the phase of supervision, clearly articulating the phase goals for each therapist, and determining what adherence and competence issues to address. The supervisor usually prepares for a session by reviewing the therapist records (in the Q-System), previous supervision ratings, and recent global therapist ratings before deciding which therapist should present a case. A general guideline is to give each therapist in the working group a chance to present a case twice a month.

Once the staffing begins, the supervisor's goal is to move from a broad discussion of the case to a specific action plan. The plan that results must propose a way to accomplish the phase goals for the family in question. The clinical supervisor structures and directs the discussion to this end, asking questions and prompting the working group to participate.

Example of Coordinating Care in an FFT SDS

The success of FFT is greatly enhanced by coordinating care among a range of organizational and community treatment and service providers. The complexity of acting-out adolescents, their families, and their situations means that FFT is but one piece of a coordinated system of care. FFT can also be enhanced by the coordinated work of different professionals working together, using the same principles for understanding clients and problems, and understanding and practicing the core principles of FFT. The real question is not if other professionals can help enhance FFT, but how their insights can be used in a coordinated and systematic SDS to accomplish that task.

The Delaware FFT Service Delivery System

Child and Families First, Inc. (CFF) is a community mental health center serving the state of Delaware. The organization has centers in both rural and urban areas. Like many organizations, CFF had a system of case managers and therapists to serve families and adolescents. The case managers helped provide for the immediate needs of the family by securing food stamps and rent assistance and providing transportation, among other things. Therapists provided the professional therapeutic services. Case managers and therapists operated as a wraparound team working simultaneously with families. Case managers would meet the family's practical needs and the therapists would focus on the family relationships. The agency quickly realized that therapists and case managers often provided overlapping services, which, while well intended, sometimes pulled families in different directions. Case managers sometimes acted as the "voice" of families with both the therapist and the community, while the therapists worked to get the family to speak for themselves. (See Figure 9.1.)

When FFT was implemented at CFF, we also started what we now call the Delaware Model: an integrated SDS that brought together case managers and FFT therapists under the same theoretical principles (FFT), organized by a data-based quality improvement system (the FFT Q-System). What is unique about the Delaware Model is that it provides an example of the ways in which care can be coordinated and specific clinical models like FFT can be extended far beyond the reach of therapy alone. The project took organizational support (from Leslie Newman, CEO), clinical support (from Vicky Kelly, clinical director), and coordinated efforts with the FFT experts (myself and Astrid van Dam, FFT clinical coordinator). The model development became a collaborative project among the case managers, who helped develop the specific instruments, manual, and training for the model. The goal was to link care specialists, therapists, and case managers together into a system of care using advanced technologies. All service providers were trained together, used the FFT lens for perspective in understanding families and their problems, and attempted to use relational skills to carry out their unique functions. A systematic treatment system emerged that took advantage of the strengths of all the available providers. The sequence of events in a particular case is described below.

Referral Management

Referrals come to the agency case managers (CMs), who conduct an initial service assessment (SA), a comprehensive review of the client's file and referral that is intended to identify the risk and assessment factors that may be present in the family context. Using the referral and any existing case records, a CM specifically considers the family's context—an area usually pushed to the generalization phase in FFT. The CM's role is to identify contextual issues early in the FFT process. Because the CM is not a therapist, this can occur without redirecting FFT away from the primary early session goals. When necessary the CM calls the school, probation office, or other referring agency and gathers further information. The

CM rarely interviews families to complete the SA. Service assessment focuses on five areas:

- Mental health (previous mental health care, last medical evaluation, current medication, and other mental health services)
- School (current attendance, specialized academic programs, transportation or peer issues related to school)
- Home environment (whether utilities are in danger of being shut off, safety issues at home or in the neighborhood, extended family, etc.)
- Juvenile justice and/or welfare involvement (history of criminal offenses, pending criminal court involvement, probation or parole)
- Peer involvement (any indication of negative peer involvement)

Case Assignment

The SA is entered into the Q-System, and the case goes into the queue for assignment to an FFT therapist. The assigned FFT therapist can review the service assessment online.

Intake Session

In the Delaware Model, the first session with the family is an intake session. Intakes are common in community mental health systems, but the Delaware FFT intake is different from most because the family, CM, FFT therapists, probation officer, school official, or welfare referral agent all attend. The goal of the intake is not to assess the family's goals or needs but instead to present the treatment team to the family and briefly review the SA. The value of this meeting is that it shows the family that there is a treatment team who all understand the goals and process of FFT. The CM also uses this meeting to complete the risk and protective factor assessment. This occurs through observation and discussion rather than questions and answers. In this meeting the FFT therapist begins the engagement and motivation process of FFT.

FFT Therapy

During FFT, therapists are the primary contact and access point for families. The role of the CM is a background one at this time, supporting FFT by helping overcome barriers to treatment (transportation, etc.). The FFT therapist is able to access the SA, which gives the therapist a broadened view of the family and frees him or her to pursue the goals of FFT.

Enhanced Generalization

When a case enters the generalization phase of FFT, the case manager is notified. The CM reviews the treatment records of the therapist, then the two meet to develop a service plan, a systematic plan for ways to help support, maintain, and generalize the FFT work into the context around the family. In the final sessions of FFT, the CM joins the conjoint family sessions and, along with the FFT therapist, begins to discuss the move to generalization. While helping alert the family to a new focus, it also provides a relational transition to the CM. The CM follows the principles of the generalization phase, using the organizing theme developed in FFT, relying on the behavior change targets developed and worked on in therapy, and keeping the principle of helping the family help themselves. When crises happen (and they do), the CM—just like the FFT therapist—doesn't change direction, but builds on the work of the FFT therapist to extend FFT further into the context and life of the family while still helping empower them to solve their own problems. Each contact the case manager makes is also logged into the Q-System and is available for the therapist's use.

The Role of the FFT Q-System

The Delaware Model project was built around the use of the FFT Q-System. The Q-System became a core tool in session planning, case management, and supervision. Each case, session, client assessment, adherence measure, and therapist's progress note was entered into the Q-System. Case, service specialist, and FFT therapist information was shared on the Q-System among those involved with each case to facilitate the transparency of treatment planning information. Data for client contact, case review, and case planning are entered and managed from the screen shown in Figure 9.3. Authorized users can select reports for a specific client, for an individual caseload, or for the entire team; reporting data are customizable. In addition, a number of reports are made available to the therapist, the supervisor, or the FFT consultant. The system also serves as a feedback tool by presenting information to therapists, supervisors, and administrators.

The reports represent feedback to the therapists based on the perspective of the client, the supervisor, and from their own session goals (see Figure 9.4). The feedback is intended to help focus attention on the areas with potential to help clients more quickly. In Figure 9.4, the therapist has selected to view information for a specific client. The client and supervisor both report high levels of model-specific adherence. Both the adolescent and parent report improvement in life and the family since therapy began. The therapist can also be informed from the measure of mental health (SDQ) areas of potential treatment planning. Those measures are available pretreatment and posttreatment. Therapist session goals, client- and supervisor-rated adherence, client outcomes, and client indications of improvement are available in real time to help the therapist plan the next session or make longer-term adjustments in the treatment plan. For the supervisor, the Q-System allows access to information regarding adherence and service delivery profiles on a teamwide basis. These data serve as the basis of supervision sessions.

CQI information is feedback to the therapist, organization, and supervisor that can be used in therapy, coordination of care, supervision, and site evaluation. For example, during the first 6 months of the project, it became apparent that two therapists had very high dropout rates (see Figure 9.7). The supervisor and coordinators were able to look at each case and determine that additional supervision would be helpful for one therapist. For the other, there were referral problems likely to account for the high dropout rate. Second, adherence ratings suggested that one therapist seemed to be having increasing difficulty delivering FFT. The supervisor was able to

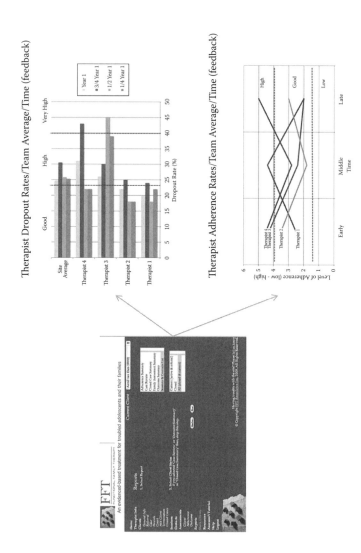

FIGURE 9.7   Therapist model adherence reports.

look more closely at the therapist's progress notes and identify specific areas where he was struggling. Therapists were able to consider what added support they might need and what organizational changes might occur for the treatment model to be more successful. Both supervisors and therapists can watch subsequent adherence scores to determine if their adjustments worked.

Delaware is currently using the cumulative reports from the Q-System to consider data-based profiles of the role of the service specialists, the FFT therapist, and other providers as well as local base-rate data (typical number of sessions, dropout rate, SDQ outcome changes, CPQ profile). Information like this is most clinically useful when it is localized through local norms and baselines for service delivery, adherence, progress, and outcome. The base-rate data can then be used to give site-specific meaning to the CQI information generated by the Q-System. This data will be the source of adaptations and changes in the Delaware Model, FFT, and many other areas of service delivery.

Conclusions

No practice stands on its own in a community-based setting. Every treatment must fit with the needs of the clients, the service delivery practices of the organization, funding, and the influence of other treatment professions and practices. Along with an effective clinical model, FFT brings into the organization the components of a service delivery system that focuses case planning, session planning, clinical supervision, and data monitoring on improving the quality of FFT services. Models for each element were developed from our experience implementing FFT in multiple systems and individual organizations.

The elements of the FFT service delivery system developed from one goal—finding ways to improve what the science told us was important: model specific adherence and therapist competence. We discovered that adhering to the model was a necessary but not sufficient condition for success; the therapist also had to demonstrate competence in applying the model to a specific family with a unique context. Given the multisystemic nature of families (discussed in Chapters 1 and 2), this was no surprise.

Over time we found FFT to function better when the broader service delivery system of the organization coordinated with FFT around three domains: session planning, clinical supervision, and ongoing data monitoring and feedback. For therapists we developed an ongoing treatment planning process (session progress notes) to help focus practice and track critical model-specific planning information. Clinical supervision partakes of the same relational qualities that are the foundation of FFT while taking on the responsibility of quality improvement for FFT services. Using information from the family, supervisor, and therapist, we used our computer system to specifically target the knowledge and performance elements of therapist adherence and competence. The system collects descriptive, process-based data for feedback to therapists to help improve their practice and to their supervisor for monitoring and supervision planning. The Q-System also aids in systematic case planning, freeing up staff time for clinical implementation. When in place, these elements form a coordinated service delivery system that integrates case planning, clinical supervision, and data monitoring. When implemented well, these domains help create and enhance the broader principles of ongoing quality improvement.

FFT began as a set of principles to engage resistant youth, grew to a process-based traditional family therapy, became an increasingly specified and clinically specific treatment model, and matured into a service delivery system. I think this evolution reflects the multisystemic and dynamically oriented nature of FFT. It is built around enduring principles that form the foundation of a clinical practice model. That model is both a conceptual map for therapists to follow and a specific yardstick for measuring areas of quality improvement. It is a model that has been and should be open to adaptation and evolution as different conceptual models and theoretical approaches emerged. The current articulation of the clinical model emphasizes the systematic yet relational nature of the change process. It is also a model that gathers data from both science and the practice field. In fact, the lessons of this final section come out of our clinical experience in implementing FFT in so many diverse organizations and service delivery systems. That is how FFT has always been—open to the science and the discoveries of ongoing practice.

References

Abrantes, A. M., Hoffman, N. G., & Anton, R. (2005). Prevalence of co-occurring disorders among juveniles committed to detention centers. *International Journal of Offender Therapy and Comparative Criminology, 49(2),* 179–193.

Alexander, J. F., & Barton, C. (1980). Intervention with delinquents and their families: Clinical, methodological, and conceptual issues. In J. Vincent (Ed.), *Advances in family intervention, assessment and theory. Greenwich*, CT: JAI Press.

Alexander, J. F. & Barton, C. (1995). Family Therapy Research. In R. Mikesell, D. Lusterman, S. McDaniel (Eds.), *Integrating family therapy: Handbook of family psychology and systems theory.* Washington DC: American Psychological Association.

Alexander, J.F., Newell, R.M., Robbins, M.S., & Turner, C.W. (1995). Observational coding in family therapy process research. *Journal of Family Psychology,* 9.

Alexander, J. F., Barton, C., Schiavo, R. S., & Parsons, B. V. (1976). Behavioral intervention with families of delinquents: Therapist characteristics, family behavior, and outcome. *Journal of Consulting and Clinical Psychology, 44,* 656–664.

Alexander, J. F., Holtzworth-Monroe, A., Jameson, P. B. (1994). The process and outcome of marital and family therapy: Research, review, and evaluation. In the *Handbook of psychotherapy and behavior change,* A. E. Bergin and S. L. Garfield (Eds.). 4th ed. Oxford, UK: Wiley, pp. 595–630.

Alexander, J. F., & Parsons, B. V. (1973). Short-term behavioral intervention with delinquent families: Impact on family process and recidivism. *Journal of Abnormal Psychology, 81,* 219–225.

Alexander, J. F., & Parsons, B. V. (1982). *Functional family therapy.* Pacific Grove, CA: Brooks/Cole.

Alexander, J. F., Pugh, C., Parsons, B., & Sexton, T. L. (2000). Functional family therapy. In D. Elliott (Series Ed.), *Blueprints for violence prevention* (2nd ed.). Golden, CO: Venture Publishing.

Alexander, J. F., Robbins, M. S., & Sexton, T. L. (2000). Family-based interventions with older, at-risk youth: From promise to proof to practice. *Journal of Primary Prevention, 21,* 185–205.

Alexander, J.F. & Sexton, T.L. (2000). Functional family therapy. OJJDP Juvenile Justice Bulletin. Rockville, MD: Juvenile Justice Clearinghouse.

Alexander, J. F., & Sexton, T. L., (2002). Functional family therapy: A model for treating high risk, acting-out youth. In J. Lebow (Ed.), *Comprehensive handbook of psychotherapy, vol. IV: Integrative/eclectic.* New York: Wiley.

Alexander, J. F., Sexton, T. L., Robbins, M. S. (2002). The developmental status of family therapy in family psychology intervention science in H.A.

Alexander, J. F., Waldron, H., Newberry, A. M., & Liddle, N. (1988). Family approaches to treating delinquents. In F. M. Cox, C. Chilman, & E. Nunnally (Eds.), *Families in trouble.* New York: Sage.

Alvarado, R., Kendall, K., Beesley, S., & Lee-Cavaness, C. (2000). *Strengthening America's families.* Washington, DC: Department of Justice, Office of Juvenile Justice and Delinquency Prevention.

American Psychological Association (2000). *Publication manual of the American Psychological Association* (4th ed.). Washington, DC: APA.

American Psychological Association (2007). Assessment of Competency Benchmarks Work Group: A developmental model for defining and measuring competence in professional psychology, June 2007. Retrieved February 2, 2009, from http://www.apa.org/ed/resources/comp_benchmark.pdf.

Andersen, R. M. (1995). Revisiting the behavioral model and access to medical care: Does it matter? *Journal of Health and Social Behavior, 36,* 1–10.

Anderson, S., Rigazio-DiGilio, S., & Kunkler, K. (1995). Training and supervision in family therapy: Current issues and future directions. *Family Relations, 44,* 489–500.

Aos, S., Barnoski, R., & Lieb, R. (1998). *Watching the bottom line: Cost-effective interventions for reducing crime in Washington.* Washington State Institute for Public Policy: RCW 13.40.500.

APA Presidential Task Force. (2006). Evidence-based practice in psychology. *American Psychologist, 61,* 271–285.

Bandura, A. (1969). *Principles of behavior modification.* New York: Holt.

Bandura, A. (1982). Self-efficacy mechanism in human agency. *American Psychologist, 37,* 122–147.

Barnoski, R. (2000). Outcome evaluation of Washington State's research-based programs for juvenile offenders. Washington State Institute for Public Policy, www.wsipp.wa.gov.

Barnoski, R. 2002a. Washington State's Implementation of Functional Family Therapy for Juvenile Offenders: Preliminary Findings. Washington State Institute for Public Policy. Olympia, WA.

Barnoski, R. (2002b). Washington state's implementation of functional family therapy for juvenile offenders: Preliminary findings. Washington State Institute for Public Policy, www.wsipp.wa.gov.

Barton, C., & Alexander, J. F. (1981). Functional family therapy. In A. Gurman & D. Kniskern (Eds.), *Handbook of family therapy.* New York: Brunner/Mazel, 403–443.

Barton, C., Alexander, J. F., Waldron, H., Turner, C. W., & Warburton, J. (1985). Generalizing treatment effects of functional family therapy: Three replications. *American Journal of Family Therapy, 13(3),* 16–26.

Bateson, G. (1972). *Steps to an ecology of mind.* San Francisco: Chandler.

Baumrind, D. (1967). Child care practices anteceding three patterns of preschool behavior. *Genetic Psychology Monographs, 75,* 43–88.

Bernal, G., & Saʹez-Santiago, E. (2006). Culturally centered psychosocial interventions. *Journal of Community Psychology,* 34, 121–131.

Bernal, G., & Scharrón del Río, M. R. (2001). Are empirically supported treatments valid for ethnic minorities? Toward an alternative approach for treatment research. *Cultural Diversity and Ethnic Minority Psychology, 7,* 328–342.

Bernard, J. M., & Goodyear, R. K. (2004). *Fundamentals of clinical supervision* (3rd ed.). Boston: Allyn & Bacon.

Berwick, D. M. (1994). Eleven worthy aims for clinical leadership of health system reform. *Journal of the American Medical Association, 272,* 797–802.

Blatt, S. J., Sanislow, C. A., Zuroff, D. C., & Pilkonis, P. A. (1996). Characteristics of effective therapists: Further analyses of data from the National Institute of Mental Health Treatment of Depression Collaborative Research Program. *Journal of Consulting and Clinical Psychology, 64,* 1276–1284.

Block, J., Block, J. H., & Keyes, S. (1988). Longitudinally foretelling drug usage in adolescence: Early childhood personality and environmental precursors. *Child Development, 59,* 336–355.

Boendermaker, L., van der Veldt, M. C., & Booy, Y. (2003). *Nederlandse studies naar de effecten van jeugdzorg.* Utrecht: NIZW.

Boendermaker, L., van Yperen, T. (2003). *Kansen in de keten. Een gemeenschappelijk referentiekader voor de justitië le jeugdinrichtingen.* Den Haag, The Netherlands: Dienst Justitië le Inrichtingen.

Boerstler, H., Foster, R. W., O'Connor, E. J., O'Brien, J. L., Shortell, S. M., Carman, J. M., et al. (1996). Implementation of total quality management: Conventional wisdom versus reality. *Hospitals and Health Services Administration, 41(2),* 143–159.

Bordin, E. S. (1979). The generalizability of the psychoanalytic concept of the working alliance. *Psychotherapy,* 16, 252–260.

Bowen, R. M. (1976). In A.C. Eringen, (Ed.), *Theory of mixtures,continuum physics,* Vol. 3. Academic Press, New York.

Bronfenbrenner, U. (1986). Ecology of the family as a context for human development: Research perspectives. *Developmental Psychology, 22(6),* 723–742.

Burlingame, G. M., Wells, M. G., Hoag, M., Hope, C., Nebeker, R., Konkel, K., et al. (1996). *Administration and scoring manual for the Youth Outcome Questionnaire (Y-OQ.1).* Wilimington, DE: American Professional Credentialing Services.

Centers for Disease Control and Prevention. (1995). *Monthly Vital Statistics* (Report 43, No. 13). Washington, DC: U.S. Public Health Service.

Centers for Disease Control and Prevention (2002). Nonfatal physical assault–related injuries treated in hospital emergency departments—United States, 2000. *Morbidity and Mortality Weekly Report, 51,* 460–463.

Centers for Disease Control and Prevention. (2010). Web-based injury statistics query and reporting system (WISQARS). Available at http://www.cdc.gov/ncipc/wisqars.

Chung, H. L., Little, M., Steinberg, L., & Altschuler, D. (2005). Juvenile justice and the transition to adulthood. Network on Transitions to Adulthood. MacArthur Foundation research network on transitions to adulthood and public policy. University of Pennsylvania Department of Sociology, 20, 2005. http://www.transad.pop.upenn.edu/downloads/chung-juvenile%20just%20formatted.pdf.

Claiborn, C. D., & Lichtenberg, J. W. (1989). Interactional counseling. *Counseling Psychologist. 17(3)*, 355–453.

Clark, R. D., & Shields, G. (1997). Family communication and delinquency. *Adolescence, 32*, 81–92.

Cleghorn, J., & Levin, S. (1973). Training family therapists by setting learning objectives. *American Journal of Orthopsychiatry, 43*, 439–446.

Community Juvenile Accountability Act. Chapter 338, Laws of 1997 RCW 13.40.540. Washington Department of Social Services, http:// www.dshs.wa.gov/pdf/EA/GovRel/leg0903/CJAA0903.pdf.

Coulehan, R. Friedlander, M., & Heatherington, L. (1998). Transforming narratives: A change event in constructivist family therapy. *Family Process, 37*, 17–33.

Crosby, Philip B. (1979). *Quality is free: The art of making quality certain.* New York: New American Library.

Dahlberg, L.L. (1998). Youth violence in the United States: Major trends, risk factors, and prevention approaches. *American Journal of Preventative Medicine, 14*, 259–272.

Datchi-Phillips, C. *Change in contexts: A critical approach to empowerment research in counseling.* Diss. Indiana University, 2009. Dissertations & Theses @ CIC Institutions, ProQuest. Web. 31 Mar. 2010.

Dawes, R. M. (1994). *House of cards: Psychology and psychotherapy built on myth.* New York: Free Press.

Diamond, G. S., Reis, B. F., Diamond, G. M., Siqueland, L., & Isaacs, L. (2002). Attachment-based family therapy for depressed adolescents: A treatment development study. *Journal of the American Academy of Child and Adolescent Psychiatry, 41*, 1190–1196.

DiClemente, R. J., Hansen, W. B., & Ponton, L. E. (1996). Adolescents at risk: A generation in jeopardy. In R. J. DiClemente, W. B. Hansen, & L. E. Ponton (Eds.), *Handbook of adolescent health risk behavior* (pp. 1–4). New York: Plenum Press.

Dishion, T. J., & McMahon, R. J. (1998). Parental monitoring and the prevention of child and adolescent problem behavior: A conceptual and empirical formulation. *Clinical Child and Family Psychology Review, 1(1)*, 61–75.

Dixon, A., Howie, P., & Starling, J. (2004). Psychopathology in female juvenile offenders. *Journal of Child Psychology and Psychiatry, 45(6)*, 1150–1158.

Dodge, K.A. (2008). Framing public policy and prevention of chronic violence in American youth. *American Psychologist, 63(7)*, 573–590.

Domalanta, D., Risser, W. L., Roberts, R. E., & Hale Risser, J. M. (2003). Prevalence of depression and other psychiatric disorders among incarcerated youths. *Journal of the American Academy of Child and Adolescent Psychiatry, 42(4),* 477–484.

Elliott, D. S. (Series Ed.). (1998). *Blueprints for violence prevention.* University of Colorado, Center for the Study and Prevention of Violence. Boulder, CO: Blueprints Publications.

Elliott, D. S., & Mihalic, S. (2004). Issues in disseminating and replicating effective prevention programs. *Prevention Science, 5,* 47–53.

Erickson, C. *The effectiveness of functional family therapy in the treatment of juvenile sexual offenders.* Diss. Indiana University, 2008. Dissertations & Theses @ CIC Institutions, Pr. Quest. Web. 31 March 2010.

Falicov, C. J. (1995). Training to think culturally: A multidimentional comparitive framework. *Family Process, 34,* 373–388.

Frank, J. D. (1969). *Persuasion and healing: A comparative study of psychotherapy.* Baltimore: Johns Hopkins University Press.

Frank, J. D., & Frank, J. B. (1991). *Persuasion and healing: A comparative study of psychotherapy* (3rd ed.). Baltimore : Johns Hopkins University Press.

Friedlander, M. L., & Heatherington, L. (1998). Assessing clients' constructions of their problems in family therapy disclosure. *Journal of Marital and Family Therapy, 24,* 289–303.

Garb, H. N. (1989). Clinical judgment, clinical training, and professional experience. *Psychological Bulletin, 105,* 387–396.

Garb, H. N. (1998). *Studying the clinician: Judgment research and psychological assessment.* Washington, DC: American Psychological Association.

Gergen, K. (1985). The social constructionist movement in modern psychology. *American Psychologist, 40,* 266–273.

Gilman, L. (2008). Supervisory interventions and treatment adherence: An observational study of supervisor interventions and their impact on therapist model adherence. Unpublished doctoral dissertation, Indiana University, Bloomington.

Glisson, C., & James, L. (1992).The interorganizational coordination of services to children in state custody. In D. Bargal & H. Schmid (Eds.), *Organizational change and development in human services organizations* (pp. 65–80). New York: Haworth.

Goldman, H. H., Ganju, V., Drake, R. E., et al. (2001). Policy implications for implementing evidence-based practices. *Psychiatr Serv.* 52:1591–1597.

Gordon, D.A. (1995). Functional Family Therapy for delinquents. In R.R. Ross, D.H. Antonowicz, & G.K. Dhaliwal (Eds.). Going straight: Effective delinquency prevention and offender rehabilitation. Ontario, Canada: Air Training and Publications.

Gordon, D. A., Arbuthnot, J., Gustafson, K., & McGreen, P. (1988). Home-based behavioral systems family therapy with disadvantaged juvenile delinquents. *American Journal of Family Therapy, 16,* 243–255.

Greenberg, L. S., & Safrin, J. D. (1990). *Emotion in Psychotherapy.* New York: Guilford Press.

Greenwood, P. W., Model, K. E., Rydell, C. P., & Chiesa, J. (1996). *Diverting children from a life of crime: Measuring costs and benefits.* Santa Monica, CA: The Rand Corporation.

Griffin, K. W., Botvin, G. J., Scheier, L. M., Diaz, T., & Miller, N. L. (2000). Parenting practices as predictors of substance use, delinquency, and aggression among urban minority youth: Moderating effects of family structure and gender. *Psychology of Addictive Behaviors, 14(2), 174–184.*

Grove, W. M., Zald, D. H., Lebow, B. S., Snits, B. E., & Nelson, C. E. (2000). Clinical vs. mechanical prediction: A meta-analysis. *Psychological Assessment, 12, 19–30.*

Gurman, A. S., & Kniskern, D. P. (Eds.). (1981). *Handbook of family therapy.* New York: Brunner/Mazel.

Gurman, A. S., Kniskern, D. P., & Pinsof, W. M. (1986). Research on the process and outcome of marital and family therapy. In S. L. Garfield & A. E. Bergin (Eds.), *Handbook of psychotherapy and behavior change* (3rd ed., pp. 565–624). New York: John Wiley and Sons.

Haas, L. J, Alexander, J. F., & Mas, C. H. (1988). Functional Family Therapy: Basic Concepts and Training Program. In H. L Liddle. Breunlin, & Schwarts (Eds). *Handbook of family therapy training and supervision.* New York: Guilford Press.

Haley, J. (1964). Research on family patterns: An instrument measurement. *Family Process, 3(1), 41–76.*

Haley, J. (1976). *Problem-solving therapy.* San Francisco: Jossey-Bass.

Hansson, K, (1998). *Functional family therapy replication in sweden: Treatment outcome with juvenile delinquents.* Paper presented to the Eighth Conference on Treating Addictive Behaviors, Santa Fe, NM.

Harrison, A., Wilson, M., Pine, C., Chan, S., & Buriel, R. (1990). Family ecologies of ethnic minority children. *Child Development, 61, 347–362.*

Hawkins, J. D. & Catalano, R. F. (1992). *Communities that care: Action for drug abuse prevention.* San Francisco: Jossey-Bass.

Hawkins, J. D., Catalano, R. F., & Miller, J. Y. (1992). Risk and protective factors for alcohol and other drug problems in adolescence and early adulthood: Implications for substance abuse preventions. *Psychological Bulletin, 112, 64–105.*

Heatherington, L., & Friedlander, M. L. (1990). Couple and family therapy alliance scales: Empirical considerations. *Journal of Marital and Family Therapy, 16(3), 299–306.*

Heatherington, L., Friedlander, M. L., & Greenberg, L. S. (2005). Change process research in couples and family therapy: Methodological challenges and opportunities. *Journal of Family Psychology, 19, 18–27.*

Henggeler, S. W. (1989). *Delinquency in adolescence.* Newbury Park, CA: Sage.

Henggeler, S. W., & Borduin, C. M. (1990). *Family therapy and beyond: A multisystemic approach to treating the behavior problems of children and adolescents.* Pacific Grove, CA: Brooks/Cole.

Henggeler, S. W., Melton, G. B., Brondino, M. J., Scherer, D. G., & Hanley, J. H. (1997). Multisystemic therapy with violent and chronic juvenile offenders and their families: The role of treatment fidelity in successful dissemination. *Journal of Consulting and Clinical Psychology, 65, 821–833.*

Henggeler, S. W., & Schoenwald, S. K. (1999). The role of quality assurance in achieving outcomes in MST programs. *Journal of Juvenile Justice and Detention Services, 14,* 1–17.

Heppner, P. P., & Claiborn, C. D. (1989). Social influence research in counseling: A review and critique. *Journal of Counseling Psychology, 36(3),* 365–387.

Henry, W. P. & Strupp, H. H. (1994). The therapeutic alliance as interpersonal process. In A. O. Horvath & L. S. Greenberg (Eds.), *The working alliance: Theory, research and practice* (pp. 51 – 84). New York: Wiley.

Hobfoll, S. E. (1991). Gender differences in stress reactions: Women filling the gaps. *Psychology and Health, 5,* 95–109.

Hoffman, L. (1981). *Foundations of family therapy.* New York: Basic Books.

Hogue, A., Liddle, H. A., Rowe, C., Turner, R. M., Dakof, G. A., & LaPann, K. (1998). Treatment adherence and differentiation in individual versus family therapy for adolescent substance abuse. *Journal of Counseling Psychology, 45,* 104–114.

Horvath, A. O. (2001). The alliance. *Psychotherapy: Theory, Research, Practice, Training, 38(4),* 365–372.

House, J., Landis, K. R., & Umberson, D. (1988). Social relationships and health. *Science, 241,* 540–545.

Huey, S. J., Jr., Henggeler, S. W., Brondino, M. J., & Pickrel, S. G. (2000). Mechanisms of change in multisystemic therapy: Reducing delinquent behavior through therapist adherence and improved family and peer functioning. *Journal of Consulting and Clinical Psychology, 68,* 451–467.

Institute of Medicine, Committee on Quality of Health Care in America. (2001). *Crossing the quality chasm: A new health system for the 21st century.* Washington (DC): National Academy Press.

Jackson, D. (1961). Interactional psychotherapy. In M. Stein (Ed.), *Contemporary psychotherapies,* (pp. 256–271). New York: The Free Press of Glenco, Inc.

Jackson, D. N., & Messick, S. (1961). Acquiescence and desirability as response determinants on the MMPI. *Educational and Psychological Measurement,* 21, 771–792.

Jones, E. E., & Nisbett, R. E. (1972). The actor and the observer: Divergent perceptions of the causes of behavior. In E. E. Jones, D. E. Kanouse, H. H. Kelley, R. E. Nisbett, S. Valins, & B. Weiner (Eds.), *Attribution: Perceiving the causes of behavior* (pp. 79–94). Morristown, NJ: General Learning Press.

Kazdin, A. E. (1987). Treatment of antisocial behavior in children: Current status and future directions. *Psychological Bulletin, 102,* 187–203.

Kazdin, A. E. (1991). Effectiveness of psychotherapy with children and adolescents. *Journal of Consulting and Clinical Psychology, 59(6),* 785–798.

Kazdin, A. E. (1997). A model for developing effective treatments: Progression and interplay of theory, research, and practice. *Journal of Clinical Child Psychology, 26,* 114–129.

Kazdin, A. E. (2001). Progression of therapy research and clinical application of treatment require better understanding of the change process. *Clinical Psychology: Science and Practice, 8(2),* 143–151.

Kazdin, A. E. (2003). Psychotherapy for children and adolescents. *Annual Review of Psychology, 54,* 253–276.

Kazdin, A. E. (2004). Evidence-based treatments: Challenges and priorities for practice and research. In B. Burns & K. Hoagwood (Eds.), *Child and adolescent psychiatric clinics of North America* (pp. 923–940). New York: Elsevier.

Kazdin, A. E. (2006). Arbitrary metrics: Implications for identifying evidence-based treatments. *American Psychologist, 61(1),* 42–49.

Kazdin, A. E. (2007). Mediators and mechanisms of change in psychotherapy research. *Annual Review of Clinical Psychology,* 3, 1–27.

Kazdin, A. E. (2008). Evidence-based treatment and practice: New opportunities to bridge clinical research and practice, enhance the knowledge base, and improve patient care. *American Psychologist, 63(3),* 146–159.

Kazdin, A. E., & Weisz, J. R. (Eds.). (2003). *Evidence-based psychotherapies for children and adolescents.* New York: Guilford Press.

Kelley, H. H. (1973). The processes of causal attribution. *American Psychologist, 28,* 107–128.

Kempton, T., & Forehand, R. (1992). Juvenile sex offenders: Similar to, or different from, other incarcerated delinquent offenders? *Behavior Research and Therapy, 30,* 533–536.

Kiesler, D. J. (1982). Interpersonal theory for personality and psychotherapy. In J. C. Anchin & D. Kiesler (Eds.), *Handbook of interpersonal psychotherapy* (pp. 3–24). Elmsford, NY: Pergamon.

Klein, K., Forehand, R., Armistead, L., & Long, P. (1997). Delinquency during the transition to early adulthood: Family and parenting predictors from early adolescence. *Adolescence, 32,* 61–80.

Klein, N., Alexander, J., & Parsons, B. (1977). Impact of family systems interventions on recidivism and sibling delinquency: A model of primary prevention and program evaluation. *Journal of Consulting and Clinical Psychology, 45,* 469–474.

Koerner, K., & Jacobson, N. S. (1994). Emotion and behavioral couple therapy. In S. M. Johnson & L. S. Greenberg (Eds.), *The heart of the matter: Perspectives on emotion in marital therapy* (pp. 207–226). New York: Brunner/Mazel.

Kogan, N. (1990). Personality and aging. In J. E. Birren & K. W. Schaie (Eds.), *Handbook of the psychology of aging* (3rd ed., pp. 330–346). San Diego, CA: Academic Press.

Kumpfer, K. L. (1999). Factors and processes contributing to resilience: The resilience framework. In M. D. Glantz & J. L. Johnson (Eds.), *Resilience and development: Positive life adaptations* (pp. 179–224). New York: Kluwer Academic/Plenum Publishers.

Kumpfer, K. L., & Turner, C. W. (1990). The social ecology model of adolescent substance abuse: Implications for prevention. *International Journal of the Addictions, 25(4A),* 435–463.

Liddle, H.A. (1985). Five factors of failure in structural-strategic family therapy: A contextual construction. In S. B. Coleman (Ed.), *Failures in family therapy* (pp. 152–189). New York: Guilford.

Liddle, H.A. (1995). Conceptual and clinical dimensions of a multidimensional, multi-systems engagement strategy in family-based adolescent treatment (Special issue: Adolescent Psychotherapy). *Psychotherapy: Theory, Research and Practice*, 32.

Liddle, H. A., Breunlin, D. C., & Schwartz, R. C. (Eds.). (1988). *Handbook of family therapy training and supervision*. New York: Guilford.

Liddle, H. A., & Dakof, G. A. (1995). Efficacy of family therapy for drug abuse: Promising but not definitive. *Journal of Marital and Family Therapy, 21(4)*, 511–543.

Loeber, R. (1991). Antisocial behavior: More enduring than changeable? *Journal of the American Academy of Child and Adolescent Psychiatry*, 30, 393–397.

Loeber, R., & Dishion, T. (1983). Early predictors of male delinquency: A review. *Psychological Bulletin, 94*, 68–99.

Loeber, R., & Stouthamer-Loeber, M. (1986). Family factors as correlates and predictors of juvenile conduct problems and delinquency. In M. H. Tonry & N. Morris (Eds.), *Crime and justice: An annual review of research*, vol. 7 (pp. 29–149). Chicago: University of Chicago Press.

Maccoby, E. E., & Martin, J. A. (1983). Socialization in the context of the family: Parent–child interaction. In P. H. Mussen & E. M. Hetherington (Eds.), *Handbook of child psychology: Socialization, personality and social development*, vol. IV (pp. 1–101). New York: Wiley.

Mahoney, M. J. (1991). *Human change processes: The scientific foundations of psychotherapy*. New York: Basic Books.

Marlatt, G. A. & Gordon, J.R. (Ed.). (1985). *Relapse prevention: Maintenance strategies in the treatment of addictive behaviors*. New York: Guilford Press.

Martin, J. R. (1997). Mindfulness: A proposed common factor. *Journal of Psychotherapy Integration, 7*, 291–312.

McGoldrick, M., & Gerson, R. (1985). *Genograms in family assessment*. New York: Norton.

Mease, A. C. & Sexton, T. L. (2005). Functional Family Therapy as a school-based mental health intervention program. In K.E. Robinson (Ed.), *Advances in school-based mental health interventions*. Kingston, New Jersey: Civic Research Institute.

Miller, T. R., Cohen, M. A., & Rossman, S. B. (1993). Victim costs of violent crime and resulting injuries. *Health Affairs, 12(4)*, 186–197.

Minuchin, S. (1979). Constructing a therapeutic reality. In E. Kaufman & P. Kaufmann (Eds.), *Family therapy of drug and alcohol abuse* (pp. 5–18). New York: Gardner.

Minuchin, S., Montalvo, B., Guemey, B. G., Rosman, B. L., & Schumer, F. L. (1967). *Families of the slums: An exploration of their structure and treatment*. New York: Basic.

Mulford, C. F., & Redding, R. E. (2008). Training the parents of juvenile offenders: State of the art and recommendations for service delivery. *Journal of Child and Family Studies, 17(5)*, 629–648.

National Institute on Drug Abuse. (1992). *National high school senior drug abuse survey 1975–1991: Monitoring the future survey*. NIDA Capsules (NIH Publication No. 99-4180). Washington, DC: U.S. Department of Health and Human Services, Alcohol, Drug Abuse, and Mental Health Administration.

Neighbors, B., Kempton, T., & Forehand, R. (1992). Co-occurrence of substance abuse with conduct, anxiety, and depression disorders in juvenile delinquents. *Addictive Behaviors, 17,* 379–386.

Nitza, A.G. (2002). The relationship of treatment adherence and outcome in functional family therapy. Unpublished doctoral dissertation, Indiana University, Bloomington.

Nitza, A.G. & Sexton, T. L. (2001). Treatment Adherence and Outcomes in Empirically Supported Treatments. Paper presented at the American Counseling Association, San Antonio, TX.

Nitza, A. G. & Sexton, T.L. (2002) The relationship of treatment adherence and outcome in functional family therapy. Unpublished doctoral dissertation, Indiana University.

Parsons, B. V., & Alexander, J. F. (1973). Short-term family intervention: A therapy outcome study. *Journal of Consulting and Clinical Psychology, 41,* 195–201.

Patterson, G. R. (1982). *Coercive family process.* Eugene, OR: Castalia.

Patterson, G. R., & Forgatch, M. S. (1985). Therapist behavior as a determinant for client noncompliance: A paradox for the behavior modifier. *Journal of Consulting and Clinical Psychology, 53(6),* 846–851.

Patterson, G. R., & Stouthamer-Loeber, M. (1984). The correlation of family management practices and delinquency. *Child Development, 55(4),* 1299–1307.

Pedersen, P. (1997). Recent trends in cultural theories. *Applied and Preventive Psychology, 6,* 221–231.

Pettit, G. S., Bates, J. E., & Dodge, K. A. (1997). Supportive parenting, ecological context, and children's adjustment: A seven-year longitudinal study. *Child Development, 68,* 908–923.

Pinsof, W. M., & Catherall, D. R. (1984). *The integrative psychotherapy alliance: Family couple and individual therapy scales.* Chicago: Center for Family Studies, Northwestern University.

Pinsof, W. M., & Wynne, L. C. (2000). Toward progress research: Closing the gap between family therapy practice and research. *Journal of Marital and Family Therapy, 26,* 1–8.

Pliszka, S. R., Liotti, M., & Woldorff, M. G. (2000). Inhibitory control in children with attention-deficit/hyperactivity disorder: Event-related potentials identify the processing component and timing of an impaired right-frontal response-inhibition mechanism. *Biological Psychiatry, 48,* 238–246.

Pliszka, S. R., Sherman, J. O., Barrow, M. V., & Irick, S. (2000). Affective disorder in juvenile offenders: A preliminary study. *American Journal of Psychiatry, 157(1),* 130–132.

Pope, C., & Feyerherm, W. (1991). Minorities in the juvenile justice system. Washington, DC: Office of Juvenile Justice and Delinquency Prevention.

Pope, C., Lovell, R., & Hsia, H. (2002). *Disproportionate minority confinement: A review of the research literature from 1989 through 2001.* Washington, DC: U.S. Department of Justice, Office of Justice Programs, Office of Juvenile Justice and Delinquency Prevention.

Prochaska, J. O. (1999). How do people change, and how can we change to help many more people? In M. A. Hubble, B. L. Duncan, & S. D. Miller (Eds.), *The heart and soul of change: What works in therapy* (pp. 227–255). Washington, DC: American Psychological Association.

Quinn, W. H., Dotson, D., & Jordon, K. (1997). Dimensions of the therapeutic alliance and their associations with outcome in family therapy. *Psychotherapy Research, 74,* 429–438.

Reiss, D., & Price, R. H. (1996). National research agenda for prevention research: The National Institute of Mental Health report. *American Psychologist, 51,* 1109–1115.

Riemer, M., Rosof-Williams, J., Bickman, L. (2005). Theories related to changing clinician practice. *Child Adolescent Psychiatric Clinics of North America*, 14:241Y254.

Robbins, M. S., Bachrach, K., & Szapocznik, J. (2002). Bridging the research-practice gap in adolescent substance abuse treatment: The case of brief strategic family therapy. *Journal of Substance Abuse Treatment*, 23, 123– 132.

Robbins, M. S., Alexander, J. F., & Turner, C. W. (2000). Disrupting defensive family interactions in family therapy with delinquent adolescents. *Journal of Family Psychology, 14(4),* 688–701.

Robbins, M. S., Mayorga, C. C., & Szapocznik, J. (2003). The ecosystemic "lens" to understanding family functioning. In T. L. Sexton, G. R. Weeks, & M. S. Robbins (Eds.), *Handbook of family therapy* (pp. 23–40). New York: Brunner-Routledge.

Robbins, M. S., Turner, C., Alexander, J. F., & Perez, G. (2003). Alliance and dropout in family therapy for adolescents with behavior problems: Individual and systemic effects. *Journal of Family Psychology, 17,* 534–544.

Robertson, A., Dill, P., Husain, J., & Undesser, C. (2004). Prevalence of mental illness and subtance abuse disorders among incarcerated juvenile offenders in Mississippi. *Child Psychiatry and Human Development, 35(1),* 55–74.

Rogers, C. (1957). The necessary and sufficient conditions of therapeutic personality change. *Journal of Consulting and Clinical Psychology, 21,* 95–103.

Rosenblatt, J. A., Rosenblatt, A., & Biggs, E. E. (2000). Criminal behavior and emotional disorder: Comparing youth served by the mental health and juvenile justice systems. *Journal of Behavioral Health Services & Research, 27(2),* 227–237.

Roth, A. D., & Fonagy, P. (1996). *What works for whom? A critical review of psychotherapy research.* New York: Guilford.

Rowe, C. L., Liddle, H. A. (2003). Substance abuse. *Journal of Marital and Family Therapy, 29,* 97–120.

Sale, E., Sambrano, S., Springer, F., & Turner, C. (2003). Risk, protection, and substance use in adolescents: A multi-site model. *Journal of Drug Education, 33(1),* 91–105.

Sapyta, J., Riemer, M., & Bickman, L. (2005). Feedback to clinicians: Theory, research, and practice. *Journal of Clinical Psychology,* 61, 145–153.

Sampson, R. J., & Laub, J. H. (1993). *Crime in the making.* Cambridge, MA: Harvard University Press.

Schoenwald, S. K., Henggeler, S. W., Brondino, M. J., & Rowland, M. D. (2000). Multisystemic therapy: Monitoring treatment fidelity. *Family Process, 39(1)*, 83–103.

Selvini-Palazzoli, M. (1978). *Self-starvation: From individuation to family therapy in the treatment of anorexia nervosa.* New York: Aronson.

Selvini-Palazzoli, M., Boscolo, L., Cecchin, G., & Prata, G. (1978). *Paradox and counterparadox.* New York: Jason Aronson.

Sexton, T. L. (2008). Evil or troubled? Treating the most difficult adolescent's mental health problems with functional family therapy. In E. De Saude Mental: O Contributo Da Terapia Funcional Familiar – Separata PSICOLOGIA FORENSE Almedina Coimbra, Portugal.

Sexton, T. L. (2009). Functional family therapy: Traditional theory to evidence-based practice. In J. Bray & M. Stanton (Eds)., *Handbook of family psychology* (pp. 327–340). Malden, MA: Wiley-Blackwell.

Sexton, T. L., & Alexander, J. F. (2002a). Family-based empirically supported interventions. *Counseling Psychologist, 30(2)*, 238–261.

Sexton, T. L., & Alexander, J. F. (2002b). Functional family therapy for at-risk adolescents and their families. In T. Patterson (Ed.), *Comprehensive handbook of psychotherapy, vol. II: Cognitive-behavioral approaches* (pp. 117–140). New York: Wiley.

Sexton, T. L., & Alexander, J. F. (2003). Functional family therapy: A mature clinical model for working with at-risk adolescents and their families. In T. L. Sexton, G. R. Weeks, & M. S. Robbins (Eds.), *Handbook of family therapy* (pp. 371–400). New York: Brunner-Routledge.

Sexton, T. L., & Alexander, J. F. (2004). *Functional family therapy clinical training manual.* Seattle, WA: Annie E. Casey Foundation.

Sexton, T. L., & Alexander, J. F. (2005). Functional family therapy for externalizing disorders in adolescents. In J. Lebow (Ed.), *Handbook of clinical family therapy* (pp. 164–194). Hoboken, NJ: John Wiley.

Sexton, T. L., Alexander, J. F., & Gilman, L. (2004). *Functional family therapy: Clinical supervision training manual.* Seattle, WA: Annie E. Casey Foundation.

Sexton, T. L., Alexander, J. F., & Mease, A. L. (2004). Levels of evidence for the models and mechanisms of therapeutic change in family and couple therapy. In M. J. Lambert (Ed.), *Bergin and Garfield's handbook of psychotherapy and behavior change* (5th ed., pp. 590–646). New York: Wiley.

Sexton, T. L., Coop-Gordon, K. Gurman, A. S. Lebow, J. L. Holtzworth-Munroe, A., & Johnson, S. (2007). *Report of the Task Force for Evidence-Based Treatments in Couple and Family Psychology.* Washington, DC: American Psychological Association.

Sexton, T. L., Gilman, L., & Johnson-Erickson, C. (2005). Evidence-based practices. In T. P. Gullotta & G. R. Adams (Eds.), *Handbook of adolescent behavioral problems: Evidence-based approaches to prevention and treatment* (pp. 101–128). New York: Springer.

Sexton, T. L., & Griffin, B. L. (Eds.). (1997). *Constructivist thinking in counseling practice, research, and training.* Counseling and development series, vol. 3. New York: Teachers College Press.

Sexton, T. L., Ostrom, N., Bonomo, J., & Alexander, J. A. (2000). *Functional family therapy in a multicultural, multiethnic urban setting.* Paper presented at the annual conference of the American Association of Marriage and Family Therapy, Denver, CO.

Sexton, T. L., Ridley, C. R., & Kleiner, A. J. (2004). Beyond common factors: Multilevel-process models of therapeutic change in marriage and family therapy. *Journal of Marital and Family Therapy, 30(2),* 131–149.

Sexton, T. L., Robbins, M. S., Hollimon, A. S., Mease, A. L., & Mayorga, C. C. (2003). Efficacy, effectiveness, and change mechanisms in couple and family therapy. In T. L. Sexton, G. R. Weeks, & M. S. Robbins (Eds.), *Handbook of family therapy* (pp. 264–301). New York: Brunner-Routledge.

Sexton, T.L., Sydnor, A.E., & Rowland, M.K. (2004). Identification and treatment of the clinical problems of childhood and adolescence (pp. 350-369) . In R. Coombs (Ed.), *Family Therapy Review: Preparing for Comprehensive and Licensing Exams.* Mahway, New Jersey: Lawrence Erlbaum Associates.

Sexton, T. L., & Turner, C. T. (in press). The Effectiveness of Functional Family Therapy for Youth with Behavioral Problems in a Community Practice Setting. *Journal of Family Psychology.*

Sexton, T. L., Turner, C. T., & Schuster, R. (in process). *Functional family therapy in a community-based setting.*

Sexton, T. L., Weeks, G. R., & Robbins, M. S. (2003). *Handbook of family therapy: The science and practice of working with families and couples.* New York: Brunner-Routledge.

Sexton, T. L., & Whiston, S. C. (1994). The status of the counseling relationship: An empirical review, theoretical implications, and research directions. *Counseling Psychologist, 22,* 6–78.

Sexton, T. L., & Whiston, S. C. (1996). Integrating counseling research and practice. *Journal of Counseling and Development, 74,* 588–589.

Sexton, T. L., & Whiston, S. C. (1998). Using the knowledge base: Outcome research and accountable social action. In C. Lee and G. Walz (Eds.), *Social action: A mandate for counselors* (pp. 241–260). Alexandria, VA: American Counseling Association.

Sexton, T. L., & Wilkenson, J. (1999). *The Functional Family Therapy Clinical Services System.* Henderson, NV: RCH Enterprises.

Sexton, T.L., Sydnor, A. E., Rowland, M. K., & Alexander, J. F. (2004). Identification and treatment of the clinical problems of childhood and adolescence. In R. Coombs (Ed.), *Family Therapy Review: Preparing for Comprehensive and Licensing Examinations* (pp. 349–369). Mahwah, NJ: Lawrence Erlbaum Associates.

Shadish, W. R., Montgomery, L. M., Wilson, P., Wilson, M. R., Bright, I., & Okwumabua, T. (1993). Effects of family and marital psychotherapies: A meta-analysis. *Journal of Consulting and Clinical Psychology, 61,* 992–1002.

Shewhart, W. A. (1931). Economic Control of Quality of Manufactured Product, New York: Van Nostrand. (Republished in 1981, with a dedication by W. Edwards Deming by the American Society for Quality Control, Milwaukee, WI.)

Snyder, H., & Sickmund, M. (1999). *Juvenile offenders and victims: 1999 national report.* Washington, DC: U.S. Department of Justice, Office of Justice Programs, Office of Juvenile Justice and Delinquency Prevention.

Snyder, J., & Patterson, G. (1987). Family interaction and delinquent behavior. In H. Quay (Ed.), *Handbook of juvenile delinquency* (pp. 216–243). New York: Wiley.

Stanton, M. & Welsh, R. (in press). Specialty competencies in couple and family psychology. In A.M. Nezu & C.M. Nezu, (Eds.), Oxford University Press series on *Specialty Competencies in Professional Psychology.* New York: Oxford University Press.

Strong, S. R. (1986). Interpersonal influence theory and therapeutic interactions. In F. J. Dorn (Ed.), *The social influence process in counseling and psychotherapy* (pp. 17–30). Springfield, IL: Charles C Thomas.

Strong, S. R., & Claiborn, C. D. (1982). *Change through interaction: Social psychological processes of counseling and psychotherapy.* New York: Wiley.

Stroul, B. A., & Friedman, R. M. (1986). *A system of care for children and youth with severe emotional disturbances.* Washington, DC: CASSP Technical Assistance Center.

Szapocznik, J., & Kurtines, W. (1989). *Breakthroughs in family therapy with drug abusing problem youth.* New York: Springer.

Szapocznik, J., Kurtines, W. M., Santiesteban, D. A., Pantin, H., Scopetta, M., Mancilla, Y., et al. (1997). The evolution of a structural ecosystemic theory for working with Latino families. In J. Garcia & M. C. Zea (Eds.), *Psychological interventions and research with Latino populations* (pp. 166–190). Boston: Allyn & Bacon.

Taylor, S. E., & Fiske, S. T. (1978). Salience, attention, and attribution: Top of the head phenomena. In L. Berkowitz (Ed.), *Advances in experimental social psychology,* vol. 11 (pp. 249–288). New York: Academic Press.

Teplin, L. A., Abram, K. M., McClelland, G. M., Dulcan, M. K., & Mericle, A. A. (2002). Psychiatric disorders in youth in juvenile detention. *Archive of General Psychiatry, 59,* 1133–1143.

Tharp, R. G. (1991). Cultural diversity and treatment of children. *Journal of Consulting and Clinical Psychology, 59,* 799–812.

U.S. Public Health Service, Office of the Surgeon General. *Youth violence: A report of the Surgeon General, 2001.* Available at http://www.surgeongeneral.gov/library/youthviolence.

Uehara, E. (1990). Dual exchange theory, social networks, and informal social support. *American Journal of Sociology, 96,* 521–557.

Ulzen, T., & Hamiton, H. (1998) The nature and characteristics of psychiatric comorbidity in incarcerated adolescents. *Canadian Journal of Psychiatry, 43,* 57–63.

Vondra, J., & Belsky, J. (1993). Developmental origins of parenting: Personality and relationship factors. In T. Luster & L. Okagaki (Eds.), *Parenting: An ecological perspective* (pp. 1–34). Hillsdale, NJ: Erlbaum.

Wahler, R. G., & Hann, D. M. (1987a). An interbehavioral approach to clinical child psychology: Toward an understanding of troubled families. In D. H. Ruben & D. J. Delprato (Eds.), *New ideas in therapy: Introduction to an interdisciplinary approach* (pp. 53–78). New York: Greenwood Press.

Wahler, R. G., Hann, D. M. (1987b). The communication patterns of troubled mothers: In search of a keystone in the generalization of parenting skills. *Education & Treatment of Children.* Vol 7(4), Fall 1984, 335–350.

Waldron, H. B., Slesnick, N., Turner, C. W., Brody, J. L., & Peterson, T. R. (2001). Treatment outcomes for adolescent substance abuse at 4- and 7-month assessments. *Journal of Consulting and Clinical Psychology, 69,* 802–813.

Waltz, J., Addis, M. E., Koerner, K., & Jacobson, N. S. (1993). Testing the integrity of a psychotherapy protocol: Assessment of adherence and competence. *Journal of Consulting and Clinical Psychology, 61,* 620–630.

Wampold, B. E. (2001). *The great psychotherapy debate: Models, methods, and findings.* Mahwah, NJ : Erlbaum.

Watzlawick, P., Weakland, J., & Fisch, R. (1974). *Change: Principles of problem formation and problem resolution.* New York: Norton.

Weisz, J. R., Huey, S. J., & Weersing, V. R. (1998). Psychotherapy outcome research with children and adolescents: The state of the art. In T. H. Ollendick & R. J. Prinz (Eds.), *Advances in clinical child psychology*, vol. 20 (pp. 49–91). New York: Plenum Press.

Weisz, V., & Tomkins, A. J. (1996). The right to a family environment for children with disabilities. *American Psychologist, 51,* 1239–1245.

Wells, M. G., Burlingame, G., Lambert, M. J., Hoag, M., & Hope, C. (1996). Conceptualization and measurement of patient change during psychotherapy: Development of the Outcome Questionnaire and Youth Outcome Questionnaire. *Psychotherapy: Theory, Research, & Practice, 33*(2), 275–283.

Westen, D., Novotny, C. M., & Thompson-Brenner, H. (2004). The empirical status of empirically supported psychotherapies: Assumptions, findings, and reporting in controlled clinical trials. *Psychological Bulletin, 130(4),* 631–663.

Whaley, A. L., & Davis, K. E. (2007). Cultural competence and evidence-based practice in mental health services: A complementary perspective. *American Psychologist, 62(6),* 563–574.

World Health Organization. (1992). *The ICD-10 Classification of Mental and Behavioral Disorders.* Geneva: World Health Organization.

Index